THE SUBLIME ARTIST'S STUDIO

GAVRIEL SHAPIRO

The
Sublime
Artist's Studio

NABOKOV AND PAINTING

NORTHWESTERN UNIVERSITY PRESS
EVANSTON, ILLINOIS

Northwestern University Press
www.nupress.northwestern.edu

This publication was prepared (in part) under a grant from the Kennan Institute
of the Woodrow Wilson International Center for Scholars, Washington, D.C. The
statements and views expressed herein are those of the author and are not necessarily those of the Woodrow Wilson Center.

Printed in the United States of America

10 9 8 7 6 5 4 3 2 1

Library of Congress Cataloging-in-Publication Data
Shapiro, Gavriel.
   The sublime artist's studio : Nabokov and painting / Gavriel Shapiro.
      p. cm.
   Includes bibliographical references and index.
   ISBN 978-0-8101-2559-9 (cloth : alk. paper)
   1. Nabokov, Vladimir Vladimirovich, 1899–1977—Knowledge—Painting.
2. Nabokov, Vladimir Vladimirovich, 1899–1977—Criticism and interpretation.
3. Art and literature. 4. Painting in literature. I. Title. II. Title: Nabokov and
painting.
   PG3476.N3Z8638 2009
   813.54—dc22

                                                                2008048247

To the memory of my father, Dr. Yaakov Shapiro,
and to my mother, Dr. Ella Leizerovsky

It is worth noting one more feature of Gogol's style: its rare picturesqueness and skillful colorfulness [. . .] The epithet "colored" begs to be uttered when one attempts to define Gogol's creative work. It seems as if the author, while composing *Dead Souls,* had transformed every drop of ink quivering on the tip of his quill into a live drop of paint. The Russian muse had not known such amazingly colored prose before. At the same time, Gogol the artist is extraordinarily diverse: now he is a luscious watercolorist, now a meticulous draughtsman, now he will enchant me in passing with a surprising miniature, with a picture on a snuffbox [. . .] It seems that one may take a pencil or a brush and illustrate each phrase of *Dead Souls*—two or three pictures per page. But I underscore: *it seems,* because in fact no artist would succeed in depicting with paints the way Gogol depicted his world with words.

—Vladimir Nabokov, "Gogol"

Contents

Note on Transliteration

A simplified version of the Library of Congress system for transliterating the Russian alphabet is employed throughout. The only exceptions are Nabokov's own transliteration of names used in his works (e.g., Fyodor, Chernyshevski) and Russian names whose spellings have become standard in English (e.g., Tolstoy, Dostoevsky), as well as transliterations in scholarly studies.

Illustrations

Figures 14–17 and 19–22 are intentionally reproduced from Richard Muther's book to show the works of art as the young Nabokov might have seen them.

Acknowledgments

I wish to thank my Cornell colleagues Robert E. Dirig, Slava Paperno, and Franklin W. Robinson. My thanks also go to various individuals and institutions that greatly assisted me in my research: Elizabeth A. Beyer, Julie S. Copenhagen, Frederick M. Muratori, Katherine Reagan, and Martha Walker of the Cornell University Library, Ithaca, N.Y.; William R. Staffeld and Margaret N. Webster of Cornell University's Knight Visual Resources Facility / College of Architecture, Art & Planning, Ithaca, N.Y.; Alice L. Birney and the staff of the Manuscript Division of the Library of Congress, Washington, D.C.; Wilma R. Slaight of Wellesley College Archives, Margaret Clapp Library, Wellesley, Mass.; Stephen Crook and the staff of the New York Public Library's Henry W. and Albert A. Berg Collection, New York City; Tanya Chebotarev and the staff of the Columbia University Library's Bakhmeteff Archive, New York City; Tricia Smith of Art Resource, New York City; Margaret Senk of the Artists Rights Society (ARS), New York City; Nikki Smith of Smith / Skolnik Literary Management, Plainfield, N.J.; Natalia Vladimirovna Tolstaia and Lidia Ivanovna Iovleva of the State Tret´iakov Gallery, Moscow; Irina Lukka and the staff of the National Library of Finland's Slavonic Collection, Helsinki; Iris Labeur and Huigen Leeflang of Rijksmuseum, Amsterdam; Hannelore John of Abteilung Bildende Kunst / Stiftung Archiv der Akademie der Künste, Berlin; Christina Schwill and Nicole Losch-Maute of Bayerische Staatsgemäldesammlungen, Munich; Sabine Gruber of Kunstmuseum Stuttgart; Caroline Berton of Les Publications Condé Nast / Vogue International, Paris; and René Guerra of Université de Nice—Sophia Antipolis.

I am thankful to the American Academy in Berlin and to the Kennan Institute of the Woodrow Wilson International Center for Scholars, Washington, D.C., for providing me with ideal conditions and an intellectually stimulating atmosphere conducive to research and writing. I am greatly indebted to Paul Barolsky, Shulamith Behr, Jessica R. Feldman, Luba Freedman, Tatiela Laake, and Leona Toker for their most beneficial advice and assistance at various stages of the project. I also wish to express my deep appreciation to Henry L. Carrigan Jr., Jenny Gavacs, Anne Gendler, Serena Brommel, and Marianne Jankowski of Northwestern University Press for their invaluable aid in turning this manuscript into a book.

Above all, I am immensely grateful to Dmitri Nabokov for his enthusiastic support, everlasting help, and insightful counsel throughout this project.

Some material, included in chapter 2, previously appeared in "Nabokov and Early Netherlandish Art," in *Nabokov at Cornell* (2003); it is reproduced here by permission of the publisher, Cornell University Press. Other segments of this same chapter appeared in *The Nabokovian* 53, 55, and 57 (Fall issues, 2004–6) and are reproduced by courtesy of the periodical. Chapters 4 and 5, in their preliminary form, appeared as "Vladimir Nabokov and *The World of Art*" and "Vladimir Nabokov and Richard Muther," in *Slavic Almanac* 6, no. 9 (2000), and 11, no. 2 (2005), respectively, and are reproduced by permission of Unisa Press.

Abbreviations

Ada	*Ada, or Ardor: A Family Chronicle.* 1969. New York: Vintage International, 1990.
AnL	*The Annotated Lolita.* Edited with preface, introduction, and notes by Alfred Appel Jr. 1970. Revised edition. New York: Vintage International, 1991.
BS	*Bend Sinister.* 1947. New York: Vintage International, 1990.
Carr	*Carrousel.* 1923. Aartswoud, The Netherlands: Spectatorpers, 1987.
CE	*Conclusive Evidence: A Memoir.* New York: Harper, 1951.
Def	*The Defense.* Translated by Michael Scammell in collaboration with the author. 1964. New York: Vintage International, 1990.
Des	*Despair.* 1966. New York: Vintage International, 1989.
En	*The Enchanter.* Translated by Dmitri Nabokov. 1986. New York: Vintage International, 1991.
EO	*Eugene Onegin: A Novel in Verse by Aleksandr Pushkin.* Translated, with a commentary, by Vladimir Nabokov. Bollingen Series 72. 4 vols. 1964. Revised edition. Princeton, N.J.: Princeton University Press, 1975.
Gift	*The Gift.* Translated by Michael Scammell with the collaboration of the author. 1963. New York: Vintage International, 1991.
Glory	*Glory.* Translated by Dmitri Nabokov in collaboration with the author. 1971. New York: Vintage International, 1991.
IB	*Invitation to a Beheading.* Translated by Dmitri Nabokov in collaboration with the author. 1959. New York: Vintage International, 1989.
KQK	*King, Queen, Knave.* Translated by Dmitri Nabokov in collaboration with the author. 1968. New York: Vintage International, 1989.

LATH   *Look at the Harlequins!* 1974. New York: Vintage International, 1990.

Laugh   *Laughter in the Dark.* 1938. New York: Vintage International, 1989.

LDQ   *Lectures on Don Quixote.* Edited by Fredson Bowers. New York: Harcourt Brace Jovanovich / Bruccoli Clark, 1983.

LL   *Lectures on Literature.* Edited by Fredson Bowers. New York: Harcourt Brace Jovanovich / Bruccoli Clark, 1980.

LoR   *Lolita* (Nabokov's Russian translation). New York: Phaedra, 1967.

LRL   *Lectures on Russian Literature.* Edited by Fredson Bowers. New York: Harcourt Brace Jovanovich / Bruccoli Clark, 1981.

Mary   *Mary.* Translated by Michael Glenny in collaboration with the author. 1970. New York: Vintage International, 1989.

NG   *Nikolai Gogol.* 1944. New York: New Directions, 1961.

NWL   *Dear Bunny, Dear Volodya: The Nabokov–Wilson Letters, 1940–1971.* Revised and expanded edition. Edited, annotated, and with an introductory essay by Simon Karlinsky. Berkeley: University of California Press, 2001.

Perepiska *Perepiska s sestroi.* Ann Arbor, Mich.: Ardis Publishers, 1985.

PF   *Pale Fire.* 1962. New York: Vintage International, 1989.

Pnin   *Pnin.* 1957. New York: Vintage International, 1989.

PP   *Poems and Problems.* New York: McGraw-Hill, 1970.

RLSK   *The Real Life of Sebastian Knight.* 1941. New York: Vintage International, 1992.

SL   *Selected Letters, 1940–1977.* Edited by Dmitri Nabokov and Matthew J. Bruccoli. New York: Harcourt Brace Jovanovich / Bruccoli Clark Layman, 1989.

SM   *Speak, Memory: An Autobiography Revisited.* 1967. New York: Vintage International, 1989.

SO   *Strong Opinions.* 1973. New York: Vintage International, 1990.

Song   *The Song of Igor's Campaign.* Translated by Vladimir Nabokov. 1960. New York: McGraw-Hill, 1975.

Ssoch   *Sobranie sochinenii russkogo perioda v piati tomakh.* 5 vols. St. Petersburg: Simpozium, 1999–2000.

Stikhi   *Stikhi.* Ann Arbor, Mich.: Ardis, 1979.

Stories   *The Stories of Vladimir Nabokov.* 1995. New York: Vintage
             International, 1997.
TRP   *Three Russian Poets.* Norfolk, Conn.: New Directions, 1944.
USSR   *The Man from the U.S.S.R. and Other Plays.* Introduced and
             translated by Dmitri Nabokov. New York: Harcourt Brace
             Jovanovich / Bruccoli Clark, 1984.

The Sublime Artist's Studio

INTRODUCTION

When we look at a painting we do not have to move our eyes in a special way even if, as in a book, the picture contains elements of depth and development. The element of time does not really enter in a first contact with a painting. In reading a book, we must have time to acquaint ourselves with it. We have no physical organ (as we have the eye in regard to a painting) that takes in the whole picture and then can enjoy its details. But at a second, or third, or fourth reading we do, in a sense, behave towards a book as we do towards a painting.

—Nabokov, *Lectures on Literature*

There comes a moment when I am informed from within that the entire structure is finished. All I have to do now is take it down in pencil or pen. Since this entire structure, dimly illumined in one's mind, can be compared to a painting, and since you do not have to work gradually from left to right for its proper perception, I may direct my flashlight at any part or particle of the picture when setting it down in writing.

—Nabokov, *Strong Opinions*

Poetry and painting have been linked, likened, and juxtaposed ever since, according to Plutarch, Simonides of Ceos proclaimed: "Poetry is a speaking picture, painting is a silent poetry." Several centuries later, Horace expressed an analogous sentiment in his famous phrase "Ut pictura poesis," most commonly rendered "As is painting so is poetry." Horace's dictum, which places the two sister arts side by side, became especially prevalent during the Renaissance, Baroque, and Romantic periods.[1] In the mid-nineteenth century, John Ruskin revitalized this concept by viewing literature and painting once again as complementary modes of expression. Ruskin's aesthetic precepts exerted a considerable influence on Russian culture at the turn of the twentieth century, in art and literature alike.[2]

Vladimir Nabokov (1899–1977) occupies an empyrean position in Russian and world literature. An apparently inexhaustible subject of research for several generations of dedicated scholars, widely taught and extensively translated, Nabokov's literary legacy has an immense and continuously growing audience. In recent years, presumably sparked by the celebrations of the writer's centenary, there have appeared, alongside the colossal literary Nabokoviana, several book-length studies on his other major passion—butterflies. In addition to assessing Nabokov's momentous entomological achievements, these studies explore the role of lepidoptera in his literary works.[3]

While the fundamental role of literature and the significance of lepidoptera in Nabokov's works are fairly recognized and have been systematically studied, the importance of the fine arts to his oeuvre has not been sufficiently addressed. Only relatively sparse scholarship, articles and book chapters, has broached the issue until not long ago.[4] Furthermore, such specialized volumes of a manifestly comprehensive nature as *The Garland Companion to Vladimir Nabokov* (1995) and *The Cambridge Companion to Nabokov* (2005) devote no attention to it whatsoever, and the multivolume sets of Nabokov's works—the Simpozium *Sobranie sochinenii* (1997–2000) and the Rowohlt *Gesammelte Werke* (1989–2004)—provide meager information concerning Nabokov's works in their relation to the fine arts. It is worth noting that Nabokov's oeuvre still awaits an academic edition with wide-ranging, in-depth annotations and commentaries that would thoroughly illuminate and exhaustively cover the writer's numerous interests and encyclopedic erudition. The importance of separate annotations and commentaries notwithstanding, they do not set out to trace specific themes throughout Nabokov's works. And finally, they do not enable one to see Nabokov's penchant for painting as a leitmotif of his creation.

Most recently, while the present study was nearing completion, there appeared a book, lavishly illustrated, that catalogues numerous occurrences of art in Nabokov's oeuvre.[5] However, when broaching Nabokov's works, save *Ada*, the book moves in rapid succession from subject to subject, from work to work, and from painting to painting, even though ostensibly focusing on several novels and one short story.

Such an incoherent approach leads to fragmentation and does not allow a more unified perspective on Nabokov's relation to art. The discussion does, however, become more viable and valid when the book turns to *Ada* (1969), Nabokov's most sizable novel, which contains numerous references to artwork that, by his own admission, "are for the most part more recent enthusiasms" (*SO* 167). (I omit a discussion of art in *Ada* since both Johnson's chapter and Ashenden's essay concentrate on the novel and cover the subject. I also omit a discussion of comic art in Nabokov's works since both Clarence Brown and I discuss it elsewhere; see the bibliography.) The altogether insufficient exposure that Nabokov scholarship has given to the subject thus far is all the more unjustified since painting has such a powerful presence in Nabokov's creative universe.

In his boyhood and early youth, Nabokov aspired to become a landscape artist. Even though he realized over time that his vocation was literature and turned from the brush to the quill, his keen sense of visual detail, nuanced perception of color, and vast knowledge of and great interest in the fine arts are all manifest in his belles lettres.[6] Furthermore, even after Nabokov realized that his vocation was literature, he retained the enthusiasm of his boyhood and early youth. He applied his draftsmanship to lepidopteral research; sketched his hallmark dedicational, luxuriant, often imaginary butterflies; and employed the acquired drawing skills in his lectures to illustrate a point. In short, he continued to engage himself in the fine arts—drawings, paintings, or watercolors, serious or humorous, or the book-length *Butterflies in Art* project—all his creative life. Moreover, Nabokov populated his literary works with painters and paintings, real and fanciful, and most importantly, he created magnificent pictorial imagery by means of another, verbal, medium of expression.

While numerous students of Nabokov's literary legacy, by and large, neglected the writer's multifaceted approach to painting, there are some historians of art who have noted and commented on his works in relation to the pictorial. Such is the distinguished Renaissance art historian Paul Barolsky, who has found it important to direct his attention to Nabokov's writings. An obvious Nabokovophile, Barolsky goes over Nabokov's partial reading list, succinctly analyzes some of his works, and briefly discusses the writer's story "La Veneziana," interpreting it as "the myth of Pygmalion" lifted "into the realm of high farce."[7]

Barolsky's pioneering endeavors are most promising, as they offer the missing art history viewpoint on the subject.

The title of this book calls for an explanation. I have borrowed the epithet "sublime" to characterize Nabokov's literary legacy from his own translation of Alexander Pushkin's poem "To Dawe, Esqr." (1828), in which the poet so dubs the "pencil," that is, the artistry, of the English portrait painter George Dawe (*EO*, 3:205).[8] The remaining portion of the title alludes to the *ut pictura poesis* simile that Nabokov tellingly employs when speaking about his writing process: "I think that what I would welcome at the close of a book of mine is a sensation of its world receding in the distance and stopping somewhere there, suspended afar like a picture in a picture: *The Artist's Studio* by Van Bock" (*SO* 72–73).

In scrutinizing Nabokov's oeuvre for its relations with painting, I take into consideration the creative legacy of the writer in all its variety—his poetry, short prose, novels, plays, memoirs, lectures, essays, interviews, and correspondence. My study, however, in no way presumes to be exhaustive. Rather, it explores and analyzes Nabokov's corpus of writings in its relation, direct and indirect, to pictorial manifestations of European art, from Old Masters to modern, first and foremost. After all, Nabokov grew up and lived most of his life in Europe, and his artistic tastes were primarily shaped by European art. This book, therefore, sets out to unravel and explore the role of some references and allusions to works of European, and particularly contemporary Russian, artists that appear in Nabokov's works. Nabokov's literary legacy, however, is so pictorially diverse that it remains wide open for exploration with regard to other periods and continents—from antiquity to the Middle Ages, from Asia to America.[9]

In structuring this book, I have been guided, most of all, by a number of themes that recur in Nabokov's prose and poetry: the authorial presence; landscape in its various roles and functions; nostalgia for the Russian past through the pictorial lens of *The World of Art;* the recollection of nineteenth-century European art through the prism of Richard Muther's influential survey, *History of Painting in the XIXth Century;* the depiction of the city, based on lessons learned from *The World of Art* and their application to the portrayal of Berlin—that other metropolis. The thematic principle makes it possible to follow a given subject matter through various literary works within each chapter, to maintain

an overarching perspective on the discussion and to generate and preserve the book's own "memory" throughout the entire study. Furthermore, I have chosen the chronological structure of the book, from Old
Masters to German Expressionists, because it allows one to discern
more distinctly the wide range of Nabokov's familiarity with various
artistic styles, from refined to "crude."

Nabokov's fascination with painting cannot be properly understood without a close inspection of his formative milieu. In chapter 1,
I look at the many aspects of his cultural development, and above all
at the atmosphere that infused his childhood home, as well as at the
wide-ranging artistic interests of his family. I consider the impact of
his private drawing masters on his artistic advancement alongside the
contribution of his excellent schooling to his aesthetic development. I
examine the ambience of St. Petersburg, the imperial capital of Russia,
where the future writer grew up. And I regard many an opportunity
the young Nabokov had to see masterpieces of art both at home and
abroad, particularly in Berlin and Paris, during his frequent boyhood
trips to western Europe.

Nabokov's exposure to art, his deep fascination with it, his aspiration to become a painter in his formative years, his brilliant mind and
scholarly propensity, all account for his multifaceted and immense artistic erudition and, specifically, for his vast knowledge and deep appreciation of the Old Masters. To a large degree, these capabilities are
part and parcel of the refined cultural and intellectual milieu to which
he belonged. Yet Nabokov possessed some distinctly unique qualities,
which I discuss in chapter 2. These are, first and foremost, the attention to the minutiae of details and the fascination with the convex
mirror that appealed to Nabokov, the verbal artist and entomologist,
in the pictorial achievements of Early Netherlandish painters—Jan
van Eyck and his younger contemporaries, Hans Memling and Petrus
Christus. In addition, Nabokov's penchant for authorial presence was
inspired by the Old Masters who not infrequently set their own images
in canvas.

Chapter 3 moves on from these unique qualities to consider the
role of landscape in Nabokov's oeuvre. The writer had an early aspiration to become a landscape artist and attached great significance
to this most pictorial and colorful of all art genres. Upon realizing,
however, that his vocation was literature, Nabokov channeled this as-

piration into the verbal medium of expression. In so doing, Nabokov endowed landscape with diverse roles and functions. Our sampling ranges from the "Russian years"—the novels *King, Queen, Knave; Glory; Invitation to a Beheading;* and *Despair;* and the short story "Cloud, Castle, Lake"—to the "American years"—the novels *Lolita* and *Pnin*—in all of which landscape, both described and seen as if pictorially rendered, plays an essential part.

Chapter 4 explores Nabokov's kinship with his favorite contemporary artists that gathered around *The World of Art,* the short-lived but very influential St. Petersburg periodical. When its publication ceased, *The World of Art* continued to function as an artistic association for approximately two more decades and left an indelible mark on the Russian culture of the turn of the twentieth century. I argue that Nabokov's kinship with these painters derives to a great extent from the writer's nostalgia: the irreversible loss of his own Russia that conflated in his mind with the loss of his happy childhood and youth. As a case in point, I select the "stylized snow" imagery, charged with longing for the irretrievable past that the writer so successfully recollected by the powers of his imagination and memory. I further reflect on the evolving relationship between Nabokov and Mstislav Dobuzhinsky, his most influential drawing master and a distinguished *World of Art* participant, and compare their tastes in contemporary Russian art to demonstrate the important role which Dobuzhinsky played in the development of Nabokov's artistic preferences, his likes and dislikes.

In chapter 5, I contemplate the probable impact of Richard Muther's *History of Painting in the XIXth Century* on the formation of Nabokov's aesthetic precepts and trace the refraction of the book's descriptive-illustrative material in Nabokov's oeuvre. This work of the German art historian was most seminal at the turn of the twentieth century throughout Europe, including Russia. The study was translated into Russian and exerted a strong influence upon *The World of Art's* many representatives, so much so that Alexander Benois, at Muther's request, felt compelled to append to it a chapter on nineteenth-century Russian art, later developing it into a separate book. I view this likely impact as an additional link between Nabokov and the artistic association, specifically because it was apparently Dobuzhinsky who introduced Muther's study to his young charge. Most importantly, Muther's book, which was part of Nabokov's familial library, provided the gifted boy with a very informative survey of nineteenth-century Western art and allowed him to see his native Russian art in the broader context.

In his boyhood, Nabokov stayed in Berlin for three months prior to World War I (1910). A decade later, as an exile, while studying at Cambridge (1919–22), the budding writer frequently visited his parents there, and afterward he himself resided in the German capital for fifteen years (1922–37). This long-term familiarity with Berlin undoubtedly accounts for the frequent occurrence of this city as the urban setting in Nabokov's interwar writings. Chapter 6 discusses the image of the *Weltstadt* and its various manifestations in Nabokov's works. To underscore Nabokov's uniqueness in his portrayal of life in Berlin, I juxtapose his verbal depiction of it with its pictorial representation by German Expressionist artists. This juxtaposition is all the more warranted since Nabokov could familiarize himself with their artwork at exhibitions, in albums, and even by way of the "hit-and-run" distribution of illustrated pamphlets on Berlin street corners.

I examine Nabokov's writings, often one and the same work, looking at them from different angles, as necessitated by references or allusions to pictorial art, thereby attempting to explore their multilayered, complex meaning. The thematic principle guiding this book offers a dynamic view of Nabokov's attitude toward a given painter, work of art, or pictorial mode of expression, thereby allowing the reader to detect stability or evolvement in the writer's artistic tastes throughout his creative life. Finally, the thematic principle offers further insights into Nabokov's text at large. Thus, tracing the persistent recurrence of the "stylized snow" motif throughout Nabokov's oeuvre draws attention to the important semantic function with which the writer endows this nostalgic imagery.

This book, to a great extent, falls into the category of *ut pictura poesis* studies, as it looks at Vladimir Nabokov's life and works in their relation to the pictorial fine arts.[10] I hope that the examination of this phenomenon will enhance our understanding of this incomparable verbal artist and of his fictional universe. I further trust that the discussion presented in this book will be of use to additional similar studies in which the interaction of the sister arts plays a significant role.

1. The Formative Milieu

Between the ages of ten and fifteen in St. Petersburg, I must have read more fiction and poetry—English, Russian and French—than in any other five-year period of my life [. . .] I was a perfectly normal trilingual child in a family with a large library.

—Nabokov, *Strong Opinions*

From conversations with my father, from daydreams in his absence, from the neighborhood of thousands of books full of drawings of animals, from the precious shimmer of the collections, from the maps, from all the heraldry of nature and the cabbalism of Latin names, life took on a kind of bewitching lightness that made me feel as if my own travels were about to begin. Thence, I borrow my wings today.

—Nabokov, *The Gift*

Vladimir Nabokov was born in St. Petersburg, the Russian imperial capital, into an aristocratic family of multifaceted aesthetic interests. His father, Vladimir Dmitrievich (1870–1922), a prominent jurist and statesman of the early twentieth century, was a great connoisseur of literature, the fine arts, theater, and music. His mother, Elena Ivanovna (née Rukavishnikov, 1876–1939), was also an amateur painter and "an industrious albeit unpublished poetess."[1] His younger brother Sergei (1900–1945) was a music aficionado and an avid piano student. His youngest brother Kirill (1911–64), whom Nabokov himself characterized as someone whose "one great reality in life was literature, especially Russian poetry" (*SM* 256), was a gifted poet.[2] As Nabokov recalls, his "parents had many acquaintances who painted and danced and made music" (*SO* 171). At their St. Petersburg residence at Bol'shaia Morskaia, 47, the Nabokovs frequently held cultural soirées, and their house "was one of the first where young Shalyapin sang" (ibid.) and where Sergei Koussevitzky, a celebrated musician and the future legendary conductor and music director of the Boston Symphony Orchestra, gave private concerts.[3] The family also had their own box at the Mariinsky Theater, where Nabokov the boy was regularly taken to opera and ballet productions.

Nicolas Nabokov (1903–78), a composer and the writer's cousin, remembers Nabokov's parents in their Berlin exile, which echoed their intensely cultured life in St. Petersburg: "Aunt Lyolya [Elena Ivanovna's family nickname] and her husband brought with them to their Berlin flat the full flavor of a wealthy, enlightened St. Petersburg home." He characterizes them, with admiration, as having "brilliant minds, quick wits, rounded educations, and strong political and cultural convictions."[4] Nicolas Nabokov also recalls that, while in Berlin, he attended general rehearsals of the Berlin Philharmonic Orchestra together with V. D. Nabokov. By Nicolas Nabokov's own admission, "it was at those Sunday-morning concerts (and the discussions with Uncle Vladimir that followed) that I received the first truly useful and lasting part of my musical education."[5]

The diverse cultural interests of the Nabokov family are manifest in V. D. Nabokov's voluminous library at their St. Petersburg residence, which contained, alongside his professional literature, books in English, French, German, Russian, and other languages on various subjects, including belles lettres and the fine arts.[6] The head of the household, Vladimir Dmitrievich, was a bibliophile who possessed great erudition in literature. This notion is supported by even such an unfavorably inclined memoirist as Kornei Chukovsky, a journalist, literary critic, and children's writer. Chukovsky, who collaborated with V. D. Nabokov in the daily *Speech* (*Rech´*), writes that Nabokov senior, the newspaper's copublisher, "knew literature by heart, especially foreign literature; in the newspaper *Speech* they were so certain of his know-it-all nature that they would turn to him for references [. . .]: where is this citation from? In what century did such and such a German poet live? And Nabokov would answer."[7] Nabokov senior's love for and knowledge of literature and his organizational talents earned him great respect among Russian literati: he was elected secretary (1909–11), deputy president (1913), and president (1914–15) of the Literary Fund.[8] In addition, from 1912 to 1914 V. D. Nabokov was a member of the All-Russian Literary Society, where he served on the committee entrusted with drafting the press legislation.[9]

In *Speak, Memory,* his English-language memoir, Nabokov recalls that his father "knew *à fond* the prose and poetry of several countries, knew by heart hundreds of verses (his favorite Russian poets were Pushkin, Tyutchev, and Fet—he published a fine essay on the latter), was an authority on Dickens, and, besides Flaubert, prized highly Stendhal, Balzac, and Zola, three detestable mediocrities from *my* point of view" (*SM* 177; italics in original).[10] And in *Other Shores,* his Russian-language memoir, Nabokov also adds Shakespeare to the list of their shared literary enthusiasms (*Ssoch,* 5:270). Even though, as can be seen from the above-quoted *Speak, Memory* passage, their literary tastes differed somewhat, there is no doubt that V. D. Nabokov, whom the future writer greatly admired and respected and who significantly influenced his cultural tastes, inculcated in his son a lifelong love for literature and was responsible for his many literary predilections, specifically for Pushkin and Tiutchev as well as for Shakespeare, Flaubert, and Dickens. For example, Nabokov reports that his father was "an expert on Dickens" and further adds: "at one time [he] read to us, children, aloud, chunks of Dickens, in English, of course" (*NWL* 268). These readings instilled in Nabokov a lasting appreciation of Dickens. In his Cornell lectures on *Bleak House,* Nabokov says of Dickens: "With Dickens we expand [. . .] In the case of Dickens the values are new. Modern authors still get drunk on his vintage [. . .] We just surrender ourselves to Dickens's voice—that is all. If it were possible I would like to devote the fifty minutes of every class meeting to mute meditation, concentration, and admiration of Dickens" (*LL* 63–64).[11]

Nabokov, however, praises Dickens with some reservations, pointing out the English writer's shortcomings: "Dickens is a good moralist, a good storyteller, and a superb enchanter, but as a storyteller he lags somewhat behind his other virtues. In other words, he is supremely good at picturing his characters and their habitats in any given situation, but there are flaws in his work when he tries to establish various links between these characters in a pattern of action" (*LL* 123). Nabokov's appraisal of Dickens echoes an article by his father in *Speech* in which he calls the English writer "a magician" and "a gripping storyteller" but at the same time notes "the improbability of the plot, the artificiality of many situations, affectedness of senses, and frequent excesses of style."[12] Furthermore, Nabokov, especially in his youth, also shared with his father a high regard for Alexander Blok. It is noteworthy that they both commemorated Blok's passing with publications that appeared side by side: V. D. Nabokov, with an article, and V. V. Nabokov, under his newly adopted pen name Sirin, with a poem.[13]

V. D. Nabokov's great love for literature and his enormous literary erudition evidently set an inspiring example for the young Nabokov. As the writer recalls, "In my boyhood I was an extraordinarily avid reader. By the age of 14 or 15 I had read or re-read all Tolstoy in Russian, all Shakespeare in English, and all Flaubert in French—besides hundreds of other books" (*SO* 46). These "hundreds of other books" included "the works of Wells, Poe, Browning, Keats, [. . .] Verlaine, Rimbaud, Chekhov, [. . .] and Alexander Blok" (*SO* 42–43). And in assessing the role of his father in his aesthetic edification, Nabokov avers: "I am also aware that my father was responsible for my appreciating very early in life the thrill of a great poem" (*SO* 46).

Aside from his high regard for and outstanding erudition in belles lettres, V. D. Nabokov loved the fine arts. Thus, during his 1916 reconnaissance trip to wartime England as part of a group of Russian literati that included the earlier mentioned Kornei Chukovsky, the journalist and writer Vasily Nemirovich-Danchenko (the older brother of the famous codirector of the Moscow Art Theater), and the novelist Alexei N. Tolstoy, Nabokov senior found time, amidst a very busy schedule, to visit the London National Gallery, where he singled out for praise the "marvelous landscapes of Claude Lorrain" and "Turner's fantastic symphonies of light."[14] V. D. Nabokov's interest in painting and his artistic taste undeniably exerted considerable influence on those of his son. We recall that young Nabokov speaks with great appreciation of Lorrain and names Turner among the painters who meant a great deal to him in his youth (see chapter 3).

It seems that V. D. Nabokov was also quite fond of the Dutch Old Masters. In the above-mentioned travel sketches about wartime England, Nabokov senior describes a newly opened room of the Dutch school of painting at the National Gallery. He writes:

> In the separate, newly opened room of the Dutch School one may feast one's eyes upon four first-rate Rembrandts, excellent pictures by [Gabriel] Metsu, [van] Ostade [Nabokov senior does

not specify whether he has Adriaen or his brother Isack in mind], two Hobbemas [works by Meindert Hobbema], and the recently acquired *Concert* (alternate title *La Collation*—"supper") by Pieter de Hooch—this admirable, unique master in his own way (my favorite).[15]

In his own compositions, Nabokov frequently refers or alludes to works of the Old Masters, particularly to those of the Dutch school. He speaks about "the rich butterflies that enliven the flowers and fruit of the old Dutch Masters" (*SO* 330), mentions van Ruysdael in *Laughter in the Dark* (*Laugh* 145)—it is not clear, though, whether the writer has Salomon or his nephew Jacob in mind—metaphorically refers to the white horses of Philips Wouwerman in "Spring in Fialta" (*Stories* 428), bestows on an *Ada* character, Lucette, love for "Flemish and Dutch oils" (*Ada* 464), and recurrently speaks of Rembrandt.

Nabokov's fascination with the works of the Old Masters (see chapter 2) and his artistic preferences were evidently shaped not only by the Hermitage Museum masterpieces that he had many an opportunity to see but also by the art collection in his familial residence, which contained a sizable number of works by Italian, Spanish, and especially Flemish and Dutch painters. After the Bolshevik coup d'état the collection was "nationalized," and its paintings in part were distributed among various art museums, including the Hermitage, and in part were sold, perhaps even abroad. The 1918 inventory lists 120 paintings in the Nabokov family art collection, the first portion of which, seventy-nine paintings in all, including sixty-one western European works of art, was "removed" from the Nabokov mansion in early September of that year.[16] Scholars have succeeded thus far in identifying only a score of works by Old Masters from the Nabokov family art collection. The most prominent among these, officially listed on the Hermitage Museum website, are *Madonna and Child* (ca. 1515) by the Venetian painter Jacopo Palma the Elder, a study of the *Head of an Old Man* (ca. 1612) for the painting *The Crown of Thorns* (*Ecce Homo*) by the illustrious Flemish painter Peter Paul Rubens, *The Entry into Jerusalem* (ca. 1620) by the Spanish Valencian-school painter Pedro de Orrente, and *Portrait of a Notary* (second half of the seventeenth century) by the Dutch Leiden-based painter Arie (Adriaen) de Vois.[17] The Hermitage Museum is apparently also in the possession of other paintings from the Nabokov family art collection, not formally listed, such as *Portrait of an Officer* (ca. 1635) by the Dutch painter Pieter Symonsz Potter and *Landscape Amidst the Rocks* (1664) by his fellow countryman Allaert van Everdingen, who made a name for himself by depicting Scandinavian scenery.

According to Petr Miagkov, the bulk of the Nabokov family art collection originated with that of the maternal ancestor Nikolai Illarionovich Kozlov (1814–89), "first president of the Russian Imperial Academy of Medicine" (*SM* 65).[18] Be that as it may, the collection's display in the house corresponded to the tastes of Nabokov's parents, and particularly to that of his father. For example, Nabokov writes that his father had in his study, together with a "mellowly illumined Perugino," "the small, honey-bright Dutch oils" (*SM* 190) which he evidently favored.

Aside from the Old Masters, the Nabokov family art collection was comprised of a large number of Russian paintings, specifically of the *World of Art* group. In his English-language memoirs, first in *Conclusive Evidence* and then in *Speak, Memory*, Nabokov mentions that in his father's study, there was hanging "right over the desk, the rose-and-haze pastel portrait" (1910) of his mother by Léon Bakst (*CE* 134 and *SM* 190), and in *Other Shores* Nabokov also describes works of the *World of Art* painters in his mother's study. There, Alexander Benois' "truly delightful rain-bloated *Bretagne* and russet-green *Versailles* neighbored by the 'delectable' (in the parlance of those times) *Turks* of Bakst and Somov's watercolor *Rainbow* amidst its wet birches."[19]

In addition to being exposed to the family art collection, Nabokov had easy access to his father's large library, which contained a sizable corpus of illustrated art books—the famous *Künstler-Monographien-Serien* that ranged from Old Masters to modern European artists, Adolf Philippi's *Kunstgeschichtliche Einzeldarstellungen*, Richard Muther's *History of Painting in the XIXth Century*, and Alexander Benois' *History of Russian Art in the XIXth Century* (for the latter two, see chapter 5).[20]

Nabokov's family, and specifically V. D. Nabokov, also possessed great enthusiasm for theater and music, which is manifest in his recollections, published in the Berlin-based periodical *Theater and Life*. Nabokov senior opens these memoirs with the following words: "I became a passionate theatergoer at the age of fourteen. As a sixth-grade schoolboy, I was mad about Russian opera, took a great interest in Russian drama and French theater. I have been carrying this passion throughout my entire life."[21] Nabokov corroborates Vladimir Dmitrievich's "very early, and lifelong, passion for the opera" (*SM* 179). He writes that his father "must have heard practically every first-rate European singer between 1880 and 1922, and although unable to play anything (except very majestically the first chords of the 'Ruslan' overture) remembered every note of his favorite operas" (ibid.). A passion for the stage is evident on Nabokov's maternal side as well. His mother's love for the theater was instilled in her by her father and his maternal grandfather, Ivan Vasil´evich Rukavishnikov (1841–1901), who, by Nabokov's own admission, had "a private theatre in his house" and "was on a friendly footing with most of the actors of the Russian stage and a regular theatregoer" (*USSR* 318).

There is no doubt that both Vladimir Dmitrievich and Elena Ivanovna inculcated in young Lody (Nabokov's Anglicized family nickname) a great appreciation for culture at large, including theater and music. Literature and the fine arts became and remained his main lifelong passions. "Although the theater always meant less to Nabokov than literature or painting," his fascination with it was also considerable.[22] While in the Crimean exile, he took part in the performance of Arthur Schnitzler's *Liebelei*. Later in Berlin he played the role of Pozdnyshev in the mock trial of the protagonist of Leo Tolstoy's *The Kreutzer Sonata* and the role of Nikolai Evreinov, an innovative stage director, theoretician of theater, and Nabokov's distant kin, in the two-act comic review *Quatsch*.[23] In addition, Nabokov's own literary legacy contains a number of theatrical works. And Nabokov displays profound understanding of stage laws and playwriting principles in his two essays "Playwriting" and "The Tragedy of Tragedy" (*USSR* 315–42).[24]

Nabokov was far less enthusiastic about music than about literature, the fine arts, and theater. But his parents were nonetheless determined to expose Nabokov the boy to the best cultural achievements of the epoch, including the classical music they both so ardently admired. For example, Nabokov recounts that he "must have attended *Ruslan* [*and Liudmila*] and *Pikovaya Dama* [*The Queen of Spades*] at least a dozen times in the course of half as many years" (*SM* 36). As a result of this exposure to music, Nabokov displays an enviably thorough knowledge and grasp of its classical, especially operatic, repertoire.[25] Nabokov's growing up in St. Petersburg, Russia's imperial capital, with its magnificent architecture and sculpture, art museums and galleries, during such a culturally splendid period as the Silver Age, which produced a plethora of superb works in literature, the fine arts, theater, and music, also contributed highly to his cultural development.[26] In this overview, I dwell on Nabokov's and his family's relation to theater and music in order to present a more complete picture of his aesthetic upbringing. Furthermore, the syncretic genres of theater, opera, and ballet include important verbal (scenarios, librettos) and visual (costume and stage designs, and lighting) components and therefore are highly relevant to the main subject of this book.

Earlier mention was made of Nabokov's parents having cultural soirées in their home and taking him as a boy to opera productions at the Mariinsky Theater. In addition, the young Nabokov attended theatrical productions staged by various innovative directors, such as Vsevolod Meyerhold and the above-mentioned Nikolai Evreinov.[27] For example, "he recalled with particular pleasure" Evreinov's staging fragments of Gogol's *Government Inspector* in his Crooked Mirror Theater "as it might appear in five different versions: in a provincial theater, in the silent movies, or as directed by Edward Gordon Craig, Max Reinhardt, or Konstantin Stanislavsky."[28] He was also apparently present at some of St. Petersburg's numerous readings of poetry and prose, and aside from "The Hermitage, St. Petersburg's Louvre," and "the Russian Museum of Emperor Alexander III" (*SM* 235), he presumably visited art exhibits, especially those of his favorite, *The World of Art.*

The Tenishev School, so named after the industrialist and benefactor Prince Viacheslav Tenishev, was founded in the autumn of 1898, only months before Nabokov's birth, and was initially located on rented premises at Zagorodnyi Prospect; in 1900 it was moved to its permanent location on Mokhovaia Street, 33–35, to the building designed by Richard Berzen.[29] This reputable and innovative school, too, played a notable role in Nabokov's aesthetic development: there he received a serious art education, studied Russian and western European literature, composed and translated poetry, which he published in the school magazine *Youthful Thought* (*Iunaia Mysl´*), and listened to Alexander Blok's poetry reading held within its walls.[30] And Nabokov, without a doubt, found beneficial the severe critique of his juvenile poetry by Vladimir Gippius (1876–1941). Himself a talented poet, or as Nabokov put it, "a wonderful poet of the [Andrei] Bely school" (*NWL* 112) and "a first-rate though somewhat esoteric poet whom I greatly admired," Gippius was Nabokov's Russian literature teacher at the Tenishev School.

Nabokov recalls that Gippius "brought a copy [of Nabokov's first, newly published, collection of poetry] with him to class and provoked the delirious hilarity of the majority of my classmates by applying his fiery criticism [. . .] to my most romantic lines" (*SM* 238). Apart from being a talented poet, Gippius was also a distinguished philologist, literary critic, and educator whom Semen Vengerov, an authority on Russian literature at the time, called "one of the most outstanding Petersburg teachers of Russian literature."[31] And it is conceivable that Gippius exerted a certain influence on the literary tastes and judgments of the young Nabokov. Andrew Field goes so far as to claim that Gippius had "a formative influence" "on the young Vladimir Nabokov as he had years earlier on Mandelstam," whereas Brian Boyd, based on Nabokov's repudiation of it, found in Nabokov's unpublished notes to Field's book, believes that there is "no reason to doubt Nabokov's denial that Gippius influenced him at all."[32]

Foreign travels apparently also played their enlightening role in the young Nabokov's aesthetic education. In particular, Nabokov recalls spending three "orthodontic" months in Berlin in the fall of 1910 (*SM* 204). Although Nabokov does not mention it specifically in his memoir, it is plausible that while in Berlin he visited the city's famous museums: the Pergamon Museum (opened in 1901), which put on display the then recently excavated Great Altar of Pergamon (whence the name of the museum), considered among the most outstanding marble masterpieces of the ancient world; the Kaiser Friedrich Museum (opened in 1904), which held a very impressive collection of Old Master paintings (now in the Gemäldegalerie); and the Alte Nationalgalerie (opened in 1876), which housed nineteenth-century German art. Nabokov also recalls at least five early visits to Paris with his family (*SM* 142), and it is very likely that he was taken to the Louvre. It is hard to imagine that this precocious youngster with artistic sensibilities would not take advantage of such remarkable opportunities.

In his boyhood and adolescence, Nabokov aspired to become a painter. By his own admission, at least "up to [his] fourteenth year," and perhaps even somewhat later, he "used to spend most of the day drawing and painting" and "was supposed to become a painter in due time" (*SO* 17). At that period, the young Nabokov studied drawing and painting privately, under the tutelage of several artists: the Englishman Henry Cumming—Nabokov calls him Mr. Cummings in his memoirs—

Stepan Iaremich, and Mstislav Dobuzhinsky.[33] But it was his mother, herself an amateur artist, who stimulated his original interest in painting. Nabokov recalls that he was "emotionally [...] still more indebted" to "the earlier color treats given me by my mother" (*SM* 92). And he elaborates elsewhere in his memoir: "How many were the aquarelles she painted for me; what a revelation it was when she showed me the lilac tree that grows out of mixed blue and red!" (*SM* 36). The latter is a very telling example of Nabokov's remarkable memory—he remembers his mother's lesson that took place at least forty years earlier—and of his propensity for the visual, and particularly for colors of objects described. It is worth noting that Nabokov also shared with his mother (and evidently inherited from her) the gift of grapheme-color synesthesia: he was able to see letters of the Cyrillic and Roman alphabets in color—the sensibility that, no doubt, contributed a great deal to his uniquely pictorial perception of the surrounding world.[34]

Henry James (also known as Genrikh Aleksandrovich) Cumming, Nabokov's first drawing master, was born in 1852 in St. Petersburg. He was a son of James Alexander Cumming, a petty merchant, and Eleonore Caroline Fröbelius. From 1869 to 1878 he audited classes at the Imperial Academy of the Fine Arts in St. Petersburg. In 1893 Cumming was awarded the title of non-class (or "free") painter that was standard for the academy's auditors, provided they fulfilled the academy program in its entirety; until the academic reform of that year, non-class painters were allowed to teach only at primary schools.[35] Although Nabokov speaks of "the meagerness of his talent" (*SM* 90), Cumming appeared to make a certain name for himself as a watercolorist. One of his watercolor drawings, *The Blue Boudoir in the Home of Count Brevern de la Gardie,* was part of the personal art collection of Nicholas II and adorned his private apartments at the Alexander Palace in Tsarskoe Selo, the favorite residence of the last Russian emperor. The drawing, taken from the palace by a German officer during World War II, was recently returned to Russia.[36]

Cumming, who earlier was a drawing master of Nabokov's mother, taught him "in 1907 or 1908" (*SM* 90). As Nabokov recalls, Cumming had worked "in the early [eighteen] nineties as foreign correspondent and illustrator for the London *Graphic*" (*SM* 90). Published between 1869 and 1932, *The Graphic* is mentioned in *Other Shores,* in the episode that describes how Nabokov as an eight-year-old boy discovered books

1. Henry Cumming, *The Railway Across the Frozen Neva*

on entomology while browsing among the "marble-bound *Graphic*" volumes.[37] As we recall, Nabokov "loaned" this exact description of the London weekly to Humbert in *Lolita:* the library of "the splendid Hotel Mirana," owned by his father, contained "marble-bound *Graphics*" (*AnL* 10 and 11).

A perusal of the periodical confirms that Cumming had indeed worked in that capacity for *The Graphic* between 1894 and 1908. Cumming's own artwork, however, was seldom reproduced in the newspaper. A rare example of it, Cumming's drawing of wintry Petersburg, is shown in figure 1. For the most part, Cumming supplied sketches of important St. Petersburg events, such as the funeral procession of Alexander III (1894), the coronation ceremony of Nicholas II (1896), and the visit of the German emperor Wilhelm II to Russia (1897), which served as the basis for actual drawings by other artists. Occasionally he provided a text as well that would serve as a drawing caption. Thus, in the October 17, 1908, issue of *The Graphic,* Cumming provided a sketch for the drawing entitled *The Cholera in St. Petersburg: A Tragic Street Incident.* In addition, the periodical, calling Cumming "our artist-correspondent," included his brief account of the event:

> While walking along the Nevsky Prospect a day or two ago, I saw a poor woman, who was going quietly down the street, suddenly fall down, her face contorted, her body writhing in agony, and her hands tearing at the pavement and the air in the spasms of an attack of cholera. Many of the passersby, among whom there were several ladies, were frightened almost out of their wits; but a *dvornik* (or doorkeeper) from a house close by came up, and with the help of a policeman got her to a cab, in which she was driven to the hospital.[38]

Judging from this expressive account, as a man of letters, Cumming possessed aptitude and skill, so much so that the periodical justifiably entrusted him with occasional descriptive dispatches.

In *The Gift* (1937–38; 1952), Nabokov mentions that Fyodor's neighbor, a painter named Carl Lorentz, who "had enjoyed before 1914 a distinguished reputation, had visited Russia to paint the Kaiser's meeting with the Tsar" (*Gift* 58). And although Nabokov most likely refers here to the 1907 imperial meeting (see *Ssoch*, 4:653), one wonders whether the writer knew of and alludes to his first drawing master's sketch of the kaiser's visit to Russia ten years earlier.

According to the address book *The Whole Petersburg/The Whole Petrograd*, Cumming had lived steadily in the Russian imperial capital from as early as 1894 until as late as 1917.[39] The same address book provides rather detailed, albeit abbreviated, information about the Englishman: he is called a watercolor painter; named the inventor of the perspectoscope, an instrument for creating enlarged views in pictures and photographs; and listed as an employee of the St. Petersburg-based *Stock Exchange Gazette* as well as an employee of and later a special artist for the London-based *Graphic* and a member of the St. Petersburg Society of Artists and of the so-called Miussar Mondays.[40]

In addition to pursuing a painterly career, Cumming, as it turns out, was very fond of music, and specifically of choral singing: he is recorded as a senior representative of the society of lovers of choir singing, Singacademie, an employee-member of the Society for Music Pedagogues and Other Music Workers, and a member of the male choir society Liedertafel.[41] From 1909, besides supporting himself by private lessons, Cumming was employed as a drawing master at the Imperial School of Jurisprudence, to which position he was, in all likelihood, recommended by V. D. Nabokov, who had taught law there from 1896 to 1904. Cumming was similarly employed at the Levitsky private school, and later at the Shipbuilding School by the Admiralty Industrial Plant.[42]

Cumming, who taught at such reputable schools and gave numerous private lessons, was undoubtedly a talented pedagogue. In the album inscription of January 27, 1910, to A. G. and M. K. Maximov, Cumming expressed his pedagogical credo as follows: "Drawing, when intelligently explained, benefits every sighted child and adult, provided they wish to learn this fascinating occupation," and he added in English: "Nobler thoughts are attained by taking interest in real art."[43]

Nabokov vividly recalls how as a boy he "was captivated by his [Cumming's] use of the special eraser he kept in his waistcoat pocket, by the manner in which he held the page taut, and afterwards flicked off, with the back of his fingers, the 'gutticles of the percha' (as he said)" (*SM* 91). Cumming, it seems, was the one who instructed the young Nabokov in the basics of drawing. To quote Nabokov, he "illustrated for me the marble laws of perspective," showed his charge how "to shade properly with smooth, merging slants" (*SM* 91), and how "when using an eraser, not to transform the paper, with a crackle, into an accordion."[44] It was Cumming, whom the writer dubs "a master of the sunset" (*SM* 91), that deserves credit for awakening Nabokov's fascination with landscape painting (see chapter 3). As a tribute to his first teacher, Nabokov has maintained that he was "emotionally [. . .] indebted to the earlier color treats given me by my mother and her former teacher [Cumming]" (*SM* 92). As Brian Boyd has perceptively remarked, "a master of the sunset," Cumming "too left a trace in the boy who would render in words so many details of so many sunsets."[45] But not only in words: Elena Vladimirovna Sikorski (née Nabokov), Nabokov's youngest sister (1906–2000), recounts in her letter to him of November 1949: "You, in Vyra [the family country estate], are painting a sunset, orange treetops from the windows of the right balcony."[46]

Nabokov's drawing master "from around 1910 to 1912" (*SM* 92), Stepan Petrovich Iaremich (1869–1939), was born into a peasant family in the village of Galaiki, Kiev province. A native of Ukraine, he received his artistic training at the School of Art by the Kievan Monastery of the Caves (1882–87) and at the Nikolai Murashko Kievan School of Drawing (1887–94). While in Kiev, Iaremich also worked with such renowned artists as Nikolai Ge and Mikhail Vrubel. In 1900 Iaremich moved to St. Petersburg, where he became an active participant in *The World of Art* and a member of the newly formed (1903) Union of Russian Artists. In 1904–7 he lived and worked abroad, mainly in Paris. As a painter, Iaremich mostly specialized in cityscapes, especially of St. Petersburg.

The artistic gifts of Iaremich appear to be relatively modest. He is mostly remembered as an art historian, art collector, museum curator, and conservation expert. He authored the first monograph on Vrubel (1911), coauthored (with Olga Forsh) a book on the painter and renowned pedagogue Pavel Chistiakov (1928), contributed three seminal chapters to a study on the eighteenth-century Russian academic school of art (1934), and published many art critiques in various periodicals.[47] For over twenty years, from 1918 until his death, Iaremich worked at the Hermitage Museum, first as the curator of its collection of drawings and engravings and later as the director of its Conservation Department.[48]

In employing "a term of the period," Nabokov calls Iaremich "the well-known 'impressionist'" and goes on to describe him as "a humorless and formless person" (*SM* 92). Apparently Iaremich, a provincial man of humble origins, who spoke Russian with a Ukrainian accent, although in Benois' words, "hardly perceptible," felt uncomfortable in the Nabokovs' aristocratic St. Petersburg home and acted in a reserved manner as the drawing master of a very precocious and gifted boy.[49] This explains why the young Nabokov's description of Iaremich as "humorless" contradicts those of him by the fellow artists who knew him intimately. Thus Dobuzhinsky writes about Iaremich: "He could sound very sardonic, but at the same time he himself would be full of the nicest disposition. Only, I often did not know whether he was speaking seriously or facetiously."[50] And Benois, Iaremich's close friend, admired the "incomparable, purely Ukrainian humor of 'Stip' [Iaremich's nickname] Iaremich."[51]

About Iaremich's teaching method Nabokov writes:

> He advocated a "bold" style, blotches of dull color, smears of sepia and olive-brown, by means of which I had to reproduce on huge sheets of gray paper, humanoid shapes that we modeled of plas-

ticine and placed in "dramatic" positions against a backcloth of velvet with all kinds of folds and shadow effects. It was a depressing combination of at least three different arts, all approximative, and finally I rebelled. (*SM* 92)

As can be seen, Nabokov thought poorly of Iaremich the teacher. What apparently irked Nabokov the most was Iaremich's disregard for detail (his being, in Nabokov's words, approximative) and his limited palette of colors. The writer, already in his boyhood, deemed detail exceptionally important (see, for example, the locomotive tender episode discussed in chapter 2) and, as we recall, professed his own great "sense of color, the love of color" (*SO* 17).

Nabokov's observation about the dullness of Iaremich's palette is corroborated by Alexander Benois, who points out that "the grayness of Iaremich's coloring was something organically inherent in him (he detested bright colors, especially the greens), and he subsequently worked out the whole doctrine that a painter could entirely manage with merely three paints: 'bone' (black paint), yellow ochre, and the whites."[52] Yet Iaremich apparently was, if not very gifted, at least a rather competent educator: in 1913, only a year after the young Nabokov's "rebellion," the renowned painter Nikolai Rerikh invited Iaremich to teach at the School of the Society for the Advancement of Arts, which he at the time directed.[53] It is obvious, however, that unlike Cumming before and Dobuzhinsky after him, Iaremich failed to establish a good rapport with the young Nabokov.

Mstislav Valerianovich Dobuzhinsky (1875–1957), who succeeded Iaremich as Nabokov's drawing master (1912–14), was born in Novgorod but grew up and spent his most formative years in St. Petersburg. He studied art at the Society for the Encouragement of the Arts in St. Petersburg (1885–87) and then privately under Lev Dmitriev-Kavkazsky (1897–99). In 1899, the year of Nabokov's birth, Dobuzhinsky, who was twenty-four years Nabokov's senior, went abroad (to Munich) for two years to continue his artistic education at the Anton Ažbe and Simon Hollósy schools of art. In 1902, a year after his return to St. Petersburg, Dobuzhinsky joined *The World of Art*.[54] By 1912, when Dobuzhinsky became the drawing master of the thirteen-year-old Nabokov, he was an accomplished painter, book illustrator, and stage designer as well as a gifted pedagogue. In 1906–11 he taught at the Elizaveta Zvantseva School of Drawing and Painting, which was also widely known as "the School of Bakst and Dobuzhinsky."

It was apparently Dobuzhinsky who prompted Nabokov to realize that his vocation was literature and to turn from the brush to the quill. Upon seeing the young Nabokov's first literary experiments, Dobuzhinsky told his pupil: "You have a talent for painting, but you must write."[55] And Dobuzhinsky was the one who trained the young Nabokov "in visual exactitude and compositional harmony,"[56] which, as the writer assessed in retrospect, he "applied gratefully [. . .] also, perhaps, to certain camera-lucida needs of literary composition" (*SM* 92). (For a detailed discussion of Dobuzhinsky's artistic career, his impact on Nabokov, and his personal and creative contacts with the writer, see chapter 4.)

* * *

Nabokov's formative milieu was that exceptionally fertile ground from which his magnificent inborn gifts sprung and evolved. First and foremost, this was due to the culturally refined and highly intellectual atmosphere that reigned in Nabokov's household, the versatility of interests of his parents, and their being at home in both Russian and western European culture. Not to a small degree, Nabokov also owes his remarkable artistic development to his growing up in St. Petersburg, the imperial capital of Russia, during the time known as the Silver Age—that spectacular epoch of cultural abundance, diversity, and spirituality—as well as to his studying at the Tenishev School, with its outstanding teachers, such as Vladimir Gippius. Finally, Nabokov's wide travels abroad during his boyhood, specifically to Paris and Berlin, where he could familiarize himself with the best examples of European art, and his lessons with Mstislav Dobuzhinsky, a distinguished artist and gifted pedagogue, who encouraged him to write, all contributed greatly to making him an intellectually, spiritually, and aesthetically refined individual, establishing his immense erudition in many fields, specifically in literature and the fine arts, and creating possibly the most illustrious writer of our modern era.

Although I have provided here a rather detailed account of Nabokov's exposure to various cultural manifestations in his formative years, I do not wish to create an impression that this phenomenon was utterly unique. Many children who grew up in Russia at the turn of the twentieth century in aristocratic and not so aristocratic households were multilingual, were exposed to the best that Russian and western European culture could offer at the time, and left a notable mark on twentieth-century Russian culture. Thus, for example, Prince Sergei Shcherbatov (1875–1962), a scion of the famous Russian aristocratic family, knew several languages, studied the fine arts abroad, and later became a painter and art patron of note; and Natalia Gershenzon-Chegodaeva (1907–77), the daughter of the renowned literary historian Mikhail Gershenzon, also knew several languages, was exposed to the best achievements in literature, art, and music, both in Russia and abroad, and eventually became a recognized art historian.[57] But it was Nabokov's remarkable memory and imagination, his innate keen senses of vision and color, his great propensity for detail, and most of all, his exceptional literary gifts and inquisitive, brilliant mind, that produced not only one of the greatest writers of the twentieth century but perhaps the last Renaissance man par excellence our civilization has ever known.

2. OLD MASTERS:
THE AUTHORIAL PRESENCE

Ogni pittore dipinge sé. [Each painter paints himself.]
—Tuscan proverb

It makes one think of the housefly an old Master would
paint on a sitter's hand to show that the person had died in
the meantime.
—Nabokov, *Look at the Harlequins!*

In chapter 1, we saw that Nabokov's interest in the art of the Old Masters was inspired in his formative years by the family's art collection
and illustrated art books, by his father's artistic tastes, and by the trea-
sures of the Hermitage and possibly those of the Kaiser Friedrich and
Louvre museums. In his adult years, Nabokov continued to display his
fascination with the art of the Old Masters. For example, while teaching at Wellesley College (1941–48), Nabokov gave a talk on Leonardo
da Vinci.[1] Leonardo had a great appeal to him on account of both
his magnificent art and his breathtaking scientific explorations—an
appeal that is manifest in Nabokov's fiction, for example, by way of
the painter's apostrophized name at the opening of Victor Wind's
poem (*Pnin* 98).[2] Owing to that same interest in science and the fine
arts, in his case lepidoptera and painting, Nabokov embarked in his
later years on the *Butterflies in Art* book project in which he intended,
among other things, to examine whether "the minutiae of evolutionary
change [can] be discerned in the pattern of a five-hundred-year-old
wing" (*SO* 168) by comparing contemporary specimens of various butterfly species to those depicted by the Old Masters.

Nabokov's oeuvre abounds with references to the art of the Old
Masters. In this regard, he is part and parcel of a long-standing literary tradition, both in Russian and western European letters. Thus, for
example, Nikolai Gogol, himself an amateur artist, speaks in his story

"The Portrait" (the 1842 redaction) of "the profundities of Raphael," the "powerful and swift brush" of Guido Reni, "the portraits by Titian," the art of Leonardo, who depicted the eyes in such a way that "the most minute, almost invisible veins were not neglected and were committed to the canvas," and referred to the old artistic schools, as for example, "the Flemish masters" or "the English school."[3] (We recall that Nabokov published a monograph on Gogol in 1944.) And Marcel Proust, Nabokov's older contemporary, although he "never touched a brush," was a great aficionado and connoisseur of painting and makes numerous allusions to artists and their artwork, specifically Old Masters, in his celebrated *In Search of Lost Time* (*À la recherche du temps perdu*, 1913–27), also known under the title *Remembrance of Things Past*.[4] (Nabokov lectured on Proust's magnum opus at Cornell University.)

Both Gogol and Proust employ references to the Old Masters and their art not merely for reference's sake but rather to advance ideas or to delineate their literary characters. For example, in mentioning Leonardo's attention to the eyes, Gogol intimates that, by contrast, the artist who created the portrait in his story went so far as to depict "alive [. . .], human eyes" that "actually destroyed the harmony of the portrait" so that "this was no longer art."[5] Harmony, then, Gogol avers, is the quintessence of art. And in *Taras Bulba* (the 1842 redaction), in the episode in which Andrii and his companion, a Tartar woman, move clandestinely through a tunnel toward the besieged Polish city of Dubno, Gogol writes that "the light grew brighter and, walking on together, now throwing a brilliant light, now casting a coal-black shadow, they resembled the paintings of Gerardo della Notte."[6] Here Gogol refers to Gerrit van Honthorst, a Dutch painter, a follower of Caravaggio, whom he calls by his Italian nickname. Honthorst, we recall, favored chiaroscuro, the interplay of light and dark, but unlike Caravaggio, he preferred night scenes (whence his nickname) with artificial light, particularly candlelight.[7] The chiaroscuro bears here a symbolic meaning. The narrator's remark about the light and dark successively enveloping Andrii together with his companion, the Tartar maidservant, reinforces the reader's impression of certain similarities between them: indeed, Andrii, a Ukrainian Cossack, like the Tartar maid, is serving the enemy. Andrii, however, does so voluntarily, a captive of his love for a Polish maiden. In addition, the light and dark in this tunnel that connects the Cossack Orthodox and the Polish Catholic worlds figuratively suggest that Andrii, abandoning his family, comrades in arms, native land, and Orthodox faith, all for his obsessive love, is crossing a moral boundary.[8]

Proust, on the other hand, employs art not so much for didactic purposes but rather to impart an impression, to evoke an association, or, to put it differently, to "set off scenes, situations, resemblances, and types that re-create or restage the art of the masters."[9] Thus, for example, Proust demonstrates Swann's dubious attempt to introduce Odette, his uncultured, philistine mistress and later his wife, "into a world of dreams and fancies which, until then, she had been debarred from entering, and where she assumed a new and nobler form" by linking her image to "Florentine painting," and particularly to Botticelli's Zipporah in his *Scenes from the Life of Moses,* or to the figure of Spring in his *Primavera.*[10] It is noteworthy in this regard that in his Cornell lectures on Proust, Nabokov points out Swann's or the narrator's ability to see "the physical appearance of this or that character in terms of paintings by famous old masters, many of them of the Florentine School" (*LL* 228).

Nabokov was an intrinsic part of this literary practice. For example, in *The Defense* (1929–30) Nabokov describes a visit by Luzhin (who apparently has never been to an art exhibit before) and his wife to Berlin's Kaiser Friedrich Museum and the protagonist's childlike reactions to paintings, to emphasize his aesthetically uncultivated personality. In addition, Nabokov shares with the reader, under the guise of Luzhin's wife, his prized observations about art schools, individual artists, and their concrete paintings. Such, for example, is a remark that "in Flanders, where they had rain and fog, painters used bright colors, while it was in Spain, a country of sunshine, that the gloomiest master of all [presumably Goya] had been born" (*Def* 190). And in *Look at the Harlequins!,* similarly to Proust's Swann, Vadim Vadimovich likens Annette to Botticelli's figure of Spring to convey the adoration of his narrator and protagonist for *his* uncultured and philistine "Odette." This heretofore unnoticed allusion to Proust, charged with subtle irony, sheds additional light on the characters (see the section on *Look at the Harlequins!* later in this chapter).[11]

At the same time, Nabokov is unique in that he makes frequent references or allusions to works of art for the sake of authorial presence, a device that has been customarily employed in various creative media,

including literature and the fine arts. This aspect of Nabokov's fascination with the Old Masters and his propensity for the device come
to the fore in his examination of Joyce's *Ulysses*. He draws his Cornell
students' attention to Joyce's "Man in the Brown Macintosh," whose
identity the writer interprets as follows:

> Do we know who he is? I think we do. The clue comes in chap-
> ter 4 of part two, the scene at the library. Stephen is discussing
> Shakespeare and affirms that Shakespeare himself is present in
> his, Shakespeare's, works. Shakespeare, he says, tensely: "He has
> hidden his own name, a fair name, William, in the plays, a super
> here, a clown there, as a painter of old Italy set his face in a dark
> corner of his canvas. . . ." and this is exactly what Joyce has done—
> setting his face in a dark corner of this canvas. The Man in the
> Brown Macintosh who passes through the dream of the book is
> no other than the author himself. Bloom glimpses his maker! (*LL*
> 319–20)[12]

As this passage indicates, Nabokov was fascinated with the authorial
presence not only in the works of other literati, his predecessors and
contemporaries, such as Shakespeare and Joyce, but also in those of
painters, specifically the Old Masters.[13] Furthermore, like the Old Masters, Nabokov tends to encode his own presence as author in his texts,
a habit that has long been noted by Nabokov scholars.[14] To be sure,
Nabokov enciphers it in many different ways, such as anagrams, his
pen name of the "Russian years" (Sirin), and his birthday that falls on
Saint George's Day. What makes Nabokov so unique is that he turns
to works of art, and specifically to the Old Masters' well-known chefs
d'oeuvre, to encode his own presence, or that of his loved ones, or to
mark an important familial event. And it is noteworthy that, in doing
so, he at times employs the works of art in which the Old Masters themselves encoded their presence or that of their loved ones.

PNIN: JAN VAN EYCK'S *MADONNA OF CANON VAN DER PAELE*

One case in point is Nabokov's novel *Pnin* (1957), in which the writer
mentions the most prominent representatives of Early Netherlandish

art, also known as the Flemish Primitives, and explicitly refers to Jan van Eyck's *Madonna of Canon van der Paele*. What Nabokov apparently found especially appealing in Early Netherlandish art was its close attention to the details of objects through their reflection in a convex mirror. Nabokov evidently possessed an innate proclivity for detail that he later perfected under the tutelage of Dobuzhinsky (see chapter 4). Already in his boyhood, Nabokov demonstrated his ability to pay close attention to the minutiae of his surroundings. Thus, he recalls that as a boy he asked his first drawing master, Henry Cumming, to draw an express train for him:

> I watched his pencil ably evolve the cowcatcher and elaborate headlights of a locomotive that looked as if it had been acquired secondhand for the Trans-Siberian line after it had done duty at Promontory Point, Utah, in the sixties. Then came five disappointingly plain carriages. When he had quite finished them, he carefully shaded the ample smoke coming from the huge funnel, cocked his head, and, after a moment of pleased contemplation, handed me the drawing. I tried to look pleased, too. He had forgotten the tender. (*SM* 93)

As this very telling passage demonstrates, Nabokov the boy pays the closest attention to minute details and exhibits distinctive attitude toward and aptitude for precision of expression. In recounting this episode, Nabokov emblematically encapsulates and drives home the vital importance of detail: a tender, as we recall, is a car attached to a locomotive for carrying a supply of fuel and water, and therefore a long-distance train without a tender cannot reach its destination.

The utmost importance that Nabokov the writer attached to detail is evident already in his early story "The Fight" (1925), at the close of which the narrator is musing: "Or perhaps what matters is not the human pain or joy at all but, rather, the play of shadow and light on a live body, the harmony of trifles assembled on this particular day, at this particular moment, in a unique and inimitable way" (*Stories* 146). And many years later, in his Cornell lectures, Nabokov taught his students to "notice and fondle details" (*LL* 1), "divine details,"[15] in order to understand better "the work of art [which] is invariably the creation of a new world" (*LL* 1). Nabokov's fascination with the convex mirror presumably originated in his passion for lepidopterous research in which the employment of a microscope, with another curviform surface, a convex lens, is essential. Nabokov scrupulously and masterfully describes the entire process of collecting and studying butterflies, including the use of the microscope, in his poem "On Discovering a Butterfly" (1943).[16]

Let us now focus on the human eye, of which the convex mirror could be considered a distant man-made variant.[17] The primary importance of the sense of vision has been known in European culture from time immemorial, so much so that scholars dubbed Western philosophy "a philosophy of light, vision, and enlightenment."[18] And it is noteworthy that Nicholas of Cusa (ca. 1400–1464), a German theologian and philosopher, and a contemporary of Early Netherlandish artists, in his treatise characteristically entitled *The Vision of God* (*De visione Dei*, 1453), describes the all-seeing God as the Infinite Eye.[19] It is telling that Nicholas of Cusa metaphorically presents his idea of the Almighty's omnivoyance by recalling, among other works, the self-portrait of his exact coeval Rogier van der Weyden, with "its face, by the painter's cunning art, being made to appear as though looking on all around it."[20]

For Nabokov, the primary importance of the eye and of the man-made convex surfaces was prompted by his aspiration in boyhood and early youth to become a painter and by his entomological studies.[21] This importance is evident in his fiction. Thus, the narrator of "Spring in Fialta" (1936) asserts:

> I am opening like an eye, amidst the city on a steep street, taking in everything at once: that marine rococo on the stand, and the coral crucifixes in a shop window, and the dejected poster of a visiting circus, one corner of its drenched paper detached from the wall, and a yellow bit of unripe orange peel on the old, slate-blue sidewalk, which retained here and there a fading memory of ancient mosaic design. (*Stories* 413)[22]

And the poem "Oculus" (1939) contains a fantasy:

> To a single colossal oculus,
> without lids, without face, without brow,
> without halo of marginal flesh,
> man is finally limited now.[23]

Nabokov expresses a very similar sentiment in his penultimate short story "The Vane Sisters" (1951): "I walked on in a state of raw awareness that seemed to transform the whole of my being into one big eyeball rolling in the world's socket" (*Stories* 619). On a more fatidic and whimsical plane, Nabokov was mindful that his surname contains the Russian word for "oculus"—*oko*. Ellendea Proffer, who designed the dust jacket for her husband Carl's *A Book of Things About Vladimir Nabokov*, conveys this notion graphically to the reader in the most ingenious manner.[24]

In addition to assigning to the eye, time and again, such a telling and prominent role in his fiction, Nabokov employs man-made convex surfaces, examples of which can already be found in his early Russian works. Thus, in the *kursaal* episode of *King, Queen, Knave*, Nabokov's second novel, febrile Martha observes that "glossy blue, red, green balloons bobbed on long strings and each contained the entire ballroom, and the chandeliers, and the tables, and herself" (*KQK* 252). (For an altogether different perception of the *kursaal* episode, see chapter 6.)

One of the primary functions that Nabokov assigns to the convex mirror is the manifestation of his authorial presence.[25] Such a manifestation is alluded to, for example, in the above-quoted *kursaal* episode in Martha's observation that the balloons' convex surfaces reflect "the entire ballroom." This "entire ballroom" in particular includes Martha's dancing partner, Blavdak Vinomori, the anagrammatized representation of Vladimir Nabokov. And toward the end of the *kursaal* episode and of the whole chapter, Franz notices that "the foreign girl in the blue dress danced with a remarkably handsome man in an old-fashioned dinner jacket" (*KQK* 254). As Franz recalls, "they had appeared to him in fleeting glimpses, like a recurrent dream image or a subtle leitmotif—now at the beach, now in a café, now on the promenade. Sometimes the man carried a butterfly net" (ibid.). To leave no doubt who this couple is, Nabokov paints a verbal portrait of his wife Véra and of himself: "The girl had a delicately painted mouth and tender gray-blue eyes, and her fiancé or husband [was] slender, elegantly balding" (ibid.). In the foreword to the English translation of the novel Nabokov admits, as he puts it, that these were "the appearances of my wife and me in the last two chapters" for "merely visits of inspection" (*KQK* viii).[26]

These strong propensities of his boyhood and early youth were what Nabokov may have bestowed in *Pnin* on the fourteen-year-old Victor Wind, a gifted, budding artist. At the same time, Nabokov endows his character with the knowledge of Early Netherlandish art that he in all probability acquired at the time of writing the novel. There is little doubt that Nabokov was familiar with *Early Netherlandish Painting*, a monumental study by Erwin Panofsky (1892–1968), an art historian of world renown.[27] It is worth noting some similarities between the lives of these two men who left an indelible mark on the culture of our time: born in the same decade into highly cultured families, both Nabokov and Panofsky grew up in turn-of-the-century Europe—Russia and Germany, respectively. Both were professionally highly regarded in their native languages and for over a decade shared Germany as their country of residence. Like Nabokov, "providentially, Panofsky escaped from Nazi Germany unscathed" to the United States, joined academia (in his case, Princeton University), and made the English language his primary medium of creative expression.[28]

Nabokov's familiarity with and great appreciation of Panofsky's work are evident in his letter to Edmund Wilson of August 7, 1957, in which he reveals that his "source for understanding *et in Arcadia ego,* meaning 'I (Death) (exist) even in Arcady,' is an excellent essay in Erwin Panofsky's *The Meaning of the Visual Arts,* Anchor Books, New York, 1955" (*NWL* 354).[29]

Panofsky's *Early Netherlandish Painting* appeared in print in 1953, when Nabokov had begun working on *Pnin.* There is a good possibility, however, that Nabokov became familiar with Panofsky's ideas on Early Netherlandish art several years prior to the book's publication. Panofsky's study in question grew out of the Norton lectures that he delivered while on his 1947–48 sabbatical leave at Harvard. That year, Nabokov still resided in Cambridge, Massachusetts (it was his last year of teaching at Wellesley College and working at the Harvard Museum of Comparative Zoology before joining Cornell University), and it is not unlikely that he attended some of Panofsky's lectures.

Nabokov credits Dobuzhinsky with teaching him to be observant of details. It is unclear, however, whether Nabokov knew at the time of studying with Dobuzhinsky that close attention to detail constitutes an important innovation of Early Netherlandish artists. But even if he did not, he certainly realized its significance at the time of writing

Pnin, most likely under the influence of Panofsky's study. In particular, Panofsky attributes to Early Netherlandish artists, especially to Jan van Eyck, that "all-embracing, yet selective, 'naturalism' which distilled for the beholder an untold wealth of visual enchantment from everything created by God or contrived by man."[30] As Panofsky maintains, "Jan van Eyck's style may be said to symbolize that structure of the universe which had emerged at his time, [. . .] he builds his world out of pigments as nature builds hers out of primary matter."[31] Following in the footsteps of Early Netherlandish artists and being familiar with their artistic innovations as described by Panofsky, Nabokov was well aware that attention to detail in his fictional universe manifests the presence of V. N., although not Visible Nature as in the paintings of his fifteenth-century predecessors, but rather the human bearer of its initials, "an anthropomorphic deity" (*BS* xii).[32]

Let us now turn to the episode in *Pnin*, central to our discussion, which reflects Victor Wind's (and apparently his creator's) fascination with Early Netherlandish painting and its artistic achievements:

> In the chrome plating, in the glass of a sun-rimmed headlamp, he [Victor] would see a view of the street and himself comparable to the microcosmic version of a room (with a dorsal view of diminutive people) in that very special and very magical small convex mirror that, half a millennium ago, Van Eyck and Petrus Christus and Memling used to paint into their detailed interiors, behind the sour merchant or the domestic Madonna. (*Pnin* 97–98)[33]

In this passage, Nabokov singles out Jan van Eyck (ca. 1395–1441), Petrus Christus (ca. 1410–75), and Hans Memling (ca. 1440–94). Upon close examination of this passage, it is possible to identify the specific paintings by these three artists that Nabokov presumably had in mind. In referring to van Eyck, Nabokov alludes, of course, to his *Arnolfini Wedding Portrait* (1434; National Gallery, London) as well as to the *Madonna of Canon van der Paele* that is named toward the end of the novel. (It is noteworthy that in his interview with Alfred Appel, conducted in September 1966, Nabokov refers to his fictional world as "*The Artist's Studio* by Van Bock" [*SO* 73]. In this phrase, aside from Nabokov's obvious self-reference—his given and last-name initials in *Van* as well as an anagrammatic allusion to his last name in *Van Bock*—there looms a possible hint to van Eyck.)[34] In these two paintings, van Eyck portrays, respectively, to quote Nabokov, "the sour merchant" (together with his bride) and "the domestic Madonna." In both of these paintings van Eyck employs convex surfaces—the mirror in the former and the polished metal of the armor in the latter—which are believed to reflect the artist's own image.[35] In the case of Petrus Christus, Nabokov evidently refers to *Saint Eligius as a Goldsmith* (1449; Metropolitan Museum of Art, New York), in which this follower and possible student of van Eyck portrays the patron saint of the goldsmiths' guild in the guise of a goldsmith (another "sour merchant") and also employs a convex mirror which reflects two figures reduced in size, or as Nabokov puts it, "diminutive people." In mentioning Memling, Nabokov alludes to the painter's *Madonna and Child with Martin van Nieuwenhove* (1487; Saint John's Hospital, Brugge). In this diptych, Memling employs a convex mirror that reflects both the Virgin and the donor, thereby "evidencing" the latter's presence at the scene.[36]

In the above-quoted passage from *Pnin*, Nabokov also highlights the three interlocking characteristics of Early Netherlandish art for which, as was mentioned earlier, he had a strong predilection in his own creative work: attention to detail, fascination with the convex mirror, and authorial presence reflected in such a mirror. As a verbal artist endowed with extraordinary visual acuity, Nabokov pays the closest attention to details by thoroughly employing in his own creative process that natural convex surface—the eye. As an accomplished entomologist he was mindful that a man-made convex surface, such as a lens in the microscope, which by the way was invented in the Netherlands some 175 years after van Eyck, also changes, and in this case enhances, the perception of objects and enables one to observe their minute, otherwise imperceptible, details. And finally, Nabokov employs the convex mirror, not unlike van Eyck, as a device for the manifestation of his authorial presence.

This presence is implied when Victor (who shares artistic sensibilities with his creator) sees himself "in the chrome plating" and by the subsequent mention of van Eyck. It becomes evident, however, only toward the end of the novel, in the protagonist's housewarming party episode, which contains a description of van Eyck's *Madonna of Canon van der Paele* (figure 2). Nabokov presents the painting in a somewhat caricatured fashion as an "ample-jowled, fluff-haloed Canon van der

2. Jan van Eyck, *Madonna of Canon van der Paele*

Paele, seized by a fit of abstraction in the presence of the puzzled Virgin to whom a super, rigged up as St. George, is directing the good Canon's attention" (*Pnin* 154). The mention of this painting occurs ostensibly because Laurence Clements, Pnin's university colleague and former landlord, bears a "striking resemblance" to the Canon (ibid.). In fact, Nabokov's mention of van Eyck's masterpiece intricately alludes to vicissitudes in the life of the title character and his pronouncements on the history of humanity, as well as to the authorial presence in the novel.

The sculptures and capital reliefs in the painting that represent episodes from the Old Testament suggest these hardships in Pnin's life.[37] Thus, *Adam and Eve, Cain Murdering Abel,* and *The Sacrifice of Isaac* illuminate Pnin's pronouncement, based in no small degree on his personal experiences—his loss of parents, close friends, and the country of his birth in the massive cataclysms that befell his native Russia and

Europe as a whole in the interwar years, as well as his heartbreaking divorce and ill treatment at the hands of his ex-wife and some colleagues at Waindell University—that "the history of man is the history of pain" (*Pnin* 168). The scenes depicting *Abraham's Victory over Chederlaomer,* *Samson Killing the Lion,* and *David Slaying Goliath,* on the other hand, foreshadow the title character's eventual triumph over his enemies when his creator-rescuer takes him along "the shining road, which one could make out narrowing to a thread of gold in the soft mist where hill after hill made beauty of distance, and where there was simply no saying what miracle might happen" (*Pnin* 191; see also chapter 3).

The key to understanding the authorial presence in the novel is not "the good Canon" but rather Saint George, his saint protector. (One might note in passing that the other saint, Saint Donatian, is pointedly absent from the novel's description of the painting.) Upon closer examination of Saint George's armor in van Eyck's painting one can discern—on a buckler, behind his left shoulder—a reflection of a human figure, which is believed to be that of the artist himself. Here van Eyck's self-portrait as a reflection in the armor of Saint George suggests Nabokov's authorial presence by way of birthday, as the writer celebrated his on April 23—Saint George's Day.[38] Van Eyck's self-representation could also draw Nabokov's attention, as it appears "on the side," in Russian *na boku,* of Saint George's armor. Further, by mentioning van Eyck's painting, Nabokov implies his own authorial presence both chromesthetically and anagrammatically: Van Eyck's vermilion hat and hose and a dark blue mantle in his image, reflected in Saint George's armor, could also attract Nabokov, since *V* and *S,* the initials of his first name, Vladimir, and of his pen name, Sirin, in the writer's chromesthetic system belong to the red and blue groups, while the Russian rendition of the color combination red-and-blue, *krasno-sinii,* anagrammatically suggests *Sirin.*[39]

The authorial presence is reinforced in this same episode when Joan Clements, Laurence's wife, ostensibly speaks of some unidentified writer but clearly refers to Nabokov: "But don't you think—haw—that what he is trying to do—haw—practically in all his novels—haw—is—haw—to express the fantastic recurrence of certain situations?" (*Pnin* 159). Joan's "fetching way" "of interrupting her sentences, to punctuate a clause or gather new momentum, by deep hawing pants" (ibid.) is designed to underscore the importance of the pronouncement and to draw the reader's attention to it. As Gennady Barabtarlo has perceptively commented, the pronouncement itself sums up "the principal feature of *Pnin's* composition and of Nabokov's novelistic art in general."[40]

Following in the footsteps of Early Netherlandish artists, particularly Jan van Eyck, Nabokov uses the convex mirror for the manifestation of his authorial presence. But while Early Netherlandish artists included their image merely reflected in the convex mirror, and not among the painting's main cast,[41] Nabokov manifests his authorial presence as "that other V. N." (*SO* 153), the deity that rules his fictional universe in a multitude of diverse ways, of which the convex mirror is but one example.

THE GIFT: REMBRANDT'S DEPOSITION FROM THE CROSS

Rembrandt and his art are frequently referred or alluded to in Nabokov's works. For example, *King, Queen, Knave* contains references to "the air of Rembrandt" and "the brightest Rembrandtesque gleam" (*KQK* 91 and 154), and "The Visit to the Museum" similarly refers to "a copper helmet with a Rembrandtesque gleam" (*Stories* 282). The latter phrase brings to mind such paintings by or attributed to Rembrandt as *The Man with the Golden Helmet* (ca. 1650; Gemäldegalerie, Staatliche Museen zu Berlin), *Mars* (1655; Art Gallery and Museum, Glasgow), and its assumed pendant *Pallas Athena* (1663; until 1930 in the Hermitage Museum, St. Petersburg; presently in the Museu Calouste Gulbenkian, Lisbon).[42] And in *Ada,* Nabokov metaphorically and most succinctly conveys the essence of Rembrandt's art in a way that outweighs many volumes written on the illustrious Dutchman: "Remembrance, like Rembrandt, is dark but festive" (*Ada* 103).

In addition to these generic references that imply Rembrandt's predilection for the interplay of light and shadow, the generally somber tones of his palette, and at the same time the gladsome nature of his art, Nabokov points to specific works by the Dutch master. Thus, Rembrandt's *Christ at Emmaus,* also known as *The Pilgrims at Emmaus,* or *Supper at Emmaus* (1648; Musée du Louvre, Paris), is mentioned in *Pnin.* In this novel, a "reproduction of the head of Christ" from this painting, "with the same, though slightly less celestial, expression of eyes and mouth" (*Pnin* 95), is hanging in the studio of Lake, Victor's art teacher. Twenty years earlier, Nabokov alludes to Christ's countenance in this painting in the description of Cincinnatus's face, with a similar emphasis on the eyes and the mouth, when speaking of "the dispersing and again gathering rays in his animated eyes" and of "the light outline of his lips, seemingly not quite fully drawn but touched by a master of masters" (*IB* 121).[43]

Another reference to Rembrandt's particular work can be found in *The Gift*. In his *Life of Chernyshevski*, Fyodor Godunov-Cherdyntsev, the protagonist of the novel, sarcastically notes that biographers viewed the author of *What Is to Be Done* as "Christ the Second" and

> mark[ed] his thorny path with evangelical signposts [. . .] Chernyshevski's passions began when he reached Christ's age. Here the role of Judas was filled by Vsevolod Kostomarov; the role of Peter by the famous poet Nekrasov, who declined to visit the jailed man. Corpulent Herzen, ensconced in London, called Chernyshevski's pillory column "The companion piece of the Cross." And in a famous Nekrasov iambic there was more about the Crucifixion, about the fact that Chernyshevski had been "sent to remind the earthly kings of Christ." Finally, when he was completely dead and they were washing his body, that thinness, that steepness of the ribs, that *dark pallor* of the skin and those long toes vaguely reminded one of his intimates of "The Removal from the Cross"—by Rembrandt, is it? (*Gift* 215; italics in original)[44]

While, as the passage indicates, Fyodor is not quite certain who painted the canvas in question, Nabokov, of course, is fully aware of Rembrandt's authorship and employs the "by Rembrandt, is it?" phrase as an emphatic, attention-drawing device.

There are at least five versions of Rembrandt's *Deposition* [*Descent*] *from the Cross* to which Fyodor hesitantly refers here: three paintings, one located at the Alte Pinakothek in Munich, the other at the Hermitage Museum in St. Petersburg (both date from 1634), and the third at the National Gallery of Art in Washington, D.C. (ca. 1651), as well as two etchings (1633; see figure 3) and *The Descent from the Cross by Torch-*

3. Rembrandt Harmensz van Rijn, *The Deposition from the Cross* (etching)

light (1654). Knowing Nabokov's penchant for the authorial presence, it is highly likely that he had the earlier etching in mind—the only variant that contains a person bearing the artist's easily recognizable features.[45] It is of course the individual standing on the ladder and supporting Christ's left arm. To Nabokov's choice points the phrase "those long toes," which look more prominent in the etching. This assertion is also validated by the novel's description of the work of art as depicting "that *dark pallor* of the skin" and "steepness of the ribs": these attributes appear more pronounced in the etching in which the body of Jesus is lit with somewhat dim and suffused backlighting. In the paintings, on the other hand, the body of Christ is shown in brighter light and therefore does not give this impression. In addition, both the National Gallery of Art painting and the later etching do not match Nabokov's description, since the "steepness of the ribs" is obscured in them by one of the individuals lowering the corpse of Jesus.

Furthermore, when referring to the *Deposition from the Cross*, Nabokov apparently also intended to invoke *Raising of the Cross* (figure 4), to which the *Deposition from the Cross* served as the pendant. In *Raising of the Cross*, Rembrandt portrayed himself once again, but this time as the soldier who helps to lift the cross to which the body of Jesus is nailed.[46] By juxtaposing these two pieces in which Rembrandt assigned such diametrically opposing roles to his own image, one may conclude that the artist wished to convey the message of collective human guilt, including his own, for the death of Jesus. At the same time, he evidently wished to show penitence when depicting himself as the sorrowful figure, in anguish, who helps lower Christ's corpse from the cross.[47] By mentioning Rembrandt's *Deposition from the Cross* and by invoking his *Raising of the Cross*, Nabokov seems to suggest a more humane role for his protagonist who is credited with the authorship of the novel about Nikolai Chernyshevsky's life.

Earlier in *The Gift*, Nabokov teaches Fyodor a lesson against stereotyping. Upon riding a tram, Fyodor is seized with prejudice against Germans, even though it was, "he knew, a conviction unworthy of an artist" (*Gift* 80). When another passenger boards the tram, Fyodor directs his hostile thoughts toward this man, discovering his more and more unattractive, "typically German," features. While Fyodor "threaded the points of his biased indictment, looking at the man who sat opposite him," all of a sudden, the fellow passenger took a copy of the Rus-

4. Rembrandt Harmensz van Rijn, *Raising of the Cross*

sian émigré newspaper from his pocket "and coughed unconcernedly with a Russian intonation" (*Gift* 82).[48] Fyodor fully comprehends the message that life, or rather his creator, sends him: "That's wonderful, thought Fyodor, almost smiling with delight. How clever, how gracefully sly and how essentially good life is!" (ibid.). This earlier ethical lesson prepares Fyodor for a more complex and benevolent world perception, so important not only in his task of writing the Chernyshevsky biography but also "the autobiography," something he will be "a long time preparing" (*Gift* 364).

The reference and allusion to Rembrandt's two pieces shed light on Fyodor's, and Nabokov's own, dual approach to "Christ the Second": on the one hand, the protagonist exhibits disdain toward Chernyshevsky, philosopher, writer, literary critic, and aesthetician; and on the other, he demonstrates compassion when admiring Chernyshevsky's personal courage and the steadfastness of his beliefs. Thus, Fyodor "began to comprehend by degrees that such uncompromising radicals as Chernyshevski, with all their ludicrous and ghastly blunders, were, no matter how you looked at it, real heroes in their struggle with the governmental order of things" (*Gift* 202–3). This dual approach clearly reflects Nabokov's own attitude toward Chernyshevsky, "whose works," as he puts it, "I found risible, but whose fate moved me more strongly than did Gogol's" (*SO* 156). In so doing, the writer advocates "mercy toward the downfallen" (*EO*, 2:311) in the compassionate tradition of Pushkin, whom he revered, and in accordance with the best liberal convictions of his own family.[49] In the spirit of Rembrandt's Passion masterpieces, Nabokov teaches his protagonist to be more benevolent and to seek redeeming features in every fellow human, no matter how "risible" he may appear.

Unlike in Joyce's *Ulysses* in which, as Nabokov puts it, "Bloom glimpses his maker" and in Nabokov's own *King, Queen, Knave,* in which Franz glimpses his, the writer does not appear in person in *The Gift,* but rather like the most creative "of his rivals" (see *SO* 32) is omnipresent and yet invisible. Nabokov's authorial presence is specifically manifest in his last Russian novel by way of references and allusions to Rembrandt's masterpieces, in which the Dutch master depicted his own persona in diametrically opposed hypostases, and through the humanity and humility lesson he teaches one of his most gifted and receptive protagonists.

LOOK AT THE HARLEQUINS!: BOTTICELLI'S *PRIMAVERA*

Nabokov's oeuvre abounds with references to Botticelli and his art. In *Laughter in the Dark,* the blind Albinus attempts in his mind "to transform the incoherent sound into corresponding shapes and colors" (*Laugh* 241), and this mental operation is described as "the opposite of trying to imagine the kind of voices which Botticelli's angels had" (*Laugh* 241–42). Here Nabokov seems to suggest Botticelli's *Virgin and Child with Eight Angels* (ca. 1481–83), the painting to which he earlier alludes in *The Defense.* We recall that Luzhin's wife guides the protagonist through Berlin's Kaiser Friedrich Museum and draws his attention to the artwork of "this one [who] liked lilies and tender faces slightly inflamed by colds caught in heaven" (*Def* 190–91 and *Ssoch,* 2:423 and 715). In this description, the painting, along with *Virgin and Child Enthroned Between Saint John the Baptist and Saint John Evangelist* (1484; both are presently at the Gemäldegalerie, Staatliche Museen zu Berlin), can be unmistakably identified. This "cold" motif resurfaces once again in *Bend Sinister* (1947) when Ember describes Ophelia and asserts that "the uncommon cold of a Botticellian angel tinged her nostrils with pink and suffused her upperlip—you know, when the rims of the lips merge with the skin" (*BS* 114). Ember's assertion is later refracted in *Look at the Harlequins!,* in Vadim Vadimovich's pronouncement that "the mad scholar in *Esmeralda and Her Parandrus* wreathes Botticelli and Shakespeare together by having Primavera end as Ophelia with all her flowers" (*LATH* 162).[50] Incidentally, Ember's assertion and Vadim's pronouncement seem to allude to John Everett Millais's *Ophelia* (1851; Tate Gallery, London), which depicts the Shakespearean heroine floating dead in the stream, covered with a multitude of flowers. It is worth noting that Millais and other Pre-Raphaelites contributed a great deal to the rediscovery of Botticelli and prepared the ground for seminal works on the illustrious Florentine by Hermann Ulmann, Herbert P. Horne, Aby Warburg, and Jacques Mesnil.[51]

In *Lolita,* when thinking of the title heroine, Humbert speaks of "those wet, matted eyelashes," evidently referring to Botticelli's *Birth of Venus* (ca.1484–86; Galleria degli Uffizi, Florence), which he names later in the novel when comparing the girl to "Botticelli's russet Venus—the same soft nose, the same blurred beauty" (*AnL* 64, 270 and 366, 439).

Humbert also points to "that tinge of Botticellian pink" (*AnL* 64 and 366) that is manifest in the Three Graces in *Primavera* (ca. 1482; Galleria degli Uffizi, Florence). In the Ur-*Lolita* novella, *The Enchanter* (written in 1939), Nabokov speaks of "a priceless original: sleeping girl, oil. Her face in its soft nest of curls, scattered here, wadded together there, with those little fissures on her parched lips, and that special crease in the eyelids over the barely joined lashes, had a russet, roseate tint where the lighted cheek—whose Florentine outline was a smile in itself— showed through" (*En* 70). The description reads like a curious cross between Botticelli's *Birth of Venus* and Giorgione's *Sleeping Venus* (ca. 1510; Gemäldegalerie, Staatliche Kunstsammlungen, Dresden).[52]

Finally, in *Look at the Harlequins!*, his last completed novel, Nabokov refers to *Primavera* directly. In his letter, which contains the marriage proposal to Annette Blagovo, Vadim Vadimovich, the bedridden protagonist of the novel, implores his addressee:

> Do not write, do not phone, do not mention this letter, if and when you come Friday afternoon; but, please, if you do, wear, in propitious sign, the Florentine hat that looks like a cluster of wild flowers. I want you to celebrate your resemblance to the fifth girl from left to right, the flower-decked blonde with the straight nose and serious gray eyes, in Botticelli's *Primavera*, an allegory of Spring, my love, my allegory. (*LATH* 107)

Contextually, this is the protagonist's love letter and marriage proposal. Metatextually, however, it may be perceived as Nabokov's own profession of love for his wife Véra. Earlier I have already discussed Nabokov's authorial presence in his oeuvre, specifically its pictorial manifestations. But is Véra, his wife, his Muse, his counsel for more than half a century, present in his works? When asked about this in one of his interviews, Nabokov responded: "Most of my works have been dedicated to my wife and her picture has often been reproduced by some mysterious means of reflected color in the inner mirrors of my books" (*SO* 191). In some cases the "reproductions" of Véra's "picture" are more discernible than in others. As I noted earlier in this chapter, Véra appears, alongside her husband, toward the end of *King, Queen, Knave* as the girl with "a delicately painted mouth and tender gray-blue eyes" which, by Nabokov's own admission, refers to "the appearances of my wife and me in the last two chapters" as "merely visits of inspection" (*KQK* 254 and viii). Véra appears once again in chapter 15 of *Speak, Memory* as the narrator's interlocutor whom he addresses as "you." Another example of Véra's presence, albeit rather surreptitious, can be detected in Nabokov's earlier poem "The Skater." We recall its final quatrain, which consists of the following lines:

> I left behind a single verbal figure,
> an instantly unfolding flower, inked.
> And yet tomorrow, vertical and silent,
> the snow will dust the scribble-scrabbled rink.[53]

These lines anagrammatically contain a dedication, as indicated by the boldfaced Cyrillic letters in the original Russian: To Véra Evseevna Slonim Vladimir Nabokov Sirin (see note 53). The poem was written on February 5, 1925, that is, a little over two months before Vladimir and Véra were married (April 15), and Nabokov evidently intended this poem as a gift to his bride.[54]

Returning to the above-quoted passage from *Look at the Harlequins!*, we may perceive it, together with the entire novel, for that matter, beyond its contextual meaning, as Nabokov's own affirmation of love for his wife of almost fifty years. It appears that Nabokov distributes Véra's traits among some of the novel's female characters. He endows **Lyubov Serafimovn**a **S**avich—whose name contains an anagram of Véra's maiden name, Véra Slonim—with Véra's excellent typing skills, her ability to recite his every poem by heart, and her remembering "thousands of enchanting minutiae scattered through all my novels" (*LATH* 83). He endows Annette Blagovo with some of Véra's attractive physical features, and bestows his adoration of Véra on the last wife of Vadim, the "you" of the novel, whom the protagonist calls "my ultimate, my immortal one" (*LATH* 122). As Brian Boyd has noted, "and it is You who helps retrieve Vadim from the realization of his worst fears, You who restores him to his self and who points beyond it [. . .] And in a very clear sense this You is also Véra Nabokov, the 'you' of *Speak, Memory*."[55] Boyd has also astutely remarked that "*Look at the Harlequins!* pays grateful homage to a woman modeled upon Véra."[56] Boyd has further observed with regard to *Look at the Harlequins!*:

A novel that appears compulsively self-referential turns out to focus on the transcendence of self; a novel that seems terminally narcissistic turns out to be a love-song, and no less passionate for all its play. And what especially interested me as a biographer was that Nabokov's career, dedicated unrelentingly to his art, and his life, devoted utterly to Véra, had begun to make a new sort of sense together.[57]

The latter assertion becomes especially pertinent if we realize that it is the virtues and talents of Véra, and her lifelong commitment to her husband, along with Nabokov's own literary brilliance, that made him one of the greatest writers of our time, in complete contradistinction to mediocre and philistine Annette, Vadim's wife of twelve years, who enjoyed reading the run-of-the-mill Galsworthy and Dostoevsky (*LATH* 98–99), and who was totally indifferent to her husband's writings. The same insurmountable distance lies between Nabokov himself and Vadim Vadimovich, whose name is merely a slur of Vladimir Vladimirovich (see *LATH* 249), Nabokov's given name and patronymic. And of course Vadim's literary talent is vastly inferior to that of Nabokov, his ultimate prototype, and his life and art are but "a parody, an inferior variant" (*LATH* 89) of those of his creator.

There are many clues in support of the notion that the novel constitutes Nabokov's homage to Véra. First of all, the novel's private nickname (*Look at the Masks!*) alludes to Vladimir's and Véra's first meeting at the charity ball where she wore a wolf mask.[58] And as Boyd intimates, "in all likelihood, the whole novel was a tribute to the kind fate that united them."[59] The very name of Botticelli's painting mentioned in the above-quoted passage, *Primavera,* Italian for "spring," as often the case with Nabokov, points to multilingual and polysemous wordplay.[60] To begin with, the title's meaning alludes to his and Véra's first and fateful meeting (May 8, 1923) as well as to their subsequent wedding (April 15, 1925), both of which took place in spring; and when Nabokov began writing the novel (late January 1973), he was presumably thinking about these two imminent golden anniversaries. Furthermore, the painting's title, divided and inverted, that is, *vera prima,* suggests "Véra the First"—the title accorded only to royalty. The word *vera,* which signifies "faith" in Russian, is also a feminine form of the Italian adjective *vero,* which means "veritable," "genuine," "thorough," "perfect." Curiously, as an Italian colloquialism, *vera* also means "a wedding ring," a connotation that nicely corresponds to the sense of the passage and to Nabokov's presumed intention of presenting the entire novel to Véra for their golden wedding anniversary.[61] And even though the protagonist compares Annette Blagovo to Flora, "the flower-decked blonde with the straight nose and serious gray eyes" metatextually implies the physical appearance of Véra Slonim, who had "gray-blue eyes" and who was "a ravishing blonde" in her younger years.[62] By mentioning Spring in the above-quoted passage, Nabokov reminds *his* beloved addressee that their first meeting (May 8) and their wedding (April 15) took place in spring.[63] Moreover, the Latin word for "spring," *ver* or *veris*, is reminiscent of Nabokov's wife's first name, whereas the Russian word for "spring"—*vesna*—is a partial anagram of her maiden name—**Véra Slonim**.

Intriguingly, this presumed intention on the part of Nabokov is consistent with the history of the painting itself: some art historians have maintained that *Primavera* had been commissioned to commemorate the 1482 wedding of Lorenzo di Pierfrancesco de' Medici and Semiramide d'Appiano. Although this hypothesis was advanced only in 1978, four years after the novel's publication, Nabokov could make this conjecture knowing that Venus, the central figure in the painting, was also recognized as the goddess of marriage and that it was long believed that the painting had been commissioned by Lorenzo di Pierfrancesco de' Medici.[64]

Thus, in *Look at the Harlequins!* Nabokov not only encapsulates, albeit in a travestied, tongue-in-cheek manner, his magnificent literary legacy, but also, most fittingly, pays a remarkable tribute to Véra—the most appropriate summation of their fifty-year marriage. And it is noteworthy that, to accentuate the message, Nabokov employs the illustrious Italian Renaissance art masterpiece whose title encodes his wife's name and conveys his tender reverence toward her.

INVITATION TO A BEHEADING:
EL GRECO'S *BURIAL OF THE COUNT OF ORGAZ*

Nabokov also occasionally encodes the presence of his only child, Dmitri (b. 1934), in his fiction. The most distinct example of such encoding may be found in the writer's last short story, "Lance" (1952). There, in its title character, Lance Boke, Nabokov, on the one hand, expresses his admiration for Dmitri's quest as an alpinist, and on the other, vents his and Véra's concerns over the dangers associated with their son's mountain-climbing pursuits.[65] (Curiously, Lance Boke, an "adventurous and boisterous" boy [*Pnin* 101] appears as a fleeting character several years later in *Pnin* as Victor's classmate and best friend.) And, of course, Dmitri is frequently referred to in chapter 15 of *Speak, Memory*, which is addressed to Véra, as "our boy" or "our child" (*SM* 298 and 306). Another, much earlier, and less conspicuous but much more striking example of Nabokov's encoding of Dmitri's presence occurs in *Invitation to a Beheading* by way of a likely reference to El Greco's painting *The Burial of the Count of Orgaz*.

El Greco is directly mentioned in *Lolita* when Humbert Humbert contemplates "the geography of the United States" and occasionally sees in it certain features reminiscent of the European landscape. He specifically envisions "a stern El Greco horizon, pregnant with inky rain, and a passing glimpse of some mummy-necked farmer, and all around alternating strips of quick-silverish water and harsh green corn, the whole arrangement opening like a fan, somewhere in Kansas" (*AnL* 152).[66] It is worth noting that Nabokov's rain-laden description of El Greco's landscape echoes those of Alexander Benois, a preeminent artist and art historian, who wrote in his *History of Painting*, an influential survey of art, primarily western European: "How characteristic of El Greco are these stormy dove-gray clouds that are found in almost all his paintings depicting open air" and specifically about El Greco's *Laocoön:* "so good is its dove-gray, stormy tone, so beautiful is the view of Toledo in the depths, behind the figures."[67]

Twenty years earlier, when composing *Invitation to a Beheading*, Nabokov does not call El Greco by name but rather alludes to his particular painting, *The Burial of the Count of Orgaz* (figure 5). The allusion appears in the pre-execution supper episode in which "a white rose [. . .] distinctly adorned his [Cincinnatus's] place" (*IB* 182). As a pictorially inclined writer and a great connoisseur of art, Nabokov, in all likelihood, alludes here to El Greco's masterpiece in which the white rose plays such a central role.

What is the purpose of adorning Cincinnatus's place with a white rose? According to folk beliefs, the flower is associated with death. If a

5. El Greco, *The Burial of the Count of Orgaz*

white rosebush unexpectedly blooms, it is a sign of death to the nearest house; and as late as the end of the nineteenth century in Wales, the flower marked the graves of young unmarried girls. These folk beliefs worked their way into the Christian church, for supposedly a white rose found by the place of a certain choir member or monk foreshadowed his impending death.[68] Thus, the flower might be seen as another carefully planted reminder of Cincinnatus's impending execution. But what M'sieur Pierre and his henchmen do not take into account—and this is one more in the series of their blunders—is that the white rose, a well-known Christian symbol of purity, strengthens Cincinnatus's connection with Christ and links him to martyrdom. We recall that in *Paradiso* Dante associates with this flower the triumph of the church and Christ's mission to humanity: "In form, then, of a white rose was shown to me the saintly host which Christ, with His own blood, made His bride" (XXXI: 1–3).[69] It is worth noting that Nabokov's direct ancestor Can Grande della Scalla, prince of Verona, sheltered the exiled Dante; the poet completed the *Inferno* and the *Purgatorio* at the court of his protector and dedicated the *Paradiso* to him (see *SO* 188).

In light of all this, the white rose that "distinctly adorn[s]" Cincinnatus's place perhaps portends not so much his oncoming physical death, as intended by his jailers, but rather his spiritual triumph over them, with his own, exemplary, mission to humanity. El Greco's *Burial of the Count of Orgaz,* in which the white rose adorns the vestment of Saint Stephen, the first Christian martyr, supports this latter meaning. (Nabokov had most likely already seen this painting in his youth, in a very crisp black-and-white reproduction from Alexander Benois' earlier mentioned *History of Painting.*)[70] Furthermore, by alluding to this painting, in which El Greco depicts the funeral of Count Orgaz, a benevolent individual, whose body is laid to rest by Saints Stephen and Augustine, but whose soul is carried into heaven by an angel, Nabokov perhaps provides the reader with the clue for the novel's deliberately dual finale. The protagonist could have been executed, but his soul, as the concluding lines, "Cincinnatus made his way in that direction where, to judge by the voices, stood beings akin to him" (*IB* 223) might be suggesting, is joining with the righteous in the Heavenly Kingdom.

This reference to El Greco's masterpiece is of interest in two other important respects. First, it has been contended that in one of the figures in the painting El Greco depicted his own image.[71] The presence of the artist's self-portrait in the painting, to which Nabokov alludes, implies the writer's authorial presence in the novel. This is substantiated by numerous contextual instances: narrative asides, such as "My poor little Cincinnatus" (*IB* 65), as well as the protagonist's deus ex machina rescue at the end of the novel.[72] Second, the boy kneeling in the left foreground, who holds the torch in one hand and points to the white rose embroidered on the sleeve of Saint Stephen's vestment with the other, is believed to be El Greco's son, Jorge Manuel. (Curiously, the artist and his son are the only two figures in the painting gazing directly at the spectator.) And the white handkerchief protruding from Jorge Manuel's pocket bears the painter's signature followed by the date of the boy's birth.[73] (This latter device is quite extraordinary, as most artists customarily inscribe on the canvas the date of the painting's completion.) Nabokov composed *Invitation to a Beheading* in 1934, the year of *his* son's birth, and therefore this likely allusion to El Greco's masterpiece could be viewed as the writer's unique tribute to this highly important event in his own personal life.[74]

Thus on the contextual plane, by alluding to El Greco's *Burial of the Count of Orgaz*, Nabokov suggests Cincinnatus's stature as a martyr and provides the clue for the novel's purposely vague, Last Judgment-like ending.[75] On the metatextual plane, the writer places himself on the same footing with the Cretan-born Spanish master by equaling his feat in the different, verbal, medium: Nabokov alludes to *his* own authorial presence and intimates the birth of *his* son in the novel he had written that year.

"LA VENEZIANA": SEBASTIANO DEL PIOMBO'S *PORTRAIT OF A YOUNG ROMAN WOMAN*

Until now, I have been focusing on Nabokov's references or allusions to paintings with multifigured compositions. The subject of the following discussion is Nabokov's short story "La Veneziana" (written in 1924), in which the writer employs a single-sitter painting—Sebastiano del Piombo's (1485–1547) *Portrait of a Young Roman Woman*, also known as *Portrait of a Girl with a Basket,* or *Dorotea* (figure 6).

Aside from "La Veneziana," in which del Piombo's masterpiece plays such a pivotal role, the painter is mentioned in *Laughter in the Dark* (1938): Albinus, the protagonist and professional art critic, wrote a "biography of Sebastiano del Piombo" (*Laugh* 129) which the cartoonist Rex calls "excellent" (ibid.).[76] Rex's only critique is that in his monograph on the artist Albinus "didn't quote his sonnets," which are "very poor" in Albinus's opinion (ibid.). Rex's suggestion to cite del

6. Sebastiano del Piombo, *Portrait of a Young Roman Woman*

Piombo's sonnets precisely because they are "very poor" and because "[T]hat's what is so charming" (*Laugh* 130) once again demonstrates the workings of his warped and sinister mind. Curiously, both Albinus and Rex err here: Sebastiano del Piombo never wrote any sonnets, good or bad. In fact, the only testimony of del Piombo's literary output is Vasari's intimation that the Venetian-born artist, in response to his close friend Francesco Berni, a comic poet, "who wrote a poem to him," "was even able to set his hand to writing humorous Tuscan verse."[77] Sebastiano's authorship of this verse, however, had been proven wrong: as late as the mid-nineteenth century, scholars discovered that it was Michelangelo who composed the reply to Berni in the name of Sebastiano.[78] Both Rex and especially Albinus should have known these facts. In the universe of Nabokov's fiction, where attention to details is essential and professional ineptitude is unpardonable, it is very telling that Rex the artist mistakenly avers that del Piombo composed sonnets and that Albinus the art critic, who wrote a biography of the Venetian-born painter, does not correct him but rather comments on their poor poetic quality. The expert incompetence of both Albinus and Rex is the writer's additional, surreptitious, scathing comment earlier in the novel on these already quite unappealing characters.

Let us now turn to "La Veneziana," in which del Piombo's painting (or rather its skillful forgery) is of such great import. Intriguingly, the Colonel in "La Veneziana," too, wrongly asserts in the beginning of the story that Sebastiano del Piombo "composed indifferent sonnets," and even though the Colonel is reportedly "inflamed by a noble passion for paintings" (*Stories* 95 and 91), like Albinus, he is unable to tell the original of del Piombo's painting from the fake.[79] He also never questions the authenticity of the painting, even though he should have known that the original had been at Berlin's Kaiser Friedrich Museum since 1885, when it was acquired from the Blenheim collection of the Duke of Marlborough—the latter provenance is apparently alluded to in the English-castle setting of the story. When the Colonel discovers that a new figure (that of Simpson) was painted into the portrait, all he cares about is to remove it as soon as possible so that he can show off the painting to the "young Lord Northwick from London" (*Stories* 113).[80] The Colonel "complacently" (*Stories* 94)—a significant and unfavorable marker in the world of Nabokov's fiction—utters platitudes about Sebastiano del Piombo in which the accurate facts are muddled with unsubstantiated anecdotes. Thus, he repeats the "legend" about the rift between Sebastiano and Raphael over "a Roman lady called Margherita, known subsequently as 'la Fornarina'" (*Stories* 95). The tale about "la Fornarina" seems to be "one of the most enduring myths," despite "the fact that there is no indication of Raphael's mistress in contemporary documents, salacious poems, or gossipy letters [which] must be taken as indicating that she did not exist."[81] The Colonel's assertion about Raphael and Sebastiano's romantic rivalry is evidently based on the existence of Raphael's *La Fornarina* (1518–19; Galleria Nazionale, Rome) and of the *Portrait of a Woman*, also known, even though incorrectly, as *La Fornarina* (1512; Galleria degli Uffizi, Florence), attributed to the Venetian-born Sebastiano. Another source of this "legend" could be the Blenheim collection's misattribution of Sebastiano del Piombo's *Dorotea* as Raphael's portrait of Fornarina.[82]

On the other hand, McGore, a "restorer, reframer, and recanvaser," is a true "old connoisseur of art" who "dedicated" his "whole life to this" (*Stories* 91 and 100). McGore's attentiveness to minute details in works of art characterizes him well in Nabokov's fictional universe. Thus upon scrupulously examining Raphael's *Virgin with the Veil* (1510–11; Musée du Louvre, Paris), McGore notes, "at a distance, two men stood by a column, calmly chatting. I eavesdropped on their conversation— they were discussing the worth of some dagger" (*Stories* 101). McGore is absolutely right: there is indeed a third person "by a column," standing near the interlocutors and ostensibly eavesdropping.

It is noteworthy that one of the sources for the story plotline—a skillful forgery mistaken for a masterpiece—could be an anecdote about Sir Joshua Reynolds (1723–92) that Richard Muther recounts in his *History of Painting in the XIXth Century*. Muther reports that while still apprenticing under Thomas Hudson, an English painter quite fashionable at the time, Reynolds already exhibited "a great skill in copying and produced many copies, especially of Guercino's paintings. During his stay in Italy he became the greatest eighteenth-century connoisseur of Old Masters." To illustrate this, Muther recounts:

> Chevalier van Loo [Muther apparently had a French portraitist, Louis-Michel van Loo, 1707–71, in mind], when he was in England in 1763, vaunted himself one day, in Reynolds' presence, upon his unfailing discrimination in telling a copy from an original. Whereupon Reynolds showed him one of his own studies of a head, after Rembrandt. The Chevalier judged it to be, indisputably, a masterpiece of the great Dutchman.[83]

This anecdote appears to be at the core of Nabokov's story "La Veneziana," in which another Englishman, Frank, fools his own father, the Colonel, ostensibly an expert on Italian Renaissance art, who mistakes his son's forgery for the original of Sebastiano del Piombo's *Dorotea*. And it is quite possible that, when composing the story, Nabokov recalled this anecdote from Muther's book. (For the impact of Muther's book on Nabokov, see chapter 5.)

Nabokov scholars have repeatedly discussed the role of *Dorotea's* description in the writer's short story and have viewed it functioning as a framing or ekphrastic device, or as an indication of otherworldliness.[84] It has apparently escaped notice, however, that the painting also manifests the authorial presence in the story, although, as Michel Niqueux has aptly observed: "The walk through the landscape with a path in the background of the portrait (this path is not in the Italian original, in del Piombo's *Dorotea*) can be interpreted [. . .] autobiographically, as a return to a child's phantasm, described in *Glory* and in *Speak, Memory*."[85]

This presence finds its expression through the description of the painting, in which the index and the middle fingers of the sitter's right hand form a "V" configuration which Nabokov evidently detected and in which he recognized his first-name, as well as his patronymic, initial. It certainly did not elude Nabokov's attention that del Piombo had created a perfect "V" configuration by altering the natural proportions of the fingers: the index and middle fingers appear in the portrait to be of equal length, whereas in reality the index finger is usually noticeably shorter than the middle one.[86]

It is noteworthy that all five of the short story's descriptions of the painting's sitter, including the one (the second) of Maureen, Dorotea's look-alike, draw the reader's close attention to the shape and position of the right-hand fingers: "with the elongated fingers of her right hand spread in pairs, she seemed to have been on the point of adjusting the falling fur"; "her shoulder, from which, as in the painting, the gray fur was slipping, and that she seemed about to pull it up, but stopped at Simpson's question, extending and twining her slender elongated fingers"; "her long fingers paused on their way to her fur wrap, to the slipping crimson folds"; "her long fingers, spread in twos, stretched toward her shoulder, from which the fur and velvet were about to fall"; and finally, an abbreviated description at the very close of the story, apparently designed to serve as the final reminder of the authorial presence: "her long fingers glowed more gently" (*Stories* 94, 99, 106, 110, and 115). When Nabokov points to the sitter's "long fingers, spread in twos" or her "extending and twining her slender elongated fingers," he clearly means the index and middle fingers of her right hand that create this "V" configuration, since her thumb is not shown, her little finger is only partially visible, and her ring finger is not stretched but rather slightly bent under the extended middle finger. The ring and the little fingers are somewhat spaced, but they can be hardly described as "spread in twos" or "stretched toward her shoulder." And Nabokov draws the reader's attention to the deliberate and contrived position of the right-hand fingers, and specifically to that of the index and middle fingers, when emphasizing that "with the elongated fingers of her right hand spread in pairs, she seemed to have been on the point of adjusting the falling fur but to have frozen motionless" and that "her long fingers paused on their way to her fur wrap" (*Stories* 94 and 99).[87]

"La Veneziana" seems to be the earliest work in which Nabokov included the "V" configuration as a manifestation of his authorial presence. Its other example, encoded through the shape of his first initial, can be found in *The Real Life of Sebastian Knight*, Nabokov's first English-language novel (1941). The "V" configuration at first appears rather inconspicuously in the description of the plotline of Sebastian Knight's novel *Success*, where "the two lines which have finally tapered to the point of meeting are really not the straight lines of a triangle which diverge steadily towards an unknown base, but wavy lines, now running wide apart, now almost touching" (*RLSK* 95). While on the surface this butterfly-fluttering description speaks of Sebastian's novel's plotline (although, on the other hand, as we recall, lepidoptery is another significant mode of Nabokov's self-encoding), it iconically alludes to the presence of the narrator V., but more importantly, to the presence of the author, the bearer of his first initial. Later in the novel, it is manifest once again, this time more overtly, through the image of the writer's first initial in the form of "a V-shaped flight of migrating cranes" (*RLSK* 137).

Several years afterward, this crane imagery reemerges in Nabokov's poem "An Evening of Russian Poetry" (1945): "On mellow hills the Greek, as you remember, / fashioned his alphabet from cranes in flight" (*PP* 158). In this programmatic poem, however, Nabokov imbues the imagery of "cranes in flight" with a new and telling meaning—*nomen est omen*. This prophetic imagery seems to intimate that Nabokov was destined to become a writer, since his first initial, "V," which resembles the "cranes in flight" from whom "the Greek" "fashioned his alphabet," lies at the base of verbal creation. (It is noteworthy that Nabokov frequently signed his dedicational inscriptions with only his *V* initial.)[88] The "cranes in flight" imagery constitutes an important milestone in Nabokov's growing self-confidence as a writer at the time of his making the English language his main medium of expression.

In addition, it is possible that by way of the portrait's "V" configuration Nabokov alludes to his future wife, Véra, whom he met in May of 1923 and married in April of 1925, only six months after composing the story. In light of this, "La Veneziana" may also be perceived as Nabokov's tribute to his bride (see the earlier mentioned poem "The Skater"), similarly to the presumed bridal portrait of the young Roman lady commissioned from Sebastiano del Piombo. To this attests "a basket of yellow fruit" (*Stories* 94)—quinces—well familiar as a matrimonial symbol. As a nuptial attribute, quinces are mentioned in Plutarch's commentaries on Solon and later in Renaissance Italy in Cesare Ripa's *Iconologia* and Andrea Alciati's *Emblematum liber,* books with which Nabokov was, no doubt, familiar.[89] Most important, the "V" configuration, "alluding to *Virtus* or to *Venus*[,] would reinforce this interpretation."[90] This bridal tribute to Véra by way of Sebastiano del Piombo's painting is all the more plausible since, as we recall, a similar tribute to her on the occasion of the Nabokovs' golden wedding anniversary, this time by means of Botticelli's *Primavera,* appears in *Look at the Harlequins!* (see the *Primavera* section in this chapter).

* * *

As an integral part of a well-established literary tradition, Nabokov frequently employs the art of the Old Masters, primarily their chefs d'oeuvre. Not unlike his predecessors and contemporaries, Nabokov describes or refers and alludes to such pictorial masterpieces in order to shed additional light on the personality and fate of his characters. For example, Luzhin's childlike reactions to Old Master canvases in *The Defense* are designed to emphasize his aesthetically uncultivated personality. And the allusion to El Greco's *Burial of the Count of Orgaz* suggests Cincinnatus's martyrdom and provides a clue for the novel's dual finale. In addition, the use of these well-known works of art enables Nabokov to employ various important narrative strategies, such as teaching his protagonist of *The Gift* a significant ethical lesson by mentioning Rembrandt's *Deposition from the Cross.*

Of special interest is Nabokov's fascination with the convex mirror, a distant optical relative of the microscope that the writer used in his entomological research. But while the microscope is employed to magnify the object, the convex mirror, with its ability to distort images, is somewhat reminiscent of the effect "the incomprehensible crazy mirror" may have when anamorphically imaging "*nonnons,*" those "incomprehensible monstrous objects" (see *IB* 135–36), that could serve Nabokov as a neat formulaic presentation and perception of fiction as refracted "reality."[91]

What makes Nabokov's use of Old Masters' works so unique, however, is that he turns to them to encrypt the presence of himself, his loved ones—his wife and son—or to mark an important familial event—his prospective marriage, his son's birth, or his own golden wedding anniversary. Nabokov often accomplishes all this by referring to a painting in which an artist himself resorted to "set[ting] his face in a dark corner of his canvas"—a device reminiscent of *mise-en-abîme*—or by referring to a memorable gesture in a painting, or to its title.[92]

The works of Old Masters discussed in this chapter extend over two centuries, from the fifteenth to the seventeenth, and form, as it happens, an almost perfect circular itinerary, from Flanders (Jan van Eyck) to Italy (Botticelli and del Piombo), to Spain (El Greco), and to the Netherlands (Rembrandt). Finally, Nabokov's employment of Old Masters' works for the encoding of his own self or that of his loved ones spans over half a century, from "La Veneziana" (1924) to *Look at the Harlequins!* (1974), thereby demonstrating the writer's propensity for this practice throughout his entire literary career.

3. LANDSCAPE:
SOME ROLES AND FUNCTIONS

I am going to show you not the painting of a landscape, but
the painting of different ways of painting a certain landscape, and I trust their harmonious fusion will disclose the
landscape as I intend you to see it.

—Nabokov, *The Real Life of Sebastian Knight*

I don't write consecutively from the beginning to the next
chapter and so on to the end. I just fill in the gaps of the picture, of this jigsaw puzzle which is quite clear in my mind,
picking out a piece here and a piece there and filling out
part of the sky and part of the landscape.

—Nabokov, *Strong Opinions*

I owe many metaphors and sensuous associations to the
North Russian landscape of my boyhood.

—Nabokov, *Strong Opinions*

In his boyhood and early youth, Nabokov aspired to become an artist,
a landscape artist. As he once told Alfred Appel Jr.: "I was really born
a landscape painter" (*AnL* 414; also see *SO* 17 and 166–67). This fascination with landscape that contains "poetic sensibility" and could be
viewed as a bridge of sorts between the fine arts and poetry, and later,
thanks to its "prosaic naturalness," to prose, may explain Nabokov's
smooth transition to and channeling his creative powers into these
verbal modes of expression.[1] Another reason for Nabokov's penchant
for landscape originates in the writer's love of colors—hence his youthful enthusiasm for the most pictorial artistic genre that constitutes
"the imitation" of "all the designs with which the Seasons paint the
meadows, and the manifestations we see in the heavens."[2] Yet another

reason for Nabokov's proclivity for landscape lies in his great interest in nature in general, his ardent passion for lepidoptery in particular, and his scientific knowledge and high appreciation of flora and fauna. Although Nabokov later shifted his mode of expression, he always maintained his fondness for landscape and frequently employed the genre in its verbal rendition.

This early aspiration of Nabokov is manifest throughout his entire oeuvre, in which landscape customarily plays an essential role, specifically in such works of the "Russian years" as *King, Queen, Knave* (1928), *Glory* (1931–32), *Despair* (1934), *Invitation to a Beheading* (1935–36), and "Cloud, Castle, Lake" (1937), as well as in such works of the "American years" as *Lolita* (1955) and *Pnin* (1957).

Nabokov's perception of landscape as a highly important part of the narrative finds its expression in his Cornell lectures, in which he criticized Fedor Dostoevsky for neglecting this pictorial genre in his works: "If you examine closely any of his works, say *The Brothers Karamazov*, you will note that the natural background and all things relevant to the perception of the senses hardly exist. What landscape there is is a landscape of ideas, a moral landscape. The weather does not exist in his world" (*LRL* 104).

It was apparently Henry Cumming, Nabokov's first drawing master, whom the writer dubs "a master of the sunset" (*SM* 91), that deserves credit for arousing Nabokov's initial interest in landscape painting. The writer recalls:

> I loved the nimble way he [Cumming] had of soaking his paintbrush in multiple color to the accompaniment of a rapid clatter produced by the enamel containers wherein the rich reds and yellows that the brush dimpled were appetizingly cupped; and having thus collected its honey, it would cease to hover and poke, and, by two or three sweeps of its lush tip, would drench the "Vatmanski" paper with an even spread of orange sky, across which, while that sky was still dampish, a long purple-black cloud would be laid. (*SM* 93)

Nabokov also recalls how Cumming "contented himself with painting under my enchanted gaze his own wet little paradises, variations of one landscape: a summer evening with an orange sky, a pasture ending in the black fringe of a distant forest, and a luminous river, repeating the sky and winding away and away" (*SM* 91). And while acknowledging that he had learned a great deal from Dobuzhinsky, Nabokov maintains that "emotionally" he is "still more indebted to the earlier color treats given me by my mother and her former teacher [Cumming]" (*SM* 92).[3]

Whom among the landscape painters did Nabokov consider significant for his artistic development? The writer admits, albeit without any elaboration, that the landscape artists that meant a great deal to him in his youth were "mostly Russian and French painters" (*SO* 166–67).

Among the Russian artists that depicted landscape, Nabokov specifically meant Isaac Levitan and some of the *World of Art* painters, such as Alexander Benois and Konstantin Somov, whom he held in great esteem. In contradistinction to Levitan and the *World of Art* painters, Nabokov thought very poorly of the Wanderers, with their emphasis on social awareness in art, and of the Academicians, with their deadening, stagnating conventionality (see chapter 4).

As for the French landscape artists, Nabokov evidently had Claude Lorrain (1600–1682) in mind, first and foremost: "So convincing was his example and so great was his influence that, by the late nineteenth century, landscape would become arguably the dominant genre of painting in Europe and America."[4] In his essay "Painted Wood" (1923), the young Nabokov pays an ardent tribute to the French landscape painter when singling him out as an example of how "art and nature mingle together—in such a wonderful way that it is difficult to say for instance whether sunsets made Claude Lorrain, or Claude Lorrain made sunsets" (*Carr* 21). Lorrain was known for his landscapes "suffused with the light of the rising and setting sun."[5] The young Nabokov's specific predilection for the French painter's sunsets apparently arises from his childhood, and therefore very vivid, recollections of his first drawing master's, Henry Cumming's, above-mentioned penchant for the depiction of sunsets. Nabokov's particular fondness for sunsets is evident in his early poem "Clouds" (1921), which contains the following admission of his lyrical "I": "I love the sunset clouds."[6] It seems that by "equating" Lorrain with sunsets Nabokov had in mind the painter's numerous depictions of that time of the day, such as *Seaport at Sunset* (1639; Musée du Louvre, Paris) and *Harbor Scene at Sunset*

(1643; Royal Collection, Windsor Castle, London). It is quite possible that when linking Lorrain's art to sunsets, Nabokov invoked the elegy "An Eventide" (1806) by the Russian Romantic poet and translator Vasily Zhukovsky, which contains pastoral imagery reminiscent of the French painter's artwork. Of particular interest is the following stanza:

> Already eventide . . . the clouds' edges grew dim,
> The last rays of sunlight are dying on the tower roofs.
> The last glinting stream in the river
> Is fading with the darkling sky

—a description that bears a close resemblance to Lorrain's landscape imagery.[7]

Several years later, Nabokov names Lorrain, this time facetiously, in *King, Queen, Knave,* when the inventor points in the corridor of Dreyer's office to the faucet "with the air of Rembrandt indicating a Claude Lorraine" (*KQK* 91).[8] He mentions the French painter once again, but this time seriously, in *Lolita* when Humbert muses about the American countryside and observes, among other things, "Claude Lorrain clouds inscribed remotely into misty azure with only their cumulus part conspicuous against the neutral swoon of the background" (*AnL* 152). The formation *Claude/clouds* is a very fitting example of the visual and semantic sign "refraction" of the landscape painter's first name in the celestial configurations; clouds in the "misty azure" once again suggest "rain"—the second half of the painter's toponymic nickname.

Another French painter that Nabokov probably had in mind was Lorrain's contemporary Nicolas Poussin (1594–1665), to whose *Et in Arcadia ego,* also known as *Les bergers d'Arcadie* (1638–40; Musée du Louvre, Paris), set amidst a wooded landscape, both Nabokov and his one-time friend Edmund Wilson refer in their correspondence (*NWL* 352–54).[9] In his letter to Wilson mentioned earlier (in chapter 2), Nabokov reveals that his "source of understanding *et in Arcadia ego*" is Panofsky's "excellent essay" (*NWL* 354), a reference to the latter's "*Et in Arcadia Ego:* Poussin and the Elegiac Tradition."[10]

Nabokov's deep knowledge of the Arcadian motif and its representation in literature is manifest in his *Lectures on Don Quixote,* in which the writer maintains:

> The Arcadian (or Pastoral) theme is closely allied to the Italian novella and to the chivalry romance, merging with them at various points. This Arcadian slant is derived from the following odd combination of notions: Arcadia, a mountainous district of legendary Greece, had been the abode of a simple contented people; so let us disguise ourselves as shepherds and spend sixteenth-century summers wandering in idyllic bliss or romantic distress about the mollified mountains of Spain. The special theme of distress pertained to chivalry stories of penitent, unhappy, or insane knights who would retire to the wilderness to live like fictitious shepherds. These Arcadian activities (minus the special distress) were later transferred to other mountainous parts of Europe by eighteenth-century writers of the so-called sentimental school, in a kind of back-to-nature movement, though actually nothing could be more artificial than the tame and coy kind of nature visualized by Arcadian writers. (*LDQ* 30)

Apparently under the influence of Panofsky's seminal article, Arcady figures especially prominently in Nabokov's works of the "American years." Thus, in *Lolita* "American wilds" are dubbed "lyrical, epic, tragic but never Arcadian" (*AnL* 168). In *Pnin,* "English shepherd dogs belonging to one of the masters" at St. Bart's "could generally be found drowsing in their private Arcadia on a lawn before the gate" (*Pnin* 93–94). In *Pale Fire* (1962), Charles Kinbote comments on John Shade's poem by employing the entire formula: "Even in Arcady am I, says Death in the tombal scripture," but later modifies it to "'Even in Arcady am I,' says Dementia, chained to her gray column" (*PF* 174 and 237). By equating Death with Dementia, Nabokov underscores Kinbote's own mental desolation and emotional misery and portends his sad fate outside the boundaries of the novel. Nabokov frequently discusses the Arcadian motif in his commentary to *Eugene Onegin* (see, for example, *EO,* 2:199, 219, 321–22, and 3:290). And finally, Nabokov repeatedly refers or alludes to Arcady in *Ada* as, for example, in the pronouncement that "nothing in world literature, save maybe Count Tolstoy's reminiscences, can vie in pure joyousness and Arcadian innocence with the 'Ardis' part of the book" (*Ada* 588).[11]

Nabokov's intimate knowledge of Poussin's art is further underscored by the writer's mention of this French painter, specifically known for his depiction of glowing silky-blue skies. This knowledge is manifest in Nabokov's verbal rendition of a New York City Central Park view as it emerged from his hotel window: "tapestry-like clumps of trees, and from the flanks, set off with lilac-colored gouache, mysterious skyscrapers under a Poussin sky."[12]

Moreover, in singling out French landscape artists, Nabokov also had in mind French Impressionists, many of whom distinguished themselves in depicting both landscapes and cityscapes of France, just as Nabokov decades later distinguished himself in depicting verbal landscapes and cityscapes of Russia (primarily flashbacks), Germany, and the United States. Nabokov's close familiarity with the French Impressionists' principal artistic achievements is manifest in *Lolita*. In his comment on the episode in which Rita, baffled by Humbert's calling the hotel blue, exclaims: "Why blue when it is white, why blue for heaven's sake?" (*AnL* 263), Nabokov remarks: "What Rita does not understand is that a white surface, the chalk of that hotel, does look blue in a wash of light and shade on a vivid fall day, amid red foliage. H.H. is merely paying a tribute to French impressionist painters. He notes an optical miracle as E. B. White does somewhere when referring to the divine combination of 'red barn and blue snow.'" And then later in his commentary, the writer adds the above-mentioned and oft-quoted phrase about his being "really born a landscape painter" (*AnL* 437). This sequence suggests that Nabokov, when paying tribute to "French painters" (*SO* 166–67), was also thinking of the impact of French Impressionists on his seminal development as a pictorial and verbal landscape artist.[13]

Nabokov's interest in landscape stayed with him throughout his creative life. It is evident from his correspondence, particularly with his wife. For example, in his letter to Véra, his future wife, from Prague of August 24, 1924, Nabokov writes:

The Management of the Western and Eastern Skies regaled us with a monstrously beautiful sunset. Up above, the sky was deep blue and only in the west was there a cloud in the shape of a lilac wing spreading its orange ribs. The river was rose, as if from a drop of port wine, and alongside it, an express train was flying from Prague to Paris. And on the extreme horizon, underneath that violet cloud trimmed with orange fuzz, a strip of sky was glowing with light greenish turquoise, within which dissolved fiery islets.[14]

This remarkably vivid description of the sunset—Nabokov's predilection for sunsets is manifest here once again—reveals his masterful painterly vision of the world, verbally expressed. The description implies depth ("on the extreme horizon") as well as shapes ("cloud in the shape of a lilac wing"), rich and nuanced colors ("deep blue," "pink," "greenish turquoise," "violet," "orange"), planes (vertical, such as "the sky" "up above" and "the river" below, as well as horizontal, with the cloud in the west), and an excellent sense of composition—all being the key components of artistic sensibility.

Nabokov describes an equally remarkable sunset in his memoir:

I recall one particular sunset. It lent an ember to my bicycle bell. Overhead, above the black music of telegraph wires, a number of long, dark-violet clouds lined with flamingo pink hung motionless in a fan-shaped arrangement; the whole thing was like some prodigious ovation in terms of color and form! It was dying, however, and everything else was darkening, too; but just above the horizon, in a lucid, turquoise space, beneath a black stratus, the eye found a vista that only a fool could mistake for the spare parts of this or any other sunset. It occupied a very small sector of the enormous sky and had the peculiar neatness of something seen through the wrong end of a telescope. There it lay in wait, a family of serene clouds in miniature, an accumulation of brilliant convolutions, anachronistic in their creaminess and extremely remote; remote but perfect in every detail; fantastically reduced but faultlessly shaped; my marvelous tomorrow ready to be delivered to me. (*SM* 213)

Unlike the instantaneous sunset description in the letter, Nabokov's depiction of the sunset in the Russian countryside is given in retrospect, as a flashback. Even though Nabokov does not base this depiction on a fresh impression but rather draws it from memory, he conveys it with the same attention to colors, shapes, planes, and composition, and does so in exquisite pictorial detail.

The writer's fascination with landscape is also evident in a review that dates from the early 1930s of the art exhibit of Iosif Matusevich (1879–1940), a fellow Russian émigré, painter, and man of letters. In this review, Nabokov calls Matusevich's landscapes of Berlin's outskirts "unique" and singles out for praise "one small watercolor of his—a truly wonderful piece: a dark beach in Ahlbeck [a Baltic Sea resort], the gray swollen skies, the ochre sail, and the red-black silhouettes of fishermen standing by murky water."[15] This brief description of Matusevich's watercolor is in itself "a truly wonderful [master]piece": here Nabokov verbally reproduces the work of art by expertly conveying in words the parallel and similarly toned and yet dynamically contrasting skies and seashore, animate figures ("fishermen") and inanimate objects ("sail"), bright ("ochre" and "red-black") and bleak ("murky") hues. This brief description is an obvious manifestation of the device of ekphrasis—that "verbal representation of visual representation"— the most distinct example of which in Nabokov's oeuvre is evident in his earlier poem "Ut pictura poesis" (1926; see chapter 4).[16] In this rare art review, Nabokov demonstrates once again the great virtuosity of his verbal palette of colors—his superb ability to paint, but with words.[17]

Nabokov's penchant for landscape found its expression in his own artwork throughout his entire life. As was already mentioned, while in Russia, Nabokov liked to paint countryside landscapes at the Vyra family estate (*Perepiska* 56). Unfortunately, none of these landscapes seem to have survived through those turbulent times. Nabokov, however, continued drawing and painting landscapes in exile. Thus, when residing in Berlin, he drew a landscape that he entitled *Autumn in Sans Souci* (figure 7). It depicts an autumnal view at the summer residence of the Prussian king Frederick the Great in nearby Potsdam. This skillful drawing is reminiscent of Alexander Benois' oil entitled *The Water Parterre* (1905–6; State Russian Museum, St. Petersburg) and other numerous works from that artist's Versailles series. It is very likely that while working on the drawing, Nabokov held Benois' magnificent series in his mind's eye. The drawing shows some traditional park scenery: in the foreground, an offset partial view of a pond, with three statues on its bank, fringed in the background by a grove of trees traversed by a

7. Vladimir Nabokov, *Autumn in Sans Souci*

footpath winding into a dense wood. (As we shall see later, a path [*tropa* or *tropinka* in Russian] winding through a wood is a common trope in Nabokov's oeuvre.)

After moving to the United States (May 1940), and while staying at the country house of his friend, the Harvard University professor of history, Mikhail Karpovich, near West Wardsboro, Vermont, in the summer of 1942, the writer painted the surrounding landscape, this time choosing watercolor as the medium of expression.[18] The watercolor depicts a typical New England countryside: an old barn in the background to the far left, a large tree stump and an automobile (an elderly small sedan) in the middle foreground, and a mature deciduous tree to the right border. More than a decade later, Karpovich's country homestead served Nabokov as the prototype for Al Cook's The Pines.[19] And perhaps, when composing *Pnin*, Nabokov used the watercolor as a visual memento. Thus, Pnin's "pale blue, egg-shaped two-door sedan, of uncertain age and in mediocre condition" (*Pnin* 112), is reminiscent of the watercolor's elderly sedan; the "quaint old barn" (*Pnin* 127) painted by Gramineev, a landscape painter, reminds one of its watercolor counterpart; and the stump in the middle of the painting is evidently at least partially responsible for Nabokov's choice of his protagonist's surname Pnin (a "stump" in Russian is *pen´*).

After settling in Montreux, Nabokov once again turned to pencil (figure 8). The drawing, which Nabokov made on an index card, shows two figures, one sitting and another standing, fishing by the reedy edge of the lake; and on the opposite side, two trees situated on hillocks fading to a gently rising tree-lined slope. The writer marked the card with the local Swiss toponyms and names: at the top, Nabokov inscribed "La Lignière," referring to the well-known sanatorium, Clinique La Lignière, founded in 1905, to which in the early 1960s his son, Dmitri, was admitted with a case of food poisoning; in the upper left corner, he parenthetically penned "Genève," with the city's area code number under it; in the upper right corner, he inscribed "Nyon," the closest to Clinique La Lignière and the largest nearby settlement, an ancient town, founded by Julius Caesar; and on the far right side, he notated

8. Vladimir Nabokov, Untitled

"Séchaud," the surname of a local grocer, who supplied their Montreux Palace apartment with food and beverages. According to Dmitri Nabokov, the five-digit number on the drawing, 9-80-61, is not a transposed date (even though the Nabokovs arrived in Montreux on August 7, 1961), but rather a telephone number.[20] Better known is Nabokov's other index-card drawing from the Montreux period, dated from August 25, 1961. It shows the Dents du Midi massif located at the western extremity of the Pennine Alps and overlooking Lake Geneva.[21]

Nabokov's lifelong fascination with landscape accounts for the pivotal role that this branch of art frequently plays in his works. The following discussion demonstrates the versatile functions with which Nabokov endows landscape. It is important to underscore that landscape is defined here as both the ekphrastic description of a specific painting, real or imaginary, and the description of natural scenery within the narrative. It is true that literature has had such a long history of resorting to this trope that it no longer automatically calls to mind a painting as such. Nabokov apparently viewed this as a challenge and, by virtue of his verbal pictorial magic, overcomes this automatism by depicting landscape in such strikingly unique, memorable ways and by endowing it with such indispensable functions that it forces the reading audience to pay its undivided attention to the genre and to view it afresh.

GLORY: THE ENTICING LANDSCAPE

Landscape plays the key role in *Glory,* running as a red thread throughout the entire novel. It first appears at the book's very beginning: it is the painting hanging in Martin's nursery room, "a watercolor depicting a dense forest with a winding path disappearing into its depths" (*Glory* 4). It is noteworthy that this watercolor and the similar fairy tale images echo Nabokov's own childhood experience. As Nabokov puts it in his memoirs, "I imagined the motion of climbing into the picture above my bed and plunging into that enchanted beechwood—which I did visit in due time" (*SM* 86).[22]

Concomitant with the nursery room watercolor, "in one of the English books that his [Martin's] mother used to read to him" "there was a story about just such a picture with a path in the woods, right above the bed of a little boy, who, one fine night, just as he was, nightshirt and all, went from his bed into the picture, onto the path that disappeared in the woods" (*Glory* 4–5).

It seems that a character's longing to step into a picture occurs in Nabokov's works as early as 1923, in his verse play *The Tragedy of Mr. Morn.* There, the title character, turning to Edmin, his aide, friend, and confidant, and pointing to a picture, exclaims:

> Look: a green meadow,
> and there, beyond, a spruce forest
> turning an oily black, and
> two clouds transfixed with slanting gold . . . and it's
> already eventide . . . and in the air, perhaps,
> the ringing of a church bell . . . midges swarm . . .
> Escape, but how? There, into this picture, amid the airy,
>   pensive grassy hues.[23]

Here Nabokov employs a well-known ekphrastic attention-drawing device, to which attests the locution "look," already familiar in antiquity. For example, the Greek Sophist Philostratus the Elder frequently utilizes it in verbal renditions of pictorial images in his *Imagines*.[24]

Soon afterward, Nabokov modified this device: in his story "La Veneziana," unlike in *The Tragedy of Mr. Morn,* where an escape into a painting is presented as merely a possibility and wishful thinking on the part of the character, this transcendental traversal does take place. There, the art restorer McGore talks about his recurrent experience of stepping into paintings: "Instead of inviting a painted figure to step out of its frame, imagine someone managing to step into the picture himself. Makes you laugh, doesn't it? And yet I've done it many a time" (*Stories* 100). Later in the story, Simpson, whom McGore tells about his experience, steps into the alleged painting by Sebastiano del Piombo that at the end of the story turns out to be an exceedingly adroit forgery by Frank, his university friend.

It is possible that Buster Keaton's film *Sherlock Jr.,* released on April 21, 1924, reminded Nabokov of this device and prompted him to employ it both in the story, whose manuscript is dated October 5 of the same year (*Stories* 646), and in the subsequent novel *Glory*. We recall that Buster Keaton's title character, a movie projectionist, falls asleep on the job and in his dream steps into the movie he is showing.

In *Glory,* both the painting in his nursery room and the corresponding description in the English book, the pictorial and the verbal hypostases of the landscape, represent Martin's Russian childhood and his
upbringing by his Anglophile mother. (They also epitomize Nabokov's
own creative shift from the pictorial to the verbal mode of expression.)
That "English book" is apparently an English translation of Hans
Christian Andersen's story "Ole Lukoie" (1841; see *Ssoch,* 3:718). The
passage in question describes this stepping into the picture as follows:

> Over the chest of drawers hung a large painting in a gilt frame.
> It was a landscape in which one could see tall old trees, flowers
> in the grass, and a large lake from which a river flowed away
> through the woods, past many castles, far out to the open sea.
> Ole Lukoie touched the painting with his magic sprinkler, and
> the birds in it began to sing, the branches stirred on the trees,
> and the clouds billowed along. You could see their shadows sweep
> across the landscape. Then Ole Lukoie lifted little Hjalmar up to
> the frame and put the boy's feet into the picture, right in the tall
> grass, and there he stood.[25]

Another pictorial source of this imagery is apparently a cover of the
children's magazine *A Path* (*Tropinka,* 1906–12).[26] The cover depicts not
only a winding path leading to a forest but also, in the foreground, a
little boy and a woman, apparently his mother, like Martin and Sofia
Dmitrievna at the time of her reading the book out loud to him, both
engrossed in the dreamy, fairy tale–like atmosphere.

When in the Crimea, while standing near an abyss overlooking the
sea, Martin watches "a full moon's wake, the 'Turkish trail' spreading
in the middle and narrowing as it approached the horizon" (*Glory* 20).
"That moon's scintillating wake" "enticed" Martin "in the same ways as
had the forest path in the nursery picture," and immediately afterward
it evokes the childhood memory of riding a train "across the French
countryside" (ibid.).[27]

In his later years, Martin perceives this nursery painting as the emblem of his unfolding life:

> When, as a youth, he recalled the past, he would wonder if one
> night he had not actually hopped from bed to picture, and if this

had not been the beginning of the journey, full of joy and anguish, into which his whole life had turned. He seemed to remember the chilly touch of the ground, the green twilight of the forest, the bends of the trail (which the hump of a great root crossed here and there), the tree trunks flashing by as he ran past them barefoot, and the strange dark air, teeming with fabulous possibilities. (*Glory* 5)

This formulaic landscape imagery accompanies Martin throughout his later years and serves as the epitome of his entire being. When he rides a train en route to southern France, this time as an adult, he imagines: "'Like this I shall travel north, exactly like this, in a coach that one cannot stop—and after that, after that—' He began to follow a forest path, the path unwound, kept unwinding" (*Glory* 156). Later that night, this imagery returns to Martin as the epitome of his life, which he first likens to riding a fast train and merely wandering "from car to car," and then sees the continuation of this journey on foot, with the corresponding landscape formula: "a forest, a winding path" (*Glory* 157).

This formulaic landscape—a winding path in the forest—comes into view throughout Nabokov's oeuvre: we find it, for example, in *The Defense,* when Luzhin the boy attempts to escape by "a beaten footpath" to "a dense wood" (*Def* 21); in *Bend Sinister,* when Adam Krug, like Vasiliy Ivanovich from "Cloud, Castle, Lake" before him, imagines getting off the train in order "to stop those speeding trees and the path twisting between them" (*BS* 13); and in *Look at the Harlequins!,* when Vadim Vadimovich, in stark contrast to Martin, who presumably fails to steal across Soviet Russia's border, successfully exits the country, following "a fairy-tale path winding through a great forest" (*LATH* 9).

Landscape also plays an essential role in Martin's self-testing of his courage in the mountains of Switzerland, the country of his paternal ancestors. We recall that earlier in the novel, Martin walks along a perilous cornice "accidentally" and could not force himself at the time to repeat this deed "deliberately" (*Glory* 87). Later in the novel, however, Martin finds it necessary to put his courage to the test once again by performing this challenging exercise:

Unhurriedly, purposefully, he ascended the slope and reached the broken gray rocks. He climbed up the stony steepness and

found himself on the same little platform from which the familiar cornice started to round the sheer cliff. Without hesitation,
obeying an inner command that could not be disregarded, he began to sidle along the narrow shelf. When it tapered to an end he
looked down over his shoulder and saw, under his very heels, the
sunny precipice and at the bottom of it the porcelain hotel [. . .]
Upon safely reaching the platform, Martin grunted with joy,
and in the same purposeful way, with a stern sense of duty fulfilled, climbed down scree and heather, *found the right path* and
descended toward the Majestic—to see what it would have to say.
(*Glory* 169–70; italics added)

The italicized phrase underscores the significance of Martin's endeav-
or.[28] This self-testing comes after Martin's walking

with springy steps through the mountainside fir forest whose
blackness was broken from place to place by the radiance of a
slender birch tree, [and] he anticipated with rapture a similar
sun-pierced thicket on a far Northern plain with spiderwebs
spread on the sunbeams, and with damp hollows choked with
willow herb, and, beyond, the luminous open spaces, the empty
autumnal fields, and the squat little white church on a hillock
tending as it were the isbas that looked on the point of wandering
away; and, encircling the hillock, there would be the bright bend
of a river brimming with enmeshed reflections. He was almost
surprised when he glimpsed an alpine slope through the coni-
fers. (*Glory* 169)[29]

The "slender birch tree" of the Swiss Alpine terrain in the very beginning of the above-quoted passage, which incidentally echoes "a
lone birch tree" (*Glory* 9) of the Crimean fauna, does not occur here
by sheer chance. Its function is to invoke in Martin the imagery of Russian landscape that he projects on his Swiss, as earlier on the Crimean,
surroundings. We recall that a lone birch as a symbol of Russia in exile
recurrently appears in Nabokov's early works, especially in his poetry.
For example, in the poem "A Birch in the Vorontsov Park," composed
in the Crimea in the spring of 1918 and later included in his verse collection *The Empyrean Path* (1923), Nabokov writes:

Amidst blooming fiery trees
a birch is grieving on the meadow,
like a captive maiden in a sparkling circle
of maidens from indigenous tribes.

And only I am friends with the lonely birch,
I share her springtime melancholy:
she seems to me to be a sister
of my faraway beloved.[30]

In *Glory,* the present Swiss alpine terrain and the Russian imaginary, recollected, landscape, reminiscent of the nursery room watercolor, converge in Martin's mind.

It seems that Martin's "glory of high adventure and disinterested achievement" (*Glory* xiii) is not only the culmination of this journey but also an attempt at recapturing and physically returning to his past, to the Russia of his childhood. When Darwin is bewildered by Martin's desire to steal across the Russian border rather than to travel there by train with a foreign passport and an officially issued visa (see *Glory* 199–200), he is evidently unaware of the nursery room watercolor that made such an indelible mark on his friend's life. How else could Martin return to the Russia of his childhood but in "his own way" (*Glory* 176), by a path in the woods reminiscent of his nursery room watercolor? To this alludes the map episode with Gruzinov in which the key phrases "a very dense wood" and "invisible footpaths" (*Glory* 177) echo "a dense forest" and "a winding path disappearing into its depths," as well as "the path that disappeared into the woods" of the nursery room watercolor and the English book story of his childhood (*Glory* 4–5).

The hazardous nature of this endeavor becomes clear from Gruzinov's mentioning, as some sort of warning, the ominous names of the border-crossing villages Carnagore, deriving from the components "carn" (the Latin *carnis* that stands for "flesh") and "gore" ("thickened blood from a cut or wound," the latter being a transliterated homonym of the Russian locution that signifies "grief" or "misfortune"), and Torturovka (obviously stemming from the word "torture"; *Glory* 177).[31] The fatal outcome of Martin's expedition is predictable not only because, on the factual plane, he attempts the dangerous border-crossing to totalitarian Soviet Russia, but also on a figurative plane, thereby demonstrating the impossibility of any physical return to one's childhood.

Contrary to his creator, who cathartically returns to his native country, the land of his childhood and early youth, time and again in his writings, by the power of his imagination and memory, Martin, whom Nabokov "was careful not to [. . .] [endow with] talent," not "to make him an artist, a writer" (*Glory* xiii), had no other way to return "into forbidden Zoorland" (*Glory* xii), but only physically, at his own peril. Therein lies the valor and merit of his deed: similarly to Prince Igor of the celebrated Russian epic "who girded his mind / with fortitude, / and sharpened his heart / with manliness" (*Song* 31), Martin, although knowing full well the mortal dangers of his expedition, embarks on it nonetheless in his "inutile deed of renown," in which he pursues no political or any other practical purpose but rather seeks "the glory of this earth and its patchy paradise," "the glory of personal pluck" (*Glory* xii–xiii). And it is noteworthy that Nabokov's translation of *The Song of Igor's Campaign* (1960), which precedes by ten years the translation of *Glory*—Nabokov's collaborative effort with his son Dmitri—contains a recurrent passage about the troops "seeking for themselves honor, and for their prince glory" and the opening line in the concluding passage that reads: "Glory to Igor son of Svyatoslav" (*Song* 33, 36, and 72), which shed additional light on the novel through its English title and on the knightly valor of its protagonist.[32]

INVITATION TO A BEHEADING: THE DECEPTIVE LANDSCAPE

In my monograph on *Invitation to a Beheading,* I discuss the significance of "flowers of evil" in the novel.[33] This significance is reinforced by the "gardens of evil" in which those flowers grow. The importance of these gardens in the world of the novel is suggested in the pre-execution supper episode by the presence among the town fathers of "the park superintendent" (in Russian, "upravliaiushchii sadami," that is "the gardens' manager" [*IB* 187; *Ssoch*, 4:163]). These "gardens of evil" accompany Cincinnatus throughout his entire life. Thus, Cincinnatus was taught to write by copying "the model words from the flower beds in the school garden" (*IB* 97). He was appointed a teacher to a kindergarten (in Russian, "detskii sad," which literally means, like the equivalent German locution, a "children's garden"; *IB* 30; *Ssoch,* 4:60). At the trial, his defendants' bench turns out to be a "park bench" (in Russian, "sadovaia skam´ia," that is, a "garden bench" [*IB* 21; *Ssoch,* 4:54]). Cincinnatus's first meeting with M'sieur Pierre is marked by flowers (peonies) "from the director's garden" (*IB* 79). (Incidentally, in referring to his native Elderbury, the executioner describes it in particular as that of "fruit orchards" [*IB* 110], "plodovye sady" [*Ssoch,* 4:112], which is literally "fruit gardens" in the original Russian.) And on his way to the scaffold, Cincinnatus rides by Garden Street (see *IB* 216).

But of course the pivotal role among all these "gardens of evil" belongs to the Tamara Gardens. Their first mention occurs early in the novel, when the incarcerated Cincinnatus goes home on an imaginary journey:

> Now and then a wave of fragrance would come from the Tamara Gardens. How well he knew that public park! There, where Marthe, when she was a bride, was frightened of the frogs and cockchafers . . . There, where, whenever life seemed unbearable, one could roam, with a meal of chewed lilac bloom in one's mouth and firefly tears in one's eyes . . . That green turfy tamarack park, the languor of its ponds, the tum-tum-tum of a distant band. (*IB* 19)

Already here we can see that Cincinnatus views the Tamara Gardens as a sanctuary to which he can escape "whenever life seemed unbearable."

Throughout the novel, he continues to perceive the Tamara Gardens as some kind of Eden to which he frequently directs his thoughts and dreams:

> And so began those rapturous wanderings in the very, very spacious (so much so that even the hills in the distance would be hazy from the ecstasy of their remoteness) Tamara Gardens, where, for no reason, the willows weep into three brooks, and the brooks, in three cascades, each with its own small rainbow, tumble into the lake, where a swan floats arm in arm with its reflection. The level lawns, the rhododendrons, the oak groves, the merry gardeners in their green jackboots playing hide-and-seek the whole day through; some grotto, some idyllic bench, on which three jok-

ers had left three neat little heaps (it's a trick—they are imitations made of brown painted tin), some baby deer, bounding into the avenue and before your very eyes turning into trembling mottles of sunlight—that is what those gardens were like! There, there is Marthe's lisping prattle, her white stockings and velvet slippers, her cool breast and her rosy kisses tasting of wild strawberries. If only one could see from here—at least the treetops, at least the distant range of hills . . . (*IB* 27–28)

In this description, the ostensibly pastoral ambience of the Tamara Gardens, with their uniform, triple, design—they contain three brooks and three cascades—is undercut and undermined by the three heaps of fake human feces on one of its benches, thereby suggesting their defiled and at the same time deceptive nature. Their illusory character is also underscored by the idleness of their gardeners who have nothing else to do but to play hide-and-seek all day long. It is noteworthy that these "merry gardeners in their green jackboots" later materialize in M'sieur Pierre, who emerges in one of his photographs "in a garden, with a giant prize tomato in his hands," in another, "with the watering can" (*IB* 83 and 84), and who for his formal presentation to Cincinnatus as his executioner wears "a velvet jacket, an arty bow tie and new, high-heeled, insinuatingly squeaking boots with glossy legs (making him somehow resemble an operatic woodman)" (*IB* 171). The Tamara Gardens, therefore, become a symbol of Cincinnatus's fallacious hopes and unfulfilled aspirations: his idyllic courtship of Marthe there, which he earlier perceived as a promise of blissful marriage, turns into constant suffering from her habitual, matter-of-fact infidelities (see *IB* 31 and 63–64).

The Tamara Gardens, as well as all the other gardens in the novel, are evil not intrinsically but because of their being fashioned and controlled by malevolent creatures, those "specters, werewolves, parodies," those "adult dummies" (*IB* 40 and 95) who make them function as the integral part of the dystopian world surrounding Cincinnatus. Until nearly the end of the novel, all these phenomena arouse no suspicion in the protagonist, who feels mesmerized by the Tamara Gardens: "Cincinnatus, his palm pressed to his cheek, in motionless, ineffably vague and perhaps even blissful despair, gazed at the glimmer and haze of the Tamara Gardens and at the dove-blue melting hills beyond them—oh, it was a long time before he could take his eyes away" (*IB* 42–43), finding them "bewitching" (*IB* 43). Cincinnatus's unheeded perception of the Tamara Gardens as "bewitching" may convey an ominous impression in the English translation and was perhaps intended by Nabokov as an early warning to his protagonist. In Russian, however, it is more conducive to Cincinnatus's blissful perception of the Tamara Gardens: "adorably."[34]

As I mentioned elsewhere, this passage in its tonality is reminiscent of one in *Prison Pastimes* (1908) by Vladimir Dmitrievich Nabokov, the writer's father. In his prison memoirs, Nabokov senior recalls the sentiments that the sight of the Tauride Palace aroused in him from his cell: "To this day, I cannot overcome my excitement at the sight of the Tauride Palace. And of course to have it before my eyes in the current situation means to see before me, as if incarnate, that brief and recent but seemingly so distant past which will be forgotten neither by us, nor by history."[35]

The apparent resemblance in intonation also reverberates semantically: both locations epitomize the lost hopes, political for Nabokov senior, since the Tauride Palace was the seat of Russia's short-lived Duma (parliament) where Vladimir Dmitrievich was one of the leaders of the Cadet (Constitutional-Democratic) parliamentary faction from May 10 to July 21, 1906, when the First Duma was dissolved; and personal for Cincinnatus.[36] Curiously, the Tauride Palace, with its garden, built in 1783–89 by the architect Ivan Starov, served as the prototype for every Russian country estate manor with its own cupola and columns.[37] This observation rings true (if not the cupola, then at least the columns) regarding the house of the Vyra country estate, where the future writer spent most of his Russian summers, and even more so regarding the mansion of the Rozh(d)estveno estate which he inherited in 1916 after the death of his maternal uncle Vasily Ivanovich Rukavishnikov. It appears that the description of the manor in which the pre-execution supper takes place, its "theatrically lighted carriage porch with whitewashed columns, friezes on the pediment," which stand "in the very thick of the Tamara Gardens" (*IB* 181 and 187), suggests such a replica of the Tauride Palace.[38] The palace was originally built for Prince Grigory Potemkin (1739–91), the all-powerful favorite of Catherine the Great. Potemkin's name is associated with the so-called Potemkin Villages, those rows of sham façades of nonexistent houses that symbolize fraud and deception. The irony that the Tauride Palace, associated with the corrupt magnate, became the site of the nascent and short-lived Russian democracy was evidently not lost on Nabokov, who employs a similar manor with the gardens as a symbol of his novel's deceitful dystopia. And Nabokov also remembered that the Tauride Palace was the seat of the Constituent Assembly, the hope of Russian postimperial democracy, to which his father was elected as the Cadet Party delegate. The Bolsheviks disbanded the Constituent Assembly by force in January 1918, by which time V. D. Nabokov, with his whole family, was already in the Crimea.

There contributes to Cincinnatus's erroneous perception of the Tamara Gardens a phonetic resemblance between their name, *Tam*ara, and the Russian *tam* ("there") to which Cincinnatus strives to escape from *tut*, "here," "the horrible 'here'" and "the dead end of this life" (*IB* 93 and 205).[39] An insight comes to Cincinnatus only toward the end of the novel when he realizes that the pre-execution supper takes place "in the very thick of the Tamara Gardens" (*IB* 187). The gardens and their surroundings turn out to be the scene of the lightbulb monogram that plays an essential role in the novel:

> And, first in the garden, then beyond it, then still further, along the walks, in groves, in glades and on lawns, singly and in clusters, ruby, sapphire, and topaz lamps lit up, gradually inlaying the night with gems. The guests began to "oh!" and "ah!" M'sieur Pierre inhaled sharply and grabbed Cincinnatus by the wrist. The lights covered an ever-increasing area: now they stretched out along a distant valley, now they were on the other side of it, in the form of an elongated brooch, now they already studded the first slopes; once there they passed on from hill to hill, nestling in the most secret folds, groping their way to the summits, crossing over them! "Oh, how beautiful," whispered M'sieur Pierre, for an instant pressing his cheek against the cheek of Cincinnatus.
>
> The guests applauded. For three minutes a good million light bulbs of diverse colors burned, artfully planted in the grass, in branches, on cliffs, and all arranged in such a way as to embrace the whole nocturnal landscape with a grandiose monogram of

"P" and "C," which, however, had not quite come off. Thereupon the lights went out all at once and solid darkness reached up to the terrace. (*IB* 189)

The inclusion of Cincinnatus's initials in the monogram is a very telling manifestation of the prison-house of language: an attempt by M'sieur Pierre and his minions to coerce the dissenter, even on the eve of his execution, by way of his initials, into becoming an integral part of the world around him.[40] And the very fact that this action takes place in the Tamara Gardens should not escape the reader's notice.

Cincinnatus neither shares M'sieur Pierre's admiration for the "beautiful" monogram nor joins the guests in their applause, thereby once again resisting his tormentors, albeit silently (*IB* 189). And the very fact that the monogram "had not quite come off" portends the protagonist's eventual flight from the surrounding world and its ultimate demolition. Shortly before the monogram episode, Cincinnatus seems to get an inkling of the Tamara Gardens' true nature when he observes their "charmed hills" "pressing against the metallic sky" and "folded in gloom" (*IB* 187)—the description that foreshadows the apocalyptic collapse of the whole world around him in the final scene of the novel.

It is, however, only after this supper, at which, ironically, the park superintendent has inquired whether he is "admiring the landscape" (*IB* 187 and 188), and after the last meeting with Marthe, that Cincinnatus finally realizes: the surrounding world, including the Tamara Gardens, from which he used to see "in the distance" (*IB* 27) "those hills which broke out in a deadly rash" (*IB* 205), could offer him no refuge or liberation.[41] Cincinnatus finds them only when he makes his way from the deceptive Tamara Gardens to the genuine "there" by walking "in that direction where, to judge by the voices, stood beings akin to him" (*IB* 223).

"CLOUD, CASTLE, LAKE": THE IDYLLIC LANDSCAPE

The very title of this story constitutes the European landscape in a nutshell. It consists of a man-made object ("castle") flanked by two natural objects ("cloud" and "lake"). (In the original Russian, this sequence is somewhat different: there, two natural objects, "cloud" and "lake," are followed by the man-made—"tower"). The title, therefore, signifies the fundamental role of landscape in the story. Its significance is proclaimed in the following, perhaps programmatic, sentence: "We both, Vasiliy Ivanovich and I, have always been impressed by the anonymity of all the parts of a landscape, so dangerous for the soul, the impossibility of ever finding out where that path you see leads—and look, what a tempting thicket!" (*Stories* 432).

In his examination of the story, Maxim Shrayer presents fascinating visual evidence of the actual locations that might have served Nabokov as the prototype for the story. He takes into account the "castle" at the spa, known then as Marienbad and now as Mariánské Lázně, where Nabokov composed the story, and considers some other Czech "castles" in which Nabokov stayed or which he could have seen at that time.[42]

Curiously, there is a linguistic detail in the story that has gone unnoticed: when Vasiliy Ivanovich, the protagonist of the story, approaches the inn, in which he intends to rent a room with the view of cloud, castle, and lake, the innkeeper is "a tall old man vaguely resembling a Russian war veteran, who spoke German so poorly and with such a soft drawl that Vasiliy Ivanovich changed to his own tongue, but the man understood as in a dream and continued in the language of his environment, his family" (*Stories* 435). This passage suggests that the innkeeper is Czech. That explains why he speaks poor German and why he understands, "as in a dream," Vasiliy Ivanovich's Russian, a kindred Slavic language, while himself switching to "the language of his environment, his family."

As convincing as Shrayer's evidence is regarding the actual Czech locations, it does not account for the spiritual aspect of the landscape that permeates the story.[43] It appears that Nabokov drew the initial stimulus for this verbal formulaic landscape from Poussin's *Landscape with Saint Matthew and the Angel* (1640; Gemäldegalerie, Staatliche Museen zu Berlin), which he could see at the time at the Kaiser Friedrich Museum. The painting contains the three title components—cloud, castle, lake. Most important are the foreground figures of Saint Matthew and of the angel who provides heavenly instruction to the apostle in his writing of the Gospel.

This divine guidance, as exhibited in Poussin's masterpiece, must have appealed to Nabokov's perception of a writer whose creative process is modeled on that of the Almighty. In a letter to his mother of October 13, 1925, while working on his first novel *Mary* (1926), Nabokov maintains: "I understand how God as he created the world found this a pure, thrilling joy. *We* are translators of God's creation, his little plagiarists and imitators, we dress up what he wrote, as a charmed commentator sometimes gives an extra grace to a line of genius"[44] (italics in cited source). And in his poem "Tolstoy" (1928), Nabokov wrote:

> Почти нечеловеческая тайна!
> Я говорю о тех ночах, когда
> Толстой творил; я говорю о чуде,
> об урагане образов, летящих
> по черным небесам в час созиданья,
> в час воплощенья . . . Ведь живые люди
> родились в эти ночи . . . Так Господь
> избраннику передает свое
> старинное и благостное право
> творить миры и в созданную плоть
> вдыхать мгновенно дух неповторимый. (*Ssoch*, 2:593–94)

> (The mystery is almost superhuman!
> I mean the nights on which Tolstoy composed;
> I mean the miracle, the hurricane
> of images flying across the inky
> expanse of sky in that hour of creation,
> that hour of incarnation. . . . For, the people
> born on those nights were real. . . . That's how the Lord
> transmits to his elected his primeval,
> his beatific license to create
> his worlds, and instantly to breathe into
> the new-made flesh a one-and-only spirit.)[45]

Following this divine model, Sebastian Knight, a writer and the title character of Nabokov's first English-language novel, when found resting on the floor after completing one of his books, explains: "I have finished building a world, and this is my Sabbath rest" (*RLSK* 88). And many years later, Nabokov averred in an interview: "A creative writer must study carefully the works of his rivals, including the Almighty" (*SO* 32).

In addition, Nabokov could have drawn his inspiration for the spiritualized landscape of "Cloud, Castle, Lake" from Caspar David Friedrich (1774–1840), the German Romantic landscape artist, whose paintings "instantly radiate the unique intensity of experiencing and expressing the impalpable mysteries of landscape"—those manifestations of the Divine.[46] Nabokov was familiar with the art of Friedrich, but presumably not until his departure from Russia. Although a sizable number of Friedrich's paintings were acquired as early as 1820 by the Russian grand duke and later emperor Nicholas I as well as by Vasily Zhukovsky, who befriended the artist and used his position as the tutor for the grand duchess (later empress) Alexandra and for their son, Czarevich Alexander, the future emperor Alexander II, to solicit monetary assistance for the financially strained painter, they were not publicly displayed until after 1917.[47] Nabokov, therefore, most likely became familiar with Friedrich's art while in Germany, both at the museums and from art books.[48] It is worth noting that in *Look at the Harlequins!* Nabokov mentions an oil painting depicting "an alpine torrent with a fallen tree lying across it" (*LATH* 18) that brings to mind Friedrich's *Rocky Gorge* (ca. 1823; Kunsthistorisches Museum, Vienna). And although the novel's narrator calls the oil "conventional" (ibid.), this pronouncement may reflect Nabokov's attitude not toward Friedrich's art as a whole but rather toward this specific painting in the early 1970s when he was at work on the novel; it may also constitute the writer's reaction to the artwork by one of Friedrich's epigones. It is noteworthy that Friedrich would frequently place a sole viewer in his ethereal landscapes as, for example, in his *Landscape with a Rainbow* (ca. 1810; formerly Staatliche Kunstsammlungen, Weimar; now lost).

Influenced by Friedrich, his fellow countryman Adrian Ludwig Richter (1803–84) also conveys a spiritualized landscape of "cloud, castle, lake" in *Crossing the Elbe River at the Schreckenstein near Aussig* (figure 9). The artist depicts a boat crossing the Elbe River by the Schreckenstein castle that stands on the top of the cliff. The passenger with the knapsack, standing in the boat, with one foot on its board, as if ready to jump out, and propping up his chin on his hands, appears totally transfixed by the sight of the castle, not unlike the protagonist of Nabokov's story who "even pressed his hand to his heart, as if to see whether his heart was there in order to give it away" (*Stories* 435). By contrast, the oarsman and the other passengers seem oblivious to the majestic sight

9. Adrian Ludwig Richter, *Crossing the Elbe River at the Schreckenstein near Aussig*

and are reminiscent of Vasiliy Ivanovich's fellow travelers, even though Richter's characters look like the stock self-absorbed Romantic figures and not the odious creatures of Nabokov's short story: "At some distance, Schramm, poking into the air with the leader's alpenstock, was calling the attention of the excursionists to something or other; they had settled themselves around on the grass in poses seen in amateur snapshots, while the leader sat on a stump, his behind to the lake, and was having a snack" (ibid.).

The fairy-tale dimension of the story, "a pure, blue lake, with an unusual expression of its water" in which "a large cloud was reflected in its entirety," as well as "an ancient black castle" that "towered" "on a hill thickly covered with verdure" (*Stories* 435), could have been suggested to Nabokov by Karl Friedrich Schinkel's *Castle by a River* (1820; Schloss Charlottenburg, Berlin), which is permeated with the dreamy atmosphere of the fairyland. Schinkel's oil, with its mysterious, dreamy atmosphere and the three main components—cloud, castle, and water—was presumably influenced by Albrecht Altdorfer's panel *Danube Landscape near Regensburg* (ca. 1520–25; Alte Pinakothek, Munich), with which Nabokov most likely also was familiar.

In his depiction of the "cloud, castle, lake," Nabokov could also have been pictorially inspired by the "castle" landscapes of J. M. W. Turner (1775–1851), the renowned English landscape artist whom the writer singles out for his impact on him in his youth (*SO* 166–67). Works which specifically come to mind are the English painter's castle watercolors, such as *Dartmouth Castle* (1822; Tate Gallery, London), which Nabokov could see on his visits to the English capital during his Cambridge years. It is worth noting that Turner's watercolor calls to mind Nabokov's story in that it depicts a group of people (a party of two sailors and their female companions) sitting with their backs to the "cloud, castle, lake" and completely ignoring the view.

Thus, in "Cloud, Castle, Lake," Nabokov has created a composite Romantic landscape image for which he could draw inspiration from several renowned landscape painters of the period. In Friedrich's and Richter's art, Nabokov might find a spiritualized landscape with the lone gazing figure that invites a spectator to share his point of view. Schinkel's oil might suggest the fairy-tale dimension to the writer. And in Turner's watercolors, Nabokov might discover a Romanticized view of the landscape with a cloud, castle, and water (lake, river, sea) combination contrasted with a company of people that takes no notice whatsoever of the majestic scenery.

The Romantic atmosphere of the spiritualized central European landscape, not unlike that in the works of Friedrich and his followers, can be found in the poetry of Fedor Tiutchev (1803–73). Already at the outset of the "pleasure trip" (*Stories* 430), as if in anticipation of this landscape, Vasiliy Ivanovich starts reading from a book of Tiutchev's poetry, and particularly his poem "Silentium!"[49] He, however, recites the poem's line "A thought pronounced is a lie" ("Mysl´ izrechennaia est´ lozh´") as "We are slime. Spoken is a lie" ("My sliz´. Rechennaia est´ lozh´").[50] Vasiliy Ivanovich's garbling of the poem's words is telling because his fellow travelers are indeed slimy. More importantly, Vasiliy Ivanovich's misreading of Tiutchev's maxim proves to be fatal when he fails to keep his discovery of the "cloud, castle, lake" landscape to himself. Instead of remaining in this idyllic place, Vasiliy Ivanovich returns to his traveling companions to tell them that he intends to abandon their joint trip and to stay in the chosen locality. As a result, his fellow "excursionists" force him to continue the trip and, while on the train ride back to Berlin, beat him with such a "great deal of inventiveness" that Vasiliy Ivanovich begs his creator "to let him go" because "he had not the strength to belong to mankind any longer" (*Stories* 437).

It is worth noting that *Glory* may also be read as an allusion to Tiutchev's "Silentium!"[51] The following passage from the novel corroborates this assertion: "From early childhood his [Martin's] mother had taught him that to discuss in public a profound emotional experience—which, in the open air, immediately evanesces and fades, and, oddly, becomes similar to an analogous experience of one's interlocutor—was not only vulgar, but also a sin against sentiment" (*Glory* 12).

The poem is no less important for the understanding of *Invitation to a Beheading*. The inner world of the novel's protagonist conveys the atmosphere of concealment that dominates Tiutchev's piece. When Cincinnatus does share his feelings with the characters around him, they mock and torment him, like the Schramms and Schultzes who mock and torment Vasiliy Ivanovich. Thus, when Cincinnatus shares his dream of escaping to freedom with M'sieur Pierre, the executioner and the prison director mock him with the "rescue" operation. Nevertheless, Cincinnatus eventually triumphs in his struggle with the surrounding world because he ultimately follows the dictum of Tiutchev's verse.[52]

It is worth comparing the role of landscape, and specifically of the Tamara Gardens, in *Invitation to a Beheading* to that in the story "Cloud, Castle, Lake," written shortly after the publication of the novel. It is especially pertinent because Nabokov demonstratively links them through the exclamation of the Cincinnatus-like Vasiliy Ivanovich: "Oh, but this is nothing less than an invitation to a beheading" (*Stories* 436). In *Invitation to a Beheading*, Cincinnatus initially perceives the Tamara Gardens as an Eden but eventually begins to see clearly their deceptive nature as well as the malevolent essence of the whole world around him. In "Cloud, Castle, Lake," Vasiliy Ivanovich finds an idyllic place, but his inability to keep this discovery to himself not only spells his demise, but also indicates that the opportunity is missed forever. It is noteworthy that when Andrew Field speculated that Vasiliy Ivanovich "will go back to the perfect and dream-like lake," Nabokov poignantly replied to his first biographer: "He will never find it again."[53]

KING, QUEEN, KNAVE; DESPAIR; LOLITA:
THE LANDSCAPE AS THE "PERFECT CRIME" SETTING

Landscape is used as the murder scene in a number of Nabokov's works, as its habitually remote setting appears to be congenial with the surreptitiousness sought by a perpetrator of this heinous crime. Furthermore, the pastoral placidity of the natural scenery stands in stark contrast to the contemplated or committed violence by man, ostensibly created in God's image, and serves as a grim warning of the moral abyss into which human nature is capable of sinking. In all these works, however, the crime is either aborted at the last moment, or its perpetration leaves enough clues to apprehend the murderer.[54]

In *King, Queen, Knave*, Martha and Franz consider various ways of murdering Dreyer, such as poisoning or shooting, but eventually abandon "elaborate combinations, complicated details, phony weapons" and decide that "the sought-for method must be absolutely natural, absolutely pure" (*KQK* 197).[55] Eventually they opt to drown him in the sea. For this purpose, while vacationing at a Baltic Sea resort, Martha challenges Dreyer to a bet: she and Franz will reach a certain Rockpoint by a rowboat faster than he will on foot (see *KQK* 236). They then lure Dreyer into the rowboat and intend to push him overboard, knowing full well that he cannot swim. It looks as if the crime scene had been perfectly chosen for its seclusion: "A delightfully compliant mist veiled the receding beach. The boat started to round the little rocky island where seagulls were the only witnesses" (*KQK* 241–42). Later, upon surveying the scene, Martha once again concludes: "Sand, rocks, and further on, heathery slopes and woods. Not a soul, not a dog ever came here" (*KQK* 244). At the last moment, however, Martha decides to postpone the realization of her villainous plan when she learns that Dreyer expects to "clinch" a very profitable "deal" the following day (*KQK* 248). Martha is certain that the situation will present itself again soon. The aborted attempt, however, spells her ruin, as the inclement rainy weather makes her fatally ill.

In *Despair*, Hermann commits the murder of Felix in the countryside that he presents as a landscape painting: "To my right, beyond the field, the wood was painted a flat grey on the backdrop of the pale sky" (*Des* 163). He aspires to commit "a prefect crime" (*Des* 123), sacrilegiously equating it with art. He maintains that "if the deed is planned and performed correctly, then the force of creative art is such, that were the criminal to give himself up on the very next morning, none would believe him, the invention of art containing far more intrinsical truth than life's reality" (*Des* 122). Hermann, however, commits two major mistakes that eventually lead to his capture: he erroneously believes that he and his victim are twins, and he forgets to dispose of the stick "branded with the owner's name: Felix Wohlfahrt [whose given name and surname ironically mean, respectively, "happy," "lucky," or "prosperous" in Latin; and "well-being" in German] from Zwickau" (*Des* 202–3). The "imperfect" crime not only points to Hermann's warped world perception and disregard for detail but also suggests that he is a failed artist. (For an examination of the subject from a different angle, see chapter 6.)

Finally, in *Lolita,* where landscape plays a crucial role, Humbert, who is plotting to kill his wife Charlotte in order to realize his long-cherished "desire" (*AnL* 44) for her daughter, turns to a landscape as the murder stage.[56] Like Martha and Franz, he considers various murder schemes and eventually sets his eyes on drowning her. Like Hermann, he strives for a "perfect" crime and believes that in the Hourglass Lake he has found "the setting [that] was really perfect for a brisk bubbling murder" (*AnL* 86). Like Martha in *King, Queen, Knave,* Humbert presumes that the place he selected for the crime is fairly secluded:

> I walked down to Hourglass Lake. The spot from which we and a few other "nice" couples (the Farlows, the Chatfields) bathed was a kind of small cove; my Charlotte liked it because it was almost "a private beach." The main bathing facilities (or "drowning facilities" as the Ramsdale *Journal* had had occasion to say) [perhaps this phrase, coined by the local periodical, gave Humbert the idea] were in the left (eastern) part of the hourglass, and could not be seen from our covelet. To our right, the pines soon gave way to a curve of marshland which turned again into forest on the opposite side. (*AnL* 85)

The only two witnesses noticed by Humbert were "on the opposite bank": "a retired policeman of Polish descent and the retired plumber" who "were engaged in building, just for the dismal fun of the thing, a wharf" (*AnL* 85–86). As Humbert sinisterly remarks, "the man **of law** and the man of water were **just near** enough to witness an accident and just **far** enough not to observe a crime" (*AnL* 86; emphasis added). Humbert, however, aborts the lethal scheme because, as he puts it, "I could not make myself drown the poor, slippery, big-bodied creature" (*AnL* 87). Little did he know at the time that there was another, undetected, witness, Jean Farlow, whose name is encoded in the above-quoted phrase and who "in a place of green concealment [. . .] [was] spying on nature [. . .], trying to finish a lakescape" (*AnL* 88).

Ironically, Jean sees both Charlotte and Humbert from her shelter and almost paints them into her "lakescape." She admits noticing something that Humbert "overlooked" (*AnL* 89)—his wristwatch—which may suggest that Jean was close enough to detect the intended "drowning." Furthermore, her remark is highly ironic because Humbert "overlooked" not so much taking off the watch (that is waterproof) but, more important, the presence of Jean in such near-proximity to their bathing. When Humbert becomes aware of this, he thanks God for saving him from committing the crime, in the act of which he would have inevitably been caught—"thank God, not water, not water!" (*AnL* 88). At the end of this episode, Humbert realizes the fallaciousness of the very idea of a perfect crime when he remarks upon learning about Jean Farlow's (note a very fitting meaningful surname = far + low-[profile]) inconspicuous, nearby presence: "Nonetheless it was a very close shave, speaking quite objectively. And now comes the point of my perfect-crime parable" (*AnL* 88). Curiously, Humbert and Charlotte not only become part of the "lakescape" by virtue of the narrator's own verbal description of it, but also nearly so pictorially as the figures that an amateur artist, Jean Farlow, in her words, "almost put [. . .] in my lake" (*AnL* 89). Here once again, as often the case with Nabokov (compare the landscape in the oil painting and its book description in *Glory*), the verbal and the pictorial representations of the landscape tend to converge.

PNIN: THE LIBERATING LANDSCAPE

Finally, the landscape plays a significant role in *Pnin*, and specifically in its closing passage. Throughout the novel, the protagonist, whom

Nabokov lovingly calls "a man of great moral courage, a pure man, a scholar and a staunch friend, serenely wise, faithful to a single love" is misunderstood and ridiculed by most of his colleagues, "many an average intellectual," to whom he seems to be merely "a figure of fun" (*SL* 182). These specifically include Jack Cockerell, who by his cruel, sadistic behavior toward Pnin is reminiscent of M'sieur Pierre, the sinister executioner in *Invitation to a Beheading*. Both Jack Cockerell and M'sieur Pierre are related through Petrushka—the crude and cynical personage of the Russian puppet theater, akin to the commedia dell'arte Pulcinella, French Polichinelle, and English Punch. Petrushka is a slighting form for Petr, the Russian equivalent of the Gallicized given name of the executioner, once called "Pyotr Petrovich" (*IB* 168). This explains why M'sieur Pierre calls the puppet "a namesake" ("tezka"; *Ssoch*, 4:130). (In the English translation, the word is rendered as "chum" [*IB* 137].) Another common, diminutive, form for Petr is Petia, which is also a regular folklore appellation for a rooster or cockerel (*petia* or *petia-petushok*), once again linking Cockerell to M'sieur Pierre.

One more Nabokov character, whom Cockerell resembles in his compulsive impersonation of Pnin, is Goryainov, a fleeting character in *The Gift,*

> who was well known for the fact that being able to imitate beautifully (by stretching his mouth wide, making moist ruminant sounds, and speaking in falsetto) a certain unfortunate, cranky journalist with a poor reputation, he had grown so accustomed to this image (which thus had its revenge on him) that not only did he also pull down the corners of his mouth when imitating other of his acquaintances, but even began to look like it himself in normal conversation. (*Gift* 195)

We recall that Cockerell "had acquired an unmistakable resemblance to the man [Pnin] he had now been mimicking for almost ten years" (*Pnin* 187). And as in the case of Goryainov, that compulsive mimicking, "this Pnin business," appears to wreak "some poetical vengeance" upon Cockerell by turning into "the kind of fatal obsession which substitutes its own victim for that of the initial ridicule" (*Pnin* 189).

Although N—, the novel's narrator, "a prominent Anglo-Russian writer" (*Pnin* 140)—not to be mistaken for the author, of whom N— is merely a travestied version, like the later Vadim Vadimovich, the protagonist of *Look at the Harlequins!*—feels "the mental counterpart of a bad taste in the mouth" (*Pnin* 189) upon hearing Cockerell's entire Pnin repertoire, he himself exhibits indiscretion and indecency toward his compatriot when quoting verbatim Pnin's "offer of marriage" to Liza Bogolepov, with whom he allegedly had an affair under the nose of his unsuspecting "good friend" (*Pnin* 182–83, 184, and 186). N— also demonstrates callousness toward Pnin when, having fun at his expense, he readily provides examples of the title character's clumsy English.[57] On the other hand, Vladimir Nabokov, Pnin's true creator, rescues the title character from the misery inflicted upon him by his tormentors in deus ex machina fashion, a device the writer has employed many a time before (see, for example, "Cloud, Castle, Lake," *Invitation to a Beheading*, and *Bend Sinister*). As a birthday gift (this occurs on February 15, Pnin's birthday), Nabokov liberates his much-loved character and, appropriately for this occasion, paints a delightful, wintry landscape of the northeastern American countryside: "The air was keen, the sky clear and burnished. Southward the empty road could be seen ascending a gray-blue hill among patches of snow" (*Pnin* 190). But he leaves the most magnificent depiction of the landscape for last when he shows how Pnin finally frees himself from all his predicaments by emblematically releasing his car from being squashed in between the two identical trucks of Past and Present: "Then the little sedan boldly swung past the front truck and, free at last, spurted up the shining road, which one could make out narrowing to a thread of gold in the soft mist where hill after hill made beauty of distance, and where there was simply no saying what miracle might happen" (*Pnin* 191).[58]

Nabokov creates here before our very eyes and those of his astounded, farcical look-alike a remarkable spiritualized space, reminiscent of that in "Cloud, Castle, Lake." Only this time, unlike in the story of twenty years earlier, Nabokov does not leave anything to chance and vigorously "intervenes" on behalf of his hero, "the more human, the more important, and, on a moral plane, the more attractive one" than "so-called 'normal' individuals" (*SL* 178). He comes to his hero's rescue in order to relocate him several years later to his other novel, *Pale Fire*, and to secure for him there a position as professor and head of the Russian Department at another, Wordsmith, college (see *PF* 155).[59]

* * *

Nabokov, who aspired to become a landscape artist in his childhood and early youth, demonstrates a propensity for this pictorial genre and puts it to good use throughout his entire oeuvre. Verbal landscape assumes numerous functions in Nabokov's works. (In this, Nabokov prefigures W. J. T. Mitchell, who views landscape as "a cultural medium," "an instrument of cultural power," that "greets us as space, as environment, as that within which 'we' [. . .] find or lose ourselves.")[60] The writer employs it at times as the leitmotif (a winding path in the forest) of the entire work in which it serves as the pictogram of the protagonist's whole life, at times as the stage at which the protagonist at first misinterprets but then gradually begins to comprehend the meaning of the world around him (the Tamara Gardens), at times as the focal scenery (cloud, castle, lake) that leads to the denouement of the story, at times as the ironically secluded scene of a "perfect crime," and at times as a spiritualized space that provides the appropriate setting for the culminating resolution of the narrative. Furthermore, Nabokov endows landscape with diverse roles, from enchanting (*Glory*), deceptive (*Invitation to a Beheading*) and perilous (*King, Queen, Knave; Despair; Lolita*), to idyllic ("Cloud, Castle, Lake") and liberating (*Pnin*).

4. THE WORLD OF ART

I prefer the experimental decade that coincided with my
boyhood—Somov, Benois [. . .], Vrubel, Dobuzhinski, etc.
—Nabokov, *Strong Opinions*

The World of Art constituted a major aesthetic phenomenon in Russian
culture at the turn of the twentieth century. It originated in early November 1898, less than six months before Nabokov's birth, with the
appearance of the first Russian art periodical, so named. The journal's benefactors were Princess Maria Tenisheva and the industrialist
Savva Mamontov, and its editor in chief was Sergei Diaghilev (1872–
1929). Even though the periodical was a rather short-lived under-
taking (its publication stopped in 1904), the name did not die out for
at least another two decades. *The World of Art* became an appellation
for the group that formed around several highly gifted St. Petersburg
painters—Alexander Benois (1870–1960), Konstantin Somov (1869–
1939), Léon Bakst (Lev Rosenberg, 1866–1924), and later Mstislav Dobuzhinsky (1875–1957).[1]

The group left an indelible mark on the Russian culture of the early
twentieth century, specifically on painting, book graphics, and stage
design.[2] As the journal's editor and the group's leader and manager,
Diaghilev played a magisterial role in familiarizing Russians with Western art, from Old Masters to contemporary, as well as with past and current trends in the art of their own country. After the periodical ceased
publication, Diaghilev, a talented impresario, continued to propagate
Russian contemporary art both at home and abroad for another quarter of a century (until his death in 1929) by means of art exhibits and
concerts, as well as opera and ballet productions.

Nabokov was fully aware of Diaghilev's significant role in Russian
culture of the early twentieth century. He writes: "Among the many
names connected with the Russian Renaissance, that of Diaghilev de-

serves honorable mention. Although not a creative genius in the precise sense of the term, his perfect taste in art, allied to a fascinating personality and to fiery energy in the promotion of what was finest in art, gives him a prominent place in the history of Russian culture."[3] Nabokov alludes to Diaghilev in "Solus Rex" (1940), in the figure of Prince Adulf, whose "physical aspect" the writer imagined "as resembling that of S. P. Diaghilev" (*Stories* 658), as well as in *Ada* (1969), in the figure of "a fat ballet master, Dangleleaf" (*Ada* 430).

Throughout his entire creative life, Nabokov held *The World of Art* in very high esteem. Even though his tastes evolved and changed considerably over the years, Nabokov nevertheless remained true to his appraisal of *The World of Art*. Thus, in his postcard of April 5, 1939, to Véra from London, Nabokov writes: "Then I dined at the most charming old Braikevichs'; they have a remarkable collection of paintings, especially the whole trove of Somov's, of which I could not get my fill."[4]

More than three decades later, in 1970, in an interview with Alfred Appel Jr., who queried Nabokov on his "feelings about" such avant-garde artists as Vasily Kandinsky, Kasimir Malevich, and Marc Chagall, the writer responds: "I prefer the experimental decade that coincided with my boyhood—Somov, Benois [. . .], Vrubel, Dobuzhinski, etc." (*SO* 170), thereby associating artistic innovation during his formative years with *The World of Art*'s chief representatives.[5] Although Vrubel did not belong to the group, he was revered by many of its participants. We recall that Stepan Iaremich, a painter and art critic closely affiliated with *The World of Art,* and Nabokov's drawing master (1910–12), published the first monograph on Vrubel in 1911, while he was giving drawing lessons to Nabokov.

What were the principal aspects of *The World of Art*'s outlook that could appeal to Nabokov? First, the group rejected the utilitarian approach to art that had dominated Russian culture since the 1860s. Among the proponents of this approach at the time were the Wanderers, an association of Russian painters, and their champion, the critic Vladimir Stasov, who placed emphasis on social awareness in art and its auxiliary role as the propagator of "reality." Thus Benois derides "the naiveté with which [Nikolai Chernyshevsky's treatise] *The Aesthetic Relations* [*of Art to Reality*, 1855] presents ill-digested thoughts of Western socialist and positivist thinkers."[6] This treatise, together with the midcentury works of Nikolai Dobroliubov, Dmitri Pisarev, and Vissarion Belinsky, laid the ideological foundations for the emergence of the Wanderers.

The *World of Art* group also rejected the stagnant conventionality of the Academicians. Curiously, some of them only a few decades earlier had been part of the Wanderers' movement that rebelled against and broke away from the stifling constraints of the Academy.[7] To quote Benois, "We were instinctively drawn to move away from [. . .] the tendentiousness of the Wanderers [. . .], as far as possible from our decadent Academism."[8] Instead, *The World of Art* declared freedom of expression and beauty as art's supreme goal and independent value.[9]

In chapter 4 of *The Gift*, similarly to Benois, Nabokov ridicules the aesthetic views of Chernyshevsky, the father of the positivist and utilitarian approach to art in Russia. In his 1940 review of a monograph on Diaghilev, Nabokov, like its subject, expressed disdain for "the utilitarian and didactic tendencies of the [eighteen] sixties and seventies."[10] And Nabokov maintained in a 1964 interview: "A work of art has no importance whatever to society" and "there can be no question that what makes a work of fiction safe from larvae and rust is not its social importance but its art, only its art" (*SO* 33).

Many of the *World of Art* painters viewed the poet Alexander Pushkin (1799–1837) as their standard and symbol, and themselves as recipients of the Pushkinian education and bearers and promulgators of the refined Pushkinian culture.[11] This explains why so many of them, including Benois (*The Bronze Horseman,* "The Captain's Daughter," "The Queen of Spades"), Dobuzhinsky (*Eugene Onegin,* "Mistress into Maid," "The Stationmaster"), and Somov (*Count Nulin*), to name only a few, drew illustrations, in the words of Benois, those "graphic commentaries" to Pushkin's works,[12] and designed stage sets and costumes for theater, opera, and ballet productions based on Pushkin's works—notably Benois (*The Feast During the Plague, Mozart and Salieri, The Stone Guest, Boris Godunov, The Queen of Spades*) and Dobuzhinsky (*Count Nulin, Boris Godunov, Eugene Onegin, The Queen of Spades*).

Nabokov expresses notions akin to those of the *World of Art* painters. A devoted and devout disciple of Pushkin, and the translator and annotator of *Eugene Onegin,* the poet's magnum opus, Nabokov maintains that "Pushkin's blood runs through the veins of modern Russian literature" and speaks about "the pride and purity of Pushkin's art" (*SO* 63 and 103). And we recall that Fyodor Godunov-Cherdyntsev, the protagonist of *The Gift,* similarly to his creator, "fed on Pushkin, inhaled Pushkin [. . .] Pushkin entered his blood" (*Gift* 97–98).

The preoccupation with Pushkin and his literary legacy, which came on the heels of his widely celebrated centenary in 1899, may also be seen as one of the facets of the *World of Art* painters' fascination with the past. Throughout their careers, they were frequently engaged in depictions of old St. Petersburg, apparently heightened by the city's bicentennial celebrations in 1903. Owing to the efforts of the *World of Art* participants, there emerged a true cult of the old Petersburg, and eventually, in 1908, a museum for the preservation of the city's historical and architectural monuments was founded.[13] This penchant for the past earned the group the nickname of "retrospective dreamers."[14]

Nabokov's attitude is analogous to that of *The World of Art:* the exiled writer recurrently depicts the St. Petersburg of his childhood and youth, which he re-creates through the power of his memory and the nostalgia for which he expresses time and again in both his poetry and prose.[15] Furthermore, it is fair to say that Nabokov in fact experienced a double nostalgia. On the one hand, he was influenced by the artists' retrospective dreaming while still living in Russia. On the other hand, their depiction of St. Petersburg and the capital's surroundings, which by the writer's own admission constituted the only Russia he knew and loved (see *SM* 250), evoked in him, especially in exile, a nostalgia for those bygone years of happiness, retrievable in neither time nor space, but only in memory.[16] Hence Nabokov's preoccupation, from the earliest days of his exile, with time, space, and memory, as demonstrates his entire oeuvre, from "The Return of Chorb" and *Mary* to *Look at the Harlequins!*

Additionally, the *World of Art* painters were well known for the keen attention to detail that may be specifically linked to their interest in various engraving techniques and book graphics. In chapters 1 and 2, I connected Nabokov's early penchant for detail to his studies with Mstislav Dobuzhinsky. It is worth noting in this regard that the school of academic painting in Europe at the turn of the twentieth century underscored the importance of elaborate detail in art. One of the chief propagators of this tenet in Russia was Vasily Maté, a professor at the St. Petersburg Academy of Arts, whose workshop

Dobuzhinsky attended in 1901 and from whom he learned various techniques of engraving. Aside from Dobuzhinsky, many other highly acclaimed artists—Isaac Levitan, Ilya Repin, Valentin Serov, and Anna Ostroumova-Lebedeva—attended Maté's workshop.[17] As pedagogues, they strove to inculcate this approach in their students. Thus, Nabokov recalls that his drawing master, Dobuzhinsky, "made me depict from memory, in the greatest possible detail, objects I had certainly seen thousands of times without visualizing them properly: a street lamp, a postbox, the tulip design on the stained glass of our own front door" (*SM* 92). Remaining true to his teacher's precepts, Nabokov attached the utmost importance to details in his writings.

Another pertinent aspect of *The World of Art* was its strong orientation toward Western culture. *The World of Art* journal familiarized its Russian readership with many western European artists, especially contemporaneous ones, such as the Frenchman Pierre Puvis de Chavannes, the Belgian Félicien Rops, and the Swede Anders Zorn. In addition, many of the *World of Art* representatives were fond of English art, from Joshua Reynolds and Thomas Gainsborough to the Pre-Raphaelites and Aubrey Beardsley.[18] This orientation was congenial to Nabokov, who grew up amid the Westernized culture of St. Petersburg and was trilingual, if not quadrilingual (Russian, English, French, and German), from an early age. He was frequently taken to western Europe as a boy by his parents and tutors and was raised in an Anglophile family. The refined taste of the *World of Art*'s chief participants corresponded to the highly cultured atmosphere that reigned in Nabokov's family (see chapter 1). Nabokov's close familiarity with western European, and specifically English, art of the eighteenth and nineteenth centuries is evident in his works. Thus, he mentions "a portrait of Lady Hamilton," presumably by George Romney (*Glory* 34), *The Blue Boy* by Gainsborough (*BS* 150), and *The Age of Innocence* by Reynolds (*AnL* 198 and 402). He names Turner among the painters who meant a lot to him in his youth (see *SO* 167), and recurrently alludes to Beardsley in *Lolita*.[19]

Finally, by means of its publications as well as its exhibits and performances, *The World of Art* served as a cultural mediator between Russia and the West and was the first group to put Russia on the cultural world map. Upholding and continuing this tradition, Nabokov not only served as a cultural liaison of sorts between Russia and the Western world but also became, as Omry Ronen has recently demonstrated, the first among Russian-born literati to attain "the interliterary stature of a world writer."[20]

Nabokov was well acquainted with the journal *The World of Art*. An avid reader, he could familiarize himself with the periodical in his father's voluminous library.[21] In his boyhood and early youth, at the time when Nabokov aspired to become a painter, he saw some of the *World of Art* representatives in person in his parental home. He recalls sighting Alexander Benois at their St. Petersburg residence (*Ssoch*, 5:172). In 1908–17 Benois was the art critic for the daily newspaper *Speech*, copublished by V. D. Nabokov (with I. I. Petrunkevich and others). As the artist's diaries indicate, he was on amiable terms with Nabokov senior and frequently visited the Nabokov residence at Bol'shaia Morskaia, 47.[22] Nabokov would catch a glimpse of Bakst in 1910 during the sessions when the artist worked on his mother's portrait. And Iaremich and Dobuzhinsky were, of course, his drawing masters (see chapter 1).

Nabokov was also thoroughly familiar with the works of the *World of Art* painters, as he was exposed to them daily at his St. Petersburg residence. Thus, in his English-language memoirs, first in *Conclusive Evidence* and then in *Speak, Memory*, Nabokov mentions that in his father's study, there was hanging "right over the desk, the rose-and-haze pastel portrait" (1910) of his mother by Bakst which the writer lovingly describes as follows: "The artist had drawn her face in three-quarter view, wonderfully bringing out its delicate features—the upward sweep of the ash-colored hair (it had grayed when she was in her twenties), the pure curve of the forehead, the dove-blue eyes, the graceful line of the neck" (*CE* 134 and *SM* 190).

As mentioned earlier, in *Other Shores*, his Russian-language memoir, Nabokov also describes works of the *World of Art* painters in his mother's study. There, Alexander Benois' "truly delightful rain-bloated *Bretagne* and russet-green *Versailles* neighbored by the 'delectable' (in the parlance of those times) *Turks* of Bakst and Somov's watercolor *Rainbow* amidst its wet birches." In *Speak, Memory*, Nabokov recalls seeing in his mother's study "a Somov aquarelle (young birch trees, the half of a rainbow—everything very melting and moist), [and] a splendid *Versailles* autumn by Alexandre Benois" (*SM* 226). It is possible that Nabokov alludes to Somov's *Rainbow* oil variant in *The Real Life of Sebastian Knight:* "A small old oil-painting, a little cracked (muddy road, rainbow, beautiful puddles)" (*RLSK* 35; compare *Ssoch*, 5:686).

Unlike the familiar present location of Elena Ivanovna Nabokov's portrait by Bakst—after the Bolshevik coup d'état, it became part of the State Russian Museum collection—the whereabouts of the paintings that adorned Nabokov's mother's study are not documented. Although, as Nabokov recalls, Alexander Benois intimated to him almost a quarter of a century later that "soon after the Soviet Revolution he had had all Bakst's works, as well as some of his own, such as the 'Rainy Day in Brittany,' transported from our house to the Alexander III (now State) [Russian] Museum" (*SM,* between 160 and 161). Based on Nabokov's description, however, it is possible to discern what they looked like. Thus, Nabokov's description of the two paintings by Benois parallels the artist's *Breton Landscape* (1906; State Russian Museum, St. Petersburg) and his *Versailles: At the Statue of Marcus Curtius* (1897; State Russian Museum, St. Petersburg) from the series *The Last Promenades of Louis XIV* (1897–98). Those "delectable" *Turks* of Bakst were apparently among "a number of watercolor sketches made for the Scheherazade ballet" (1910) that, as Nabokov remembers, his "parents possessed" (*SM,* between 160 and 161), such as the one for the role of Shahriar (Thyssen-Bornemisza Collection, Madrid);[23] whereas Somov's watercolor *Rainbow* could be visualized by means of its probable variant (1908; State Tret´iakov Gallery, Moscow).[24]

THE "STYLIZED SNOW" OF *THE WORLD OF ART*

In light of all these affinities, it is not surprising that Nabokov refers or alludes to works of the *World of Art* painters in his fiction. A case in point is a very specific description of snow that recurrently emerges in Nabokov's works. This description is suggested in *The Gift,* where it is characterized as "the snow of *The World of Art*" ("sneg 'Mira Iskusstva'"). In the English translation, however, apparently out of concern for the reader's unfamiliarity with Russian culture, it is rendered merely as "stylized snow" (*Ssoch,* 4:376; *Gift* 196). Many years later, Nabokov elaborated on this image in *Other Shores* where he speaks of "the vertically falling oversized snowflakes of *The World of Art.*"[25]

This image harkens back to Nabokov's poem "The Skater," whose last stanza consists of the following lines:

I left behind a single verbal figure,
an instantly unfolding flower, inked.
And yet tomorrow, vertical and silent,
the snow will dust the scribble-scrabbled rink.[26]

As we saw earlier (chapter 2), the poem, which was composed on February 5, 1925, that is, a little over two months before Nabokov's marriage to Véra Slonim (April 15), is dedicated to her by means of an anagrammatic inscription.[27] In "The Skater" Nabokov re-creates the wintry atmosphere of St. Petersburg, his and Véra's native city.[28] This is suggested by the description of snow as "vertical and silent" (literally, "noiseless"), which once again may be linked to the recurrent *World of Art* image.[29]

This image reemerges in *Mary*, on which the writer started working in the spring of 1925, shortly after composing "The Skater."[30] In Ganin's recollection of his meetings with Mary, set in St. Petersburg, there is a reference to "soft oversized snowflakes [that] came down vertically in the gray, mat-glass air" (*Mary* 69).[31] This "snow falling," "that special snow of oblivion, abundant and soundless snow," also appears in *The Defense* (*Def* 31). Later, in the partly autobiographical story "Orache" (1932), also set in St. Petersburg, a similar imagery—"oversize, irregularly shaped, hastily modeled snowflakes"—is mentioned (*Stories* 328). And the somewhat autobiographical *The Gift* contains a similar sentence: "Farewell forever: on a winter day, with large snowflakes falling since morning, drifting anyhow—vertically, slantwise, even upwards" (*Gift* 153–54).

What is the source of this persistent imagery that Nabokov links to *The World of Art*? The writer sheds some light on it in *Speak, Memory*, where he associates "the stylized snowscape of the 'Art World,'" *Mir Iskusstva*," with "Dobuzhinski, Alexandre Benois," who, as he puts it, were "so dear to me in those days" (*SM* 236).

In linking the "stylized snowscape" to Dobuzhinsky and Benois, Nabokov invokes such paintings by these artists as *A Little House in St. Petersburg* (1905; State Tret´iakov Gallery, Moscow) and *Parade Under Paul I* (1907; State Russian Museum, St. Petersburg), which depict vertically falling, oversized snowflakes.

It seems that in *Mary*, however, Nabokov alludes to yet another work by Benois. This is evident in the section that immediately precedes the earlier quoted "snow" sentence: "Mary did not move to St. Petersburg until November. They met under the same arch where Liza dies in Tchaikovsky's *The Queen of Spades*" (*Mary* 69).[32] Although Nabokov refers here to Tchaikovsky's opera—he never misses an opportunity to mock "cloying banalities" of his music and especially his "hideous and insulting" libretti (*SO* 266) (in these remarks Nabokov, however, specifically refers to another of Tchaikovsky's operas, *Eugene Onegin*)—he suggests here Pushkin's eponymous tale, and specifically, with this snow image, the episode of Hermann's waiting by the Countess's house.[33] This episode of Pushkin's tale contains a description of horrendous weather during which "wet snow fell in large flakes."[34] In the corresponding illustration, *Hermann at the Countess's Driveway* (1905), Benois depicts snow as falling vertically and in large-size flakes. Nabokov could see this piece any time after 1905 when Benois painted it. More likely, however, the writer saw it in the 1911 and 1917 publications of Pushkin's masterpiece accompanied by Benois' illustrations.

It is noteworthy that Dobuzhinsky regards the falling snow as an important component of the St. Petersburg cityscape image that helps to evoke his remembrances of the imperial capital. In a letter of January 28, 1957, to A. M. Elkan, a friend and collector of his works, Dobuzhinsky writes:

> I made a copy from your "Peter and Isaac" [Dobuzhinsky presumably refers here to his cityscape that contains the views of the equestrian statue of Peter the Great, widely known as the Bronze Horseman, and Saint Isaac's Cathedral] right before the exhibition, but it greatly differs from the original itself, where there is much *charcoal* and little *paint*. Here I worked with gouache and added the falling snow, so that it is not a duplicate at all. And I am only grateful to you that, making this piece, I was able to reminisce and immerse myself in our Petersburg moods . . . And how to forget them? When everything is emerging as if it were yesterday.[35] (italics in original)

While for Dobuzhinsky the snow imagery is an essential component of his bygone years in St. Petersburg, for Nabokov it seems to epitomize his entire Russian past. This is evident in the section of *Speak, Memory* in which the writer recalls Mademoiselle, his French governess, "rolling into our [his and his brother Sergei's] existence in December 1905" (*SM* 95). The description ends with the following digression, which echoes the story "The Visit to the Museum" (1939) and the poem "To Prince S. M. Kachurin" (1947):

> Very lovely, very lonesome. But what am I doing in this stereo-scopic dreamland? How did I get here? Somehow, the two sleighs have slipped away, leaving behind a passportless spy standing on the blue-white road in his New England snowboots and storm-coat. The vibration in my ears is no longer their receding bells, but only my old blood singing. All is still, spellbound, enthralled by the moon, fancy's rear-vision mirror. The snow is real, though, and as I bend to it and scoop up a handful, sixty years crumble to glittering frost-dust between my fingers. (*SM* 99–100)[36]

As can be seen, the "stylized snow" imagery serves Nabokov as an important metonymic device that encapsulates his Russian past and enables him to express nostalgia for the bygone years of his golden childhood and youth. In this regard, the *World of Art* painters and their art, with which Nabokov familiarized himself at that blissful period of his life and to which he felt a close bond, and specifically Dobuzhinsky, his drawing master from that period, and his artistic legacy, became especially dear to Nabokov, as he viewed this quintessential imagery through the prism of their pictorial portrayal of his beloved city.

NABOKOV AND DOBUZHINSKY:
FROM PUPIL AND TEACHER TO COEQUALS AND FRIENDS

In the example of the "stylized snow" imagery, I have demonstrated Nabokov's kinship to *The World of Art* at large and its most prominent artists, especially Benois and Dobuzhinsky. We now turn to focus on Nabokov's creative affinity with Dobuzhinsky, one of the most distinguished members and characteristic representatives of *The World of Art*'s aesthetics, and the drawing master of his boyhood and early youth, and on the dynamics of their relationship, which evolved from one of pupil and teacher to that of coequals and friends. I shall put side by side their familial and cultural backgrounds, their common interests, and discuss their artistic association and personal contacts, as these developed throughout their creative lives.

As I mentioned earlier (in chapter 1), Vladimir Nabokov was born in St. Petersburg, the Russian imperial capital, into an aristocratic family with multifaceted aesthetic interests. He received an excellent education, first at home by various tutors and governesses, and then between 1910 and 1917 at the highly regarded Tenishev School, which also numbered the poet Osip Mandelstam, the philologist Viktor Zhirmunsky, the nuclear physicist Dmitri Skobel´tsyn, and the art historian Vladimir Levinson-Lessing among its earlier graduates.[37] In his boyhood and early youth, Nabokov showed great interest in painting, but later, around the age of fifteen, turned from the pictorial to the verbal mode of expression. Between 1919 and 1922 Nabokov studied at Cambridge University, from which he graduated with honors, majoring in French and Russian literature.

Mstislav Dobuzhinsky, like Nabokov almost a quarter of a century after him, was born into a highly cultured family. His mother Elizaveta Timofeevna (née Sofiiskaia) was an opera singer. His father, Valerian Petrovich, a military officer who eventually attained the rank of major general, was a music lover, an amateur draftsman, and a connoisseur of zoology. The artist's paternal uncle Fedor was a noted jurist with whom V. D. Nabokov was apparently acquainted; his other paternal uncle, Evstafy, like Nabokov's maternal ancestors N. I. Kozlov, his daughter Praskovia, and her husband, V. M. Tarnovsky, was a physician and author of several medical studies.

Dobuzhinsky, too, received an excellent education, first in several schools (gymnasia) of St. Petersburg, Kishinev, and Vilna, among which he had to migrate because of his father's military appointments, and then, from 1895 to 1899, at St. Petersburg University, where he majored in law. He showed a great fascination with painting from his early boyhood, and it eventually became his lifelong vocation. As mentioned earlier (in chapter 1), Dobuzhinsky studied art at the Society for the Encouragement of the Arts in St. Petersburg (1885–87) and then privately under Dmitriev-Kavkazsky (1897–99). In 1899, the year of Nabokov's birth, upon graduating from the St. Petersburg University Law School, Dobuzhinsky went for two years to Munich to continue his artistic education at the Ažbe and Hollósy schools of Art.[38] In 1902, a year after his return to St. Petersburg, he joined *The World of Art*.[39] By 1912, when Dobuzhinsky became the drawing master of the thirteen-year-old Nabokov, he was an accomplished painter, book illustrator, and stage designer.

The writer and the artist shared a variety of interests and sensibilities: aptitude for pedagogy, attention to details, propensity for painting and writing, fascination with the comic, predilection for the past, and love of St. Petersburg, some of which Nabokov either acquired from or developed under his mentor's guidance.[40]

Curiously, Dobuzhinsky also collected butterflies in his boyhood. But while for him it was a passing fascination, for Nabokov lepidoptery remained a lifelong passion, second only to literature.[41] Dobuzhinsky's childhood fascination with butterflies finds its expression in *The Provinces in the 1830s* (1907–9; State Russian Museum, St. Petersburg), in which a little white butterfly, apparently a cabbage white, is depicted on a street lamp pole. One wonders whether Dobuzhinsky ever spoke about this childhood fascination of his with Nabokov.

Before teaching the young Nabokov, Dobuzhinsky had acquired a great deal of educational experience and excelled as a pedagogue. As mentioned in chapter 1, in 1906–11 he taught at the Zvantseva School of Drawing and Painting; and in 1922–23 he also taught at the State Free Art Workshops. Among his many students were Nikolai Akimov, Marc Chagall, Elena Guro, Ohel Mané-Katz, Georgy Narbut, and Georgy Vereisky.[42] Nabokov, too, was a very gifted pedagogue. His students recall that he taught them "how to read, how to see" and that "he was a fabulous teacher."[43]

Attention to detail, both in his profession and in everyday life, was very typical of Dobuzhinsky. A striking example of Dobuzhinsky's intolerance of approximation in art and of disregard for details is evident in his 1947 review of Sergei Eisenstein's movie *Ivan the Terrible* (Part I, 1944), poignantly entitled "A Sugary Film." Commenting on the movie, Dobuzhinsky writes:

> What is surprising is the inexplicable plethora of falsehood and historical inaccuracies with which the movie abounds. There, in Moscow, at the Armory and in the Historical Museum, there is at hand the entire wealth of all kinds of relics of that epoch. And one ought to admit the lack of tact and of elementary conscientious-

ness, let alone taste, on the part of the producers if they could stuff the movie, alongside credible things, with what is called a cock-and-bull story. Neither in theater nor in film do there exist trifles, and it is bad if they say: "The public will not notice this." Those who have eyes will always see mistakes and shortcomings.[44]

Dobuzhinsky's pedantic attitude to details, so distinctive of him throughout his life, is also evident in his comments on Benois' memoirs. In a letter to Benois, a close friend, on January 10, 1957, Dobuzhinsky writes: "I noticed only one mistake: the Empire-style house on Nevsky Prospect, between Liteinaia and Nadezhdinskaia Streets, where exhibits were held—is not the house of Radokonaki, as you write, but of *Bernardakki* (or Bernardazzi)—I am certain of it. And one more thing—military doctors did not have golden epaulettes but silver ones (my uncle was a military doctor, and so I remember it well)"[45] (italics in original).

It appears that aside from his natural pedagogical aptitude, Nabokov taught *his* many students at Stanford, Wellesley, Harvard, and Cornell what he learned from his drawing master—specifically to be attentive to details. In particular, Nabokov taught them that "the moonshine of generalization" should come "*after* the sunny trifles of the book have been lovingly collected" (*LL* 1; italics in original). Nabokov's attitude toward details is confirmed in his Cornell University sample exam questionnaires on Dickens's *Bleak House* and Flaubert's *Madame Bovary*. Thus, Nabokov asked his students to "give at least four descriptive details" of Bleak House, or to "describe Emma's eyes, hands, sunshade, hairdo, dress, shoes" (*LL* 383 and 385).

Even though Dobuzhinsky was steadfast in his pursuit of the career of a painter, whereas Nabokov switched from the brush to the quill in his early youth, they both tried their hands in each other's respective fields: Dobuzhinsky, who possessed a literary talent, wrote an elegant prose, to judge from his correspondence and memoirs; Nabokov continued drawing throughout his life, both as an entomologist and as an amateur artist.

Both men showed great penchant for the comic, and one wonders whether Nabokov amplified it further under his mentor's guidance. It is noteworthy that as a painter Dobuzhinsky started by contributing humorous drawings to the magazine *Jester*. And all throughout his artistic career, he had been drawing friendly (Igor Grabar, Sergei Diaghilev, Viacheslav Ivanov) and not so friendly (Nicholas II) caricatures. Of special interest in this regard is his remarkable rebus entitled "A Hundred Mugs" (1918), which "portrayed" a hundred of the most notable figures of Russian culture at the time.[46] In a letter to his father, V. P. Dobuzhinsky, on February 25, 1907, the artist admits: "Going over my child's drawings, I am indeed amazed at how early I revealed the sense of comicality: there are obvious grotesques already in my three-year-old drawings."[47] Nabokov's fascination with the comic and grotesque is evident in his oeuvre, specifically in *Laughter in the Dark, Despair, Invitation to a Beheading, The Gift* (as, for example, in the episode describing the assembly of the Society of Russian Writers in Germany), and *The Waltz Invention.*[48]

Both Dobuzhinsky and Nabokov were much interested in the past, and perhaps it was Dobuzhinsky, once again, who instilled or encouraged this interest in his gifted pupil. This interest is manifested in their fondness for genealogy, as both men speak at length in their memoirs about their maternal and paternal ancestors. Dobuzhinsky even went so far as to draw his genealogical trees for both sides of the family.[49] Nabokov drew the family tree for his *Ada* protagonists, Ada and Van. And both wrote memoirs in which childhood and youth play the most central role.[50]

It is noteworthy that both Dobuzhinsky and Nabokov turned to publishing their memoirs in earnest about the same time, late 1940s to early 1950s. Dobuzhinsky serialized them in Russian-language periodicals, mainly in *The New Review,* whereas Nabokov published his in both Russian-language and English-language periodicals, such as *The New Review* and *Experiments* as well as *The New Yorker* and *Partisan Review,* respectively. Dobuzhinsky's memoirs were published in book form only posthumously (1976), whereas Nabokov first published his English *Conclusive Evidence* (1951), then the Russian *Other Shores* (1954), and afterward the revised version of his English recollections, *Speak, Memory* (1967). Nabokov held Dobuzhinsky's memoirs in high regard. He wrote to his one-time teacher: "Your memoirs about *The World of Art* are charming: this is genuine Dobuzhinsky. These ovals, as if drawn into the text, with the portraits of Somov, Bakst, Benois, Grabar [. . .] are extraordinarily good." And he then goes on to give a bit of literary advice to his former drawing master: "One small cavil: avoid quotation marks! Words do not need typographic scaffolding."[51]

Dobuzhinsky's fascination with the past was shaped by his residing in his early years in such old cities as Novgorod, where he was born; Vilna, the ancient capital of his paternal Lithuanian ancestors; and of course St. Petersburg. For example, the artist recalls that as a child, upon his visits to his maternal grandparents in Novgorod, he "lived amidst legends." "It was also interesting to walk around the monument to the Millennium of Russia across from the [Saint Sophia] cathedral and to recognize on it various tsars and heroes in hauberk and armor."[52] It is noteworthy that this caring attitude toward the past was prevalent in the Dobuzhinsky family: his father was the founder of the Lithuanian Society for the Preservation of Antiquities, and the artist himself supported the Russian Society for the Preservation of Monuments of Art and Antiquity.[53] Nabokov's outlook, on the other hand, was primarily shaped by the architectural ensemble of the then two-hundred-year-old Russian imperial capital.

Both Nabokov and Dobuzhinsky loved St. Petersburg. The city, together with its countryside, was the only locale Nabokov ever cared for and considered his own (*SM* 73 and 250). Dobuzhinsky viewed St. Petersburg as his "home town," himself "a *native* Petersburgian" (italics in original), and repeatedly professed his love for the city.[54] The artist's fascination with St. Petersburg is reflected in his numerous depictions of the city. Nabokov used St. Petersburg as the setting for a number of his prose works (in flashbacks in *Mary* and *The Defense;* in his memoirs, *Speak, Memory* and *Other Shores;* and in imaginary returns in "The Visit to the Museum," "To Prince Kachurin" and *Look at the Harlequins!* to name only a few) and dedicated many of his poems to the city. There is, however, an essential difference between their perceptions of St. Petersburg that stems from their life circumstances.

Dobuzhinsky lived in St. Petersburg at least half of his adult life, departing from the city in December 1924, when he was almost fifty years old. His depictions of the Russian imperial capital were mainly carried out on-site, not from memory, and included the devastation and desolation that the city experienced in the early years of the Soviet regime, as reflected in the artist's series *Petersburg in 1921.* Most important, as the artist himself recalled, he introduced a new vision of the city: while at times portraying it in all its majestic imperial glory, he primarily focused his attention on the beauty of its humdrum life, on its odd, incongruous, and at times fanciful aspects, or on its inner seamy side, as he called it. Thus, in a letter to E. E. Klimov on October 1–3, 1955, he sums up his unique approach to the depiction of the city: "From the very beginning (1901) I had been mostly interested in 'the inner seamy side of the city' [. . .] and I drew 'Pieter,' its corners; I feasted my eyes upon the beauties of Petersburg but felt no urge to draw them. This Ostroumova did, and in part Benois and Lanseré, and I took it upon myself [to depict] the 'splendrous' St. Petersburg incidentally, merely at the insistence of my friends and 'clients.'" Curiously, Dobuzhinsky goes on to write in the same letter: "I became disgusted when I was proclaimed some sort of '[artistic] bard of Petersburg.'"[55]

Nabokov, on the other hand, left the city in 1917, at the age of eighteen, and except for some nightmarish visions of his imaginary return to so-called Leningrad, like the one in "The Visit to the Museum," no doubt affected by Dobuzhinsky's *Petersburg in 1921* series, he usually looked at the city from afar through the lyrical nostalgia for his childhood and youth, as can be seen, for example, in his poems "Petersburg" (1921 and 1923), and in the eponymous three-sonnet cycle (1924).[56] It is Berlin, where Nabokov resided as an adult for fifteen years (1922–37), which he observes and depicts time and again in his Russian works (see chapter 6).

Concomitant with Dobuzhinsky's interest in the past was his fascination with folk art. Since his youth, Dobuzhinsky had collected *lubok* pictures (broadsides) as well as clay and carved toys.[57] Nabokov shared this attraction to Russian folk art with his drawing master, as his essays "Laughter and Dreams" and "Painted Wood" (both 1923) demonstrate. Thus, the writer recalls, for example, "a set of a dozen round wooden 'babas' (peasant women) each one a shade smaller than the next and hollow inside, so that they fitted one into another," as well as "brightly painted round-bellied little dolls loaded with lead so that no force on earth could make them lie quietly on one side," and he observes "the connection between wooden Russian toys and the bright damp mushrooms and berries found in such profusion in the dark rich depths of northern forests" (*Carr* 19 and 21).

Although both Dobuzhinsky and Nabokov were shaped considerably by Russian culture, they were well familiar with other cultures. Dobuzhinsky was proud of and drew upon his Lithuanian paternal heritage, and he traveled widely in Europe in pre-Soviet years, including his art studies in Germany (1899–1901). Upon his departure from Soviet Russia in 1924, he resided in Lithuania, France, England, and the United States. He was well read, knew French, German, and later English, and as a graduate of St. Petersburg University Law School, was well versed in ancient Greek and Latin. It was Dobuzhinsky's father who instilled in him a propensity for multiculturalism. In a letter to Benois on November 3–6, 1956, Dobuzhinsky recalls that his father, to whom he felt "entirely indebted" for his development, used to tell him already in his childhood that he wanted him to become "a European."[58]

Nabokov was trilingual, if not quadrilingual, from his early childhood: aside from Russian, he was fluent in English and French, and possessed a reading knowledge of German that he specifically needed in his entomological studies. He grew up in an Anglophile family and was an avid reader of his father's voluminous library. In his formative years, he traveled abroad extensively (western Europe) with his family and tutors. After leaving Russia in 1919, Nabokov studied French and Russian literature at Cambridge University in England. Upon his graduation from Cambridge, he resided in Germany and France, then in the United States, and afterward in Switzerland.

Thanks in no small degree to their versatile upbringing and life circumstances, Dobuzhinsky and Nabokov were very much at home in both Russia and the West and were, each in his respective area, cultural liaisons of sorts between the two worlds. Especially telling is their work on Pushkin's novel in verse: Dobuzhinsky worked for over ten years (1926–37) on his illustrations for *Eugene Onegin*, whereas Nabokov spent about the same period of time on translating Pushkin's magnum opus into English and providing it with a copious commentary.

Dobuzhinsky left an indelible mark on Nabokov's world perception. To this Nabokov himself points in his memoirs:

> He tried to teach me to find the geometrical coordinations between the slender twigs of a leafless boulevard tree, a system of visual give-and-takes, requiring a precision of linear expression, which I failed to achieve in my youth, but applied gratefully, in my adult instar, not only to the drawing of butterfly genitalia during my seven years at the Harvard Museum of Comparative Zoology, when immersing myself in the bright wellhole of a microscope to

record in India ink this or that new structure; but also, perhaps, to certain camera-lucida needs of literary composition. (*SM* 92)

Nabokov, perhaps with excessive modesty, affirmed that as a painter he did not have "any real talent"; nevertheless all his life he undeniably possessed "the sense of color, the love of color" (*SO* 17). It was evidently Dobuzhinsky who prompted Nabokov to realize that his vocation was literature. As mentioned earlier, upon seeing young Nabokov's first literary experiments, Dobuzhinsky told his pupil: "You have a talent for painting, but you must write."

Nabokov speaks very highly of Dobuzhinsky, whom he calls "that unique master of the line" (*NG* 154). Upon receiving postcards with reproductions of Dobuzhinsky's works, Nabokov exclaims: "What a caress it is for the eye, what enchantment for the memory!"[59]

Nabokov maintained amicable relations with Dobuzhinsky throughout the years. In April 1926, at Dobuzhinsky's exhibition in Berlin, Nabokov reconnected with his former drawing master, this time as an adult, and from that time on they never lost sight of each other.[60] In a letter to his wife, Elizaveta Osipovna, on June 8, 1926, shortly after the exhibit, Dobuzhinsky asks her for Nabokov's address, which he admits inadvertently leaving behind in Berlin.[61] Under the impression of Dobuzhinsky's exhibit, Nabokov composed the poem "Ut pictura poesis," which he dedicated to his former teacher (see the discussion below). In the 1930s, the artist and the writer had numerous opportunities to see each other, particularly in Paris, where in the spring of 1937 Dobuzhinsky drew a portrait of Nabokov (figure 10). Thus, in his letter of April 7, 1937, to Véra, Nabokov writes: "Yesterday, I sat with Benois and Somov at the most charming Dobuzhinsky's." Shortly afterward, on April 23, Nabokov writes to his wife: "I am spending my birthday as follows: I shall breakfast at the Tatarinovs', then—some sun, then I shall go to Sylvia Beach, then to *Candide* with Doussia, then to the Léons', and if I have time, to Dobuzhinsky who is doing my portrait." Three days later he reports to Véra: "Dobuzhinsky did my portrait; in my opinion, it's a good likeness."[62]

In the fall of 1939, at the outbreak of World War II, Nabokov turned to Dobuzhinsky with "a very big request" to assist him in obtaining an affidavit necessary for emigration to the United States, and Dobuzhinsky promptly responded to Nabokov's plea.[63] Throughout the 1930s

10. Mstislav Dobuzhinsky, *Portrait of Vladimir Nabokov*

and 1950s, Nabokov and Dobuzhinsky maintained very warm personal relations and even collaborated on Nabokov's play *The Event,* for which Dobuzhinsky designed the stage set and costumes. (The American premiere of the play took place at the Heckscher Theatre in New York City on April 4, 1941.) Soon after the staging of the play, Nabokov lets Dobuzhinsky know that "our living room is decorated by . . . Dobuzhinsky: We hung the 'photographs' and the 'plate' from *The Event* along the walls, creating a kind of turn-of-the-century boudoir."[64]

The warmth and closeness between Nabokov and Dobuzhinsky are attested to by their epistolary exchange as well as by their mentioning each other to different correspondents. Thus, shortly after his arrival in the United States, in early June 1940, Nabokov concludes a letter to Dobuzhinsky by writing: "I am most eager to shake your big intelligent hand." In his turn, in a letter to Nabokov on April 4, 1943, Dobuzhinsky exclaims: "I often think what a void there is [in my life] because you are not here."[65] In the above-quoted letter to Véra of April 7, 1937, Nabokov refers to Dobuzhinsky as "the most charming." In a letter to Alexander Benois on June 8, 1945, Dobuzhinsky names "Vlad. Nabokov-Sirin" among those with whom he is "especially friendly" and who, "as ill luck would have it, live not in New York City." And in another letter to Benois on October 25–27, 1951, Dobuzhinsky laments his loneliness and once again names Nabokov among those friends and acquaintances that do not reside in New York City, calling the situation fatal. In particular, he reports to his correspondent that "Vlad. Nabokov-Sirin had also left [the city] long ago (he is in 'Ithaca,' at the university, gives lectures on Russian literature and writes *merely* in English)" (italics in original).[66]

Dobuzhinsky had already inspired Nabokov in his choice of subject matter and visual imagery in the writer's youth. This may be discerned in Nabokov's poem "Peter [the Great] in Holland" (ca. 1919), particularly in its backdrop first half, which calls to mind Dobuzhinsky's eponymous sketch (figure 11):

> Из Московии суровой
> он сюда перешагнул.
> Полюбил он моря гул,
> городок наш изразцовый;
>
> и бродил вдоль берегов,—
> загорелый, грубый, юный.
> Ветер. Пепельные дюны.
> Стук далеких топоров.
>
> Разноцветные заплаты
> парусов над рябью вод.
> Стая чаек. Небосвод,—
> как фаянс, зеленоватый. (*Ssoch,* 1:493)
>
> (Out of Muscovy's fierce rigor
> He crossed hither in one stride.
> To roaring seas he took a liking,
> And to our tile-clad little town;

All along the shores he wandered,
Sunburnt, rough-hewn, full of youth.
Wind. The ashen-tinted dunes.
The pounding of some axes yonder.

The motley colors of the patchwork
Of sails upon the rippled seas.
A flock of gulls, the heav'nly vault,
Greenish, like a faience glaze.)[67]

As can be seen, the three quatrains quoted here include some descriptive parallels with the Dobuzhinsky sketch, such as "ashen-tinted dunes," "axes," and "wind" as suggested by the moving clouds. These common details may be perceived, nevertheless, as sheer coincidences, especially because the poem also contains some details—"motley colors of the

11. Mstislav Dobuzhinsky, *Peter the Great in Holland*

patchwork," "a flock of gulls," Peter's wandering "all along the shores"—not found in the Dobuzhinsky sketch, but which evince Nabokov's own poetic vision of this episode in the life of Peter the Great.[68] There is one rather unique detail, however, that points to Nabokov's familiarity with Dobuzhinsky's sketch: "the heav'nly vault, / Greenish, like a faience glaze," indeed a distinctive image. Here, Nabokov draws on Dobuzhinsky's firsthand depiction of the scenery, since the artist went to the Netherlands after having been commissioned to paint a panel for the St. Petersburg School House named after Peter the Great.[69] Furthermore, Nabokov's mention of faience adds to the *couleur locale* of the poem since Delft, a city located in southern Holland, halfway between The Hague and Rotterdam, was an important pottery center from the mid-seventeenth through the eighteenth century. While the hallmark of Delft faience is blue and white (whence the term Delft Blue), the city's ceramics industry was also known for its polychrome products. The latter became widespread at the turn of the eighteenth century, that is, around the time when Peter the Great studied shipbuilding and carpentry in the navy yard of the Dutch East India Company at Saardam (or Zaandam), near Amsterdam. (Incidentally, the Dutch East India Company, founded in 1602, imported Chinese ceramics that had a great impact on the development of Delft faience.) Such, for example, is an oval plaque with Chinese-style decoration on black background with the prevalent emerald, "greenish," tint.[70]

In addition to faience, Nabokov, the art lover and entomologist, could be mindful of Delft as the birthplace of the remarkable painter Jan Vermeer, as well as of Antony van Leeuwenhoek, who was the first to apply the microscope to biological studies. And Nabokov was undoubtedly fascinated by the account of Peter the Great's meeting in Delft with the Dutch scientist, who explained the use of the microscope to the tsar.[71]

Reportedly written on March 30, 1919, in the Crimean exile, about two weeks before Nabokov left Russia forever, the poem is indicative of his nostalgia for his native city, from which he had been separated by that time for well over a year.[72] Its main subject is Peter the Great, the founder of the city. We recall that in his "Foreword" to *The Bronze Horseman*, Pushkin dubbed St. Petersburg "Peter's own creation" and the "Metropolis of Peter."[73] Further, in his poem Nabokov describes the episode in Peter's life when in 1697, as part of his fifteen-month-long Grand Embassy tour in western Europe, the young monarch studied shipbuilding and carpentry near Amsterdam. It was Amsterdam that served the tsar as one of the two models for his new city connected by canals and bridges (the other being Venice). And it is very telling that the tsar "called it Sankt Pieter Burkh, pronouncing the words in the Dutch fashion."[74]

While "Peter in Holland" points to the initial impulse and the isolated concrete image that a specific sketch by Dobuzhinsky invoked, the poem "Ut pictura poesis," which Nabokov composed under the impression of Dobuzhinsky's Berlin art exhibit in April 1926, constitutes Nabokov's tribute to the artist and to his portrayal of his native city. Nabokov not only inscribed the poem to his former drawing master—to M. V. Dobuzhinsky—but also dedicated it to him in each stanza anagrammatically. The boldfaced Cyrillic letters form a dedication that reads: to Mstislav Dobuzhinsky Vladimir Nabokov Sirin.[75]

Воспоминанье, острый луч,
преобрази мое изгнанье,
пронзи меня, воспоминанье
о баржах петербургских туч
в небесных ветреных просторах,
о закоулочных заборах,
о добрых лицах фонарей . . .
Я помню, над Невой моей
бывали сумерки, как шорох
тушующих карандашей.

Все это живописец плавный
передо мною развернул,
и, кажется, совсем недавно
в лицо мне этот ветер дул,
изображенный им в летучих
осенних листьях, зыбких тучах,
и плыл по набережной гул,—
во мгле колокола гудели—
собора медные качели . . .

Какой там **двор** зна**комый есть,**
ка**кие тум6ы! Х**орошо бы
туда перешагнуть, пролезть,
там **по**стоять, где **спят** су**гробы,**
и плотно **сл**ожены **дрова,—**
или под аркой, **на** канале,
где нежно в каменном овале
синеют **крепость и Нева.** (*Ssoch*, 2:555)

(O recollection, piercing beam,
transfigure my exile,
transfix me, recollection
of Petersburg's clouds, barge-like,
'midst windswept heavenly expanses,
of unfrequented back-road fences,
of street lamps with expressions kind . . .
O'er my Neva, there come to mind
those twilights like the rustling
of obliquely shading pencils.[76]

All this the smoothly stroking painter
in front of me unfolded, and
I had the sense that only lately
this very wind my face had fanned,
which he'd depicted by the flying
autumn leaves, by the untidy clouds,
and down the quay a humming flowed,
the bells in the penumbra dinned—
the cathedral's bronzen swings . . .

What a familiar courtyard stands nearby,
what stony posts! If I could only
step across, clamber inside,
stand for a while where snow-banks slumber,
and where logs lie, compactly stacked,
or 'neath the arch on the canal,
where on the stony oval, tinted blue,
shimmer fortress and Neva.)[77]

In this tribute to Dobuzhinsky, Nabokov employs the device of ekphrasis. He creates verbal pictures that harken back to concrete pictorial images recognizable in Dobuzhinsky's corpus of works about St. Petersburg and its surroundings. For example, the phrase "flying autumn leaves" evokes the artist's *Tsarskoe Selo: The Gates of the Cameron Gallery* (1907; State Russian Museum, St. Petersburg); "back-road fences" suggests *In the Company Headquarters: Winter in the City* (1904; State Russian Museum, St. Petersburg); "a familiar courtyard" is reminiscent of *Backyard* (1903; State Tret´iakov Gallery, Moscow); both of the latter works are called to mind by "logs lie, compactly stacked"; "street lamps with expressions kind" suggests *A Barbershop Window* (1906; State Tret´iakov Gallery, Moscow) and *Night in St. Petersburg* (1924; State Tret´iakov Gallery, Moscow); and "barge-like" and "untidy clouds" invoke the drawing *SS. Peter and Paul Fortress* (1922) from the series *Petersburg in 1921*, whereas "'neath the arch on the canal, where on the stony oval, tinted blue, shimmer fortress and Neva" suggests Dobuzhinsky's stage design for Tchaikovsky's opera *The Queen of Spades* (figure 12).[78]

The "slumber[ing]" "snow-banks" in the last stanza are also noteworthy in that they, once again, point to Nabokov's special fascination with the wintry St. Petersburg that we witnessed earlier by way of his metonymic formula of *The World of Art*. Nabokov remembers the city primarily in wintertime because he would customarily spend summers either on the family estates or abroad.[79] And it is noteworthy that in his depiction of the city, both in poetry and prose, as for example in the earlier poems "Petersburg" (1923) and "Exodus" (1924) and the later story "The Visit to the Museum," Nabokov most often depicts the wintry city. It is also worth noting the decreasing number of lines in each consecutive stanza—ten, nine, eight—as if the images are gradually receding after being put on paper and as though each remembrance of the past consumes so much of the poet's breathing power and emotional energy as to leave less and less for the next one.

The poem is not only Nabokov's tribute to Dobuzhinsky and his St. Petersburg cityscape artistry. It is also a demonstration of the budding artist-turned-poet to his former teacher that he did not forget their lessons, that he learned a great deal from them, especially in noticing minute details, and that he can verbally convey the quintessence of his art.[80] Nabokov also apparently wished to show to the drawing

12. Mstislav Dobuzhinsky, *The Zimniaia Kanavka Embankment*

master of his boyhood and early youth that he had followed his advice to paint, but with words. At the same time, knowing Nabokov's competitive spirit, it is quite possible that in this poem, by way of ekphrasis, he engaged himself in an artistic contest of sorts with his former mentor.[81]

Dobuzhinsky held this poem in very high regard. On the margin of his above-quoted letter to Nabokov of April 4, 1943, the artist inscribes the following note: "Once you wrote a small-size poem dedicated to me. I do not have it, and I much value it as a badge of distinction. For me, it is *a Vladimir of the 1st* Class and with a crown. If you find it or remember, send me this regalia"[82] (italics in original). Here Dobuzhinsky plays upon the parallel between the order's name and Nabokov's first name. In addition, the artist apparently alludes to the fact that individuals were not entitled to this order by birthright, but merely by personal merit—distinguished military or civilian state service.[83] Furthermore, unlike some other orders, such as that of Saint Anna, which included a crown, the order of Saint Vladimir did not. Thus Dobuzhinsky, who knew much about military regalia, since his father was a general, emphasizes his view of the poem as a most unique, one of a kind, award.[84]

In all likelihood, Dobuzhinsky also facetiously invokes here the title of Nikolai Gogol's dramatic fragment, *Vladimir of the Third Class.*

Another possible reference to the art of Dobuzhinsky may be found in *Other Shores.* The writer recalls that at the age of six he could read in English but not in Russian, with the exception of the word *kakao* (*Ssoch,* 5:152–53).[85] This example contains a peculiar aberration: aside from Russian, *kakao* is spelled with two *k*'s in German, but not in English, or for that matter in French, in which the word is spelled with two *c*'s— *cacao.*[86] It is very likely, however, that the word flashed through Nabokov's mind because he recalled Dobuzhinsky's watercolor *City Grimaces* (figure 13). The watercolor presents a city street on a sleety day. In the foreground it depicts an organ grinder, a cap in his hand, and his trained monkey wearing a red dress and holding a feathered cap. With their caps removed, this amusing circuslike duo pays its respects to a funeral procession. This scene appears even more contradictory, if not grotesque (hence the title), because in the background, in sharp opposition to the somberness of the procession, there is an advertisement that portrays a smiling red-cheeked female in a tight bodice, and a large pointing hand that presumably calls upon passersby to drink cocoa.[87] It is worth noting that at the time *kakao,* apparently a less common beverage than tea or coffee, was vigorously advertised. For example, the St. Petersburg daily *The New Time* (*Novoe Vremia*) for 1908 includes cocoa ads of three different Dutch companies: Bensdorp, Blooker, and Van Guten.

Yet another possible reference to Dobuzhinsky's St. Petersburg cityscape comes into view in "The Visit to the Museum." Toward the end of the story, the narrator finds himself, with shocking unexpectedness, in the contemporaneous, Soviet, St. Petersburg, renamed Leningrad, which he characterizes as "hopelessly slavish and hopelessly my own native land" (*Stories* 285). Nabokov chooses to place his narrator- "semiphantom" in one of three well-known city localities, "somewhere on the Moyka or the Fontanka Canal, or perhaps on the Obvodny" (ibid.). The mention of Moika alludes, first and foremost, to Pushkin, whose last residence was on Moika Quay, 12. The name of Fontanka evokes, of course, a popular ditty: "Siskin, siskin, where were you? I was drinking vodka on Fontanka."[88] The name could also have been on Nabokov's mind because Fontanka, 6, was the address of the Imperial School of Jurisprudence, where his grandfather D. N. Nabokov and his

13. Mstislav Dobuzhinsky, *City Grimaces*

uncles S. D. and D. D. Nabokov had studied and where his father V. D. Nabokov had taught.[89] In addition, the mention of the street perhaps points to Fontanka, 21, the building where *The World of Art*'s editorial office was located.[90] Furthermore, the mention of Moika and Fontanka side by side is self-referential, as both sites figure next to each other in Nabokov's earlier mentioned longer poem "Petersburg," which includes the following lines: "Skating rinks, skating rinks—on Moika and Fontanka Streets, / in the Iusupov silver paradise."[91]

Of special interest in the aforementioned quotation from "The Visit to the Museum" is the Obvodny Canal, which suggests an allusion to Dobuzhinsky. Many other *World of Art* painters—Alexander Benois, Evgeny Lanseré, and Anna Ostroumova-Lebedeva, for example—frequently portrayed St. Petersburg. But it was only Dobuzhinsky, to the best of my knowledge, who drew all three of these localities and depicted (even twice) the Obvodny Canal: *The Obvodny Canal in St. Petersburg* (1902; State Russian Museum, St. Petersburg) and *A Kitchen Garden at the Obvodny Canal* (1922; State Russian Museum, St. Petersburg). Dobuzhinsky's repetitive depiction of the Obvodny Canal clearly indicates that the artist was fond of this site. Evidence of this may be found in the artist's memoir: he recalls that as a child he accompanied his father to the Nevsky paper mill, located in the area, and retained a very bright recollection of this event.[92] Dobuzhinsky's works, which Nabokov saw at the Berlin exhibit, evidently triggered the writer's own remembrances of his St. Petersburg childhood and youth, to which he returns time and again in both his poetry and prose. When reminiscing about St. Petersburg, Nabokov envisioned, alongside his own recollections, Dobuzhinsky's portrayal of his native city.

NABOKOV AND DOBUZHINSKY:
SOME COMPARISON OF THEIR ARTISTIC TASTES

In this section, I attempt to compare Nabokov's and Dobuzhinsky's artistic tastes in contemporary Russian art, which may highlight not only Nabokov's kinship with but also his certain indebtedness to his former drawing master and mentor. I shall base my comparison on their assessment of the most notable Russian artistic groups, such as the Academicians, the Wanderers, and *The World of Art*, as well as some individual painters, from Ilya Repin to Natalia Goncharova. In my comparison, I look at the artistic tastes of Nabokov and Dobuzhinsky in their entirety, as if at two mosaic panels. While the similarity between the color and inlay of one pebble in each mosaic may be incidental, a multitude of such little stones that shape the respective panels, when placed side by side, bear witness to their unmistakable affinity. Whilst all Dobuzhinsky's assertions transpire directly from his memoirs and correspondence, Nabokov's "strong opinions" on art, by and large, can be found in his fiction, and therefore are more difficult to discern. They may often be gleaned only from a carefully considered context, as for instance the appraisal of Maliavin's art in *The Defense* demonstrates (see below).

An innovative artist, Dobuzhinsky did not think highly of the Academicians, with their deadening, stagnating conventionality. Thus, the works of Genrikh Semiradsky, known for his canvases on mythological subjects, and of Ivan Aivazovsky, the seascape artist, that he saw in the Museum of Alexander III (State Russian Museum, St. Petersburg) seemed to him "saccharine and false."[93]

Similarly to Dobuzhinsky, Nabokov also thought very poorly of the Academicians. In *The Gift,* Nabokov disdainfully speaks of Semiradsky's art in general when describing how "the social writer Garshin saw 'pure art' in the paintings of Semiradski" and dubbing him "a rank academician" (*Gift* 238). He also twice sneeringly mentions Semiradsky's *Phryne at Poseidon's Festival in Eulesis* (1889; State Russian Museum, St. Petersburg) in *The Defense* (*Def* 38 and 40).[94] The writer talks about Aivazovsky in *Speak, Memory* as "the well-known seascape painter" (*SM* 67); in *Other Shores,* however, he calls him "a very mediocre but very famous seascape painter of that time."[95] In his Russian-language memoir, Nabokov also scornfully refers to the Academic landscape artist Albert Benois, the elder brother of Alexander (Nabokov dubs Albert's watercolors "dead stuff"), and to Konstantin Kryzhitsky's "A Thawed Patch," apparently having in mind his *Beginning of Warm Days* or a variant of *An Early Spring* (1905; State Tret'iakov Gallery, Moscow).[96]

Nabokov conveys his attitude toward Academic art in *Pnin* by portraying Ivan Ilyich Gramineev, whose name and patronymic evoke the mediocre protagonist of Leo Tolstoy's celebrated story "The Death of Ivan Ilyich" (1887). Gramineev is described as "a well-known, frankly academic painter, whose soulful oils—'Mother Volga,' 'Three Old

Friends' (lad, nag, dog), 'April Glade,' and so forth—still graced a museum in Moscow" (*Pnin* 127). (We recall that Moscow, which Nabokov never visited, was for him a paragon of provinciality and poor taste.)[97] Gramineev's reputation as a painter becomes evident from a dialogue between Pnin and Chateau: when Pnin confirms to Chateau that "Liza's boy," Victor, "has an extraordinary talent for painting" and expresses his regret that Victor has not come with him to The Pines, thereby missing "the splendid opportunity of being coached by Gramineev," Chateau "softly rejoined": "You exaggerate the splendor" (*Pnin* 127). Curiously, Gramineev demonstrates his inobservance of nature. As an artist who paints outdoors, Gramineev is nevertheless incapable of distinguishing between various types of clouds: he presumed that "the day will continue as overcast as it had begun," and "came out with an unprotected head" (*Pnin* 126), apparently not realizing that the clouds, evidently so-called fair weather cumulus, should dissipate in the course of the day and will, therefore, expose him to the torrid sun. Such inobservance by Gramineev, an expert landscape painter, speaks poorly of his professionalism.

The Wanderers, with their emphasis on a social "message" in art, did not fare much better with Dobuzhinsky and Nabokov either. Thus, Dobuzhinsky maintains that "the ideological content and tendentiousness of the Wanderers invariably pushed the artistic objectives to the secondary plane. Owing to the homilies of Chernyshevsky and Pisarev, all 'aesthetics' was banned, and the 'realism' of the Wanderers was devoid of any artistic sentiment."[98] Toward the end of his life, however, Dobuzhinsky somewhat reevaluated his attitude toward the group. Two days before his death, in an interview on Radio Liberty, Dobuzhinsky opines in a conciliatory fashion: "Many find certain merits in them [the Wanderers], mainly because they quite attentively depicted purely realistic details of everyday life."[99]

Although, by and large, Nabokov's sentiments toward the Wanderers correspond to those of Dobuzhinsky, the writer, unlike his former teacher, did not see any redeeming features in their art. As I mentioned earlier in this chapter, Nabokov expressed disdain for "the utilitarian and didactic tendencies of the [eighteen] sixties and seventies."[100] It is not surprising, then, that Nabokov thought poorly of the Wanderers, who were promoting social awareness in art. Thus, in *Other Shores*, he scornfully mentions *The Surf*, "an enormous, slicked-down" painting by Vasily Perov, a painter of genre and social commentary and the founding member of the Wanderers movement.[101] Later in his Russian memoir, Nabokov contemptuously refers to works by two other Wanderers: *Clearing in a Pine Forest* by Ivan Shishkin, whose last name he slightingly misspells as Shishkov in his Russian memoir, apparently alluding to the conservative linguist Admiral Alexander Shishkov, and *The Head of a Gypsy Boy* by Alexei Kharlamov, whose paintings he dubs in his English-language memoir "repellently academic" (*Ssoch*, 5:288 and 709; *SM* 235).

Dobuzhinsky appreciated the art of Ilya Repin (1844–1930), the most talented and accomplished among the Wanderers, albeit with some reservations. He thought that Repin was "a truly talented painter, even though he would shock at times by his lack of taste."[102] Nabokov, on the other hand, was more categorical in his assessment of Repin's art. The writer apparently held Repin's art in low esteem primarily because of his illustrations for *Eugene Onegin*, which the painter evidently based not on Pushkin's novel in verse but on Tchaikovsky's eponymous opera, which was not true to Pushkin's magnum opus. Hence, Nabokov's scornful remark: "that totally talentless painting of the talentless Repin in which the forty-year-old Onegin is taking aim at the curly-haired Sobinov."[103]

Mikhail Vrubel (1856–1910) was possibly the most gifted and genuine Russian representative of Symbolism, the late nineteenth-century trend characterized by heightened sensitivity and tendency toward the supernatural.[104] Dobuzhinsky admired Vrubel's art, both his paintings and ceramics.[105] In a letter to Alexander Benois on April 2, 1911, he compares the recent untimely death of the Lithuanian painter and composer Mikalojus Čiurlionis to that of Vrubel, laments the fact that there were very few people at the first anniversary of Vrubel's death, and concludes that both painters had "the same vision of other worlds and almost the same end, and both are lonesome in art."[106]

Nabokov thought highly of Vrubel, whom he lists among the painters of "the experimental decade" he preferred (*SO* 170). The writer repeatedly mentions or alludes to Vrubel in his works. The name of the artist appears in the phrase "Vrublyov's frescoes"—"an amusing cross between two Russian painters (Rublyov and Vrubel)" (*Gift* 39). This "amusing cross" (pun likely intended) between Mikhail Vrubel, who in the earlier years of his artistic career became known for decorating churches and cathedrals, such as the Saint Vladimir Cathedral in Kiev, and Andrei Rublev (ca.1370–ca.1430), the renowned Russian icon painter, was designed to demonstrate Yasha Chernyshevski's ignorance of art and to set him apart from the protagonist: "no, he could not have loved painting as I do" (ibid.). Later in the novel, Nabokov mentions Pan, the Greek god of shepherds. The writer apparently has Vrubel's eponymous canvas in mind, and by way of the year of its composition (1899)—his own birth year—alludes to his authorial presence.[107] Vrubel and his paintings are also referred to in Nabokov's earlier and later works—*Despair, Ada,* and *Look at the Harlequins!* In *Despair,* a "lady in lilac silks" (*Des* 4) invokes Vrubel's portraits of his wife: *Lady in a Violet Dress* (1901; State Tret´iakov Gallery, Moscow) as well as *Portrait of Nadezhda Zabela-Vrubel on the Edge of a Birch Grove* (1904; State Russian Museum, St. Petersburg). "Vrubel's wonderful picture" of Demon, Ada's and Van's father, is mentioned in *Ada* (509). Vrubel's Demon imagery also reverberates in *Look at the Harlequins!* in which Vadim Vadimovich claims that his father's "society nickname was Demon" and that "Vrubel has portrayed him with his vampire-pale cheeks, his diamond eyes, his black hair" (*LATH* 96).[108]

Dobuzhinsky held the art of Isaac Levitan (1860–1900), who exhibited with the Wanderers but never formally joined their association, in high regard. He names Levitan, together with Konstantin Korovin and Valentin Serov, as among "the first new true, heartfelt Russian landscape painters" and credits *The World of Art* with their discovery.[109]

Nabokov, too, thought highly of Levitan's art. In his earlier essay "Laughter and Dreams," he mentions him in the same breath with Pushkin: "For if Russian head-gears and cupolas are marvelously bright-coloured there is another side of the Russian soul which has been expressed by Levithan [*sic*] in painting and by Pushkin (and others) in poetry" (*Carr* 20). In the story "Natasha" (ca. 1924), the title heroine observes the countryside in her European exile and recalls Levitan.[110] In *The Gift,* "the wall calendar with a Russian landscape by Levitan on it" is mentioned (*Gift* 89). And in *Look at the Harlequins!* Nabokov is more specific: he names "Levitan's *Clouds above a Blue River* (the Volga [. . .]), painted around 1890" (*LATH* 164), apparently referring to the artist's famous *Evening on the Volga River* (1887–88; State Tret´iakov Gallery, Moscow).[111]

Though initially associated with the Wanderers, Valentin Serov

(1865–1911) was an innovative painter who gradually turned away from their tendentiousness and social awareness in art and became closer and closer in spirit to the experimentation of *The World of Art*.[112] Dobuzhinsky always spoke highly of Serov's art. He calls him "a remarkable man" and "an extraordinary toiler in art" and remarks that "in spite of the duration wherein his pieces were created, they were beautiful namely because of their unusual freshness."[113] Dobuzhinsky's admiration for Serov's art goes back to his formative years. Dobuzhinsky recalls that in his boyhood, "to see once again Serov's *Girl with Peaches*, we would set out (while on a visit to Moscow over the Christmas holidays) in fierce cold, in poorly heated train cars, and then in a sledge, to [Savva] Mamontov's 'Abramtsevo' [the industrialist's country estate]. And what a disappointment it was when (by the instructions of the absent owners) we were not even admitted into the empty house."[114]

Nabokov never expressed any explicit opinion concerning Serov's art but mentions his paintings, actual or fictionalized, in several of his works. Thus, he refers to Serov's artwork in his story "A Russian Beauty" (1934). In the protagonist's room there is "a postcard of Serov's portrait of the Tsar" (*Stories* 386). Serov painted Tsar Nicholas II more than once. Most likely, however, Nabokov suggests here the best-known portrait of the tsar sitting at the table in the uniform tunic of the Preobrazhensky Regiment (1900; State Tret´iakov Gallery, Moscow). And in *Look at the Harlequins!* Nabokov refers to two fictionalized canvases by the artist, "a resplendent portrait by Serov, 1896, of the notorious beauty, Mme. de Blagidze, in Caucasian costume" and "Serov's *Five-petaled Lilac*, oil" (*LATH* 50 and 169). The first quotation seems to imply a composite reference to Serov's and Savely Sorin's portraits of female beauties (see below). The second quotation is a thinly disguised allusion to the artist's aforementioned oil painting *A Girl with Peaches* (1887; State Tret´iakov Gallery, Moscow). Nabokov describes the painting, which he playfully and mock-misleadingly places in "the Hermitage Museum in Leningrad," as depicting "a tawny-haired girl of twelve or so sitting at a sun-flecked table and manipulating a raceme of lilac in search of that lucky token" (*LATH* 169).[115] Serov's model, Véra Mamontova (1875–1907), a daughter of the earlier mentioned wealthy industrialist and benefactor Savva Mamontov, was indeed twelve at the time of Serov's painting her.[116] Like Nabokov's fictitious painting, Serov's depicts a girl "sitting at a sun-flecked table." Unlike Ada Bredow's hair in Nabokov's last completed novel, Véra Mamontova's hair in Serov's painting is not tawny but dark chestnut. Véra Mamontova is not "manipulating a raceme of lilac" but holds a peach in her hands, while three others are placed beside her on the table. Nabokov's mentioning Serov on several occasions and even depicting his paintings verbally, albeit somewhat fictionalized, suggest the writer's interest in and perhaps appreciation of the painter's artwork.

As was demonstrated earlier, Nabokov held in highest regard the chief representatives of *The World of Art* (Benois, Somov, Bakst, and of course Dobuzhinsky), who all played an important role in shaping his artistic tastes during his formative years. (Curiously, Nabokov lists these painters—Somov, Benois [. . .], Vrubel, Dobuzhinski [*SO* 170] in the order very similar to that of his mentor: Somov, Alexander Benois, Bakst, Serov, Vrubel.)[117] And it is hardly surprising that Dobuzhinsky always spoke very highly of his fellow *World of Art* members and close friends. It is more indicative to see how some lesser-known members of *The World of Art*, such as Savely Sorin, Filipp Maliavin, and Natalia Goncharova, fared with the writer and his artistic mentor.

A lesser-known participant of the *World of Art* exhibitions, Savely Sorin (1878–1953) made a name for himself as a portraitist. In the years prior to the Bolshevik takeover, he painted many famous representatives of the artistic world and the aristocracy: Eleonora Duse, Anna Akhmatova, and Prince Sergei M. Volkonsky; and his works were frequently reproduced in such periodicals as *Apollo* and *The Sun of Russia*. In 1917–18 Sorin lived in Yalta, and in 1919–20 in Tiflis, Batum, and Baku before leaving for France and, at the outbreak of World War II, for the United States.[118]

Dobuzhinsky, although he liked Sorin personally, did not hold his art in high regard. In a letter to Benois on October 25–27, 1951, Dobuzhinsky writes: "Sorin came back, but I have not seen him yet. He continues to be a good friend, but as you yourself understand—his art means nothing to me."[119]

In *Speak, Memory*, Nabokov singles out "a well-known painter called Sorin" (*SM* 248) among those whom he recalls seeing in his Crimean exile. And it is quite possible that Nabokov would later encounter Sorin, a mutual acquaintance of Benois and Dobuzhinsky, in Paris and New York City.[120] It appears that Nabokov alludes to Sorin, alongside Serov, in his aforementioned fictitious reference to "a resplendent portrait by

Serov, 1896, of the notorious beauty, Mme. de Blagidze, in Caucasian costume" (*LATH* 50). In this playful pastiche, Nabokov seems to conflate the two portraitists, **Valentin A. Serov** and **Savely A. Sorin**, whose names bear a strong phonetic and visual resemblance. Furthermore, both Serov and Sorin painted the same personalities, such as Fedor Shaliapin (1905 and 1943) and Maxim Gorky (1905 and 1902). Both painters were also known for their portrayals of famous beauties and even depicted the same models: Princess Olga Orlova (1911 and 1917), as well as the renowned ballerinas Anna Pavlova (1909 and 1922, both showing her in the Mikhail Fokine ballet *Les Sylphides*) and Tamara Karsavina (1909 and 1910).

Among Serov's female models with the Caucasian link there is only Maria Akimova (1908; the Picture Gallery of America, Erevan), the daughter of a rich Moscow philanthropist of Armenian origin, V. I. Kananov. This is not the case with Sorin. The French noble particle and the Georgian name of the illusory female sitter mentioned in *Look at the Harlequins!* suggest Sorin's portraits of several Georgian princesses whom he painted during his Caucasian period: Salomeia Andronikova, Melita Cholokashvili (Sorin completed her portrait in Paris in 1927), Meri Shervashidze, and Eliso Dadiani—all four well known for their remarkable beauty. Andronikova was the lyrical addressee of Osip Mandelstam's poem "A Little Straw" and of his octave that begins and ends with the lines "Komnena, the daughter of Andronik, / the daughter of Byzantine glory!" (both poems were written in 1916). Shervashidze was the purported heroine of Galaktion Tabidze's poems "Meri" (1915) and "On the Road" (1916); she won a beauty contest held in Constantinople in 1921 and was, together with Cholokashvili, the top Chanel model in Paris of the 1920s.[121]

Nabokov was familiar with Sorin's portraiture, as it was reviewed and occasionally reproduced in the Berlin-based émigré periodical *Firebird* (*Zhar-ptitsa*) to which he was a frequent contributor. Thus, Sergei Makovsky published there a survey article about Sorin's portraiture.[122] And Sorin's portrait of Eliso Dadiani, for example, was reproduced in the first issue of the magazine (1921). Characteristically, Sorin did not portray Dadiani in Caucasian costume.

A few words about Nabokov's choice of the fictional sitter's name— de Blagidze. Blagidze is a commoner's Georgian name, and therefore its appearance in combination with the French noble particle "de" is amusing in its incongruity. (Curiously, there were some Russian émigrés in France who, to emphasize their noble origin, would add "de" to their surname.)[123] The surname apparently came to Nabokov's attention because of his interest in chess. There was a chess master named Alexander Blagidze (b. 1923) who was active on the Soviet and international chess scene between the mid-1940s and the early 1960s.[124]

An additional strand in the intricate collage that provides the Caucasian costume dimension is Karsavina's portrait by the American artist John Singer Sargent (1856–1925), whose middle and last names somewhat resemble the surnames of both Russian painters. Sargent depicted the famed ballerina and beauty in the title role of the legendary Georgian Princess, in traditional Caucasian costume, in the Fokine ballet *Thamar,* performed in Paris in the Théâtre du Châtelét in May 1912. In 1942 this charcoal drawing became part of Harvard University's Fogg Art Museum collection, with which Nabokov presumably familiarized himself while residing at Cambridge, Massachusetts (1941–48).

Dobuzhinsky did not have much respect for the art of Filipp Maliavin (1869–1940). In a letter to his wife on October 29, 1935, from London, Dobuzhinsky wrote: "There is a Maliavin exhibit here; Dodia and I were there on Saturday. What a horror it is, what bad taste, simply a disgrace [. . .] What a fool—he is a disgrace to Russian art!"[125]

Nabokov, on the other hand, never expressed any overt opinion on Maliavin and his art. In *The Defense,* the narrator mentions "a large, vivid oil painting" in the anteroom of Luzhin's in-laws' residence (*Def* 119). In that painting, "a village girl in a red kerchief coming down to her eyebrows was eating an apple, and her black shadow on a fence was eating a slightly larger apple. 'A Russian *baba*,' said Luzhin with relish and laughed" (ibid.). As we know, Luzhin was habitually imperceptive of anything other than chess and was rather unsophisticated with regard to art. (We are mindful that later in the novel his wife takes him to Berlin's Kaiser Friedrich Museum, and there is a strong sense, judging from the tone of her explanations, that Luzhin had never been to an art museum before [*Def* 190–91].) Why, then, did this large oil painting attract Luzhin's attention? In the original Russian, it sounds rather gaudy and obtrusive, that is, it literally "was striking in the eyes."[126] "Luzhin, who normally did not notice such things, gave his attention to it because it was greasily glossed with electric light and the colors dazed him, like a sunstroke" (*Def* 119). The narrator notices that in the apartment itself there were "more country girls in flowered kerchiefs" (*Def* 119–20).

Curiously, the tenth issue (1923) of *Firebird* contains several examples of Maliavin's art, including his *Peasant Women* (1914), along with Sergei Makovsky's article about the painter. It looks like Nabokov was familiar with Makovsky's piece, as some textual parallels between the article and the novel indicate. Makovsky's description of Maliavin's early *baba*, whose "sarafan is like a red calico fire" and whose "sharp, blackish-blue shadow on her forehead, almost improbable shadow—one has to get used to it,"[127] turn in the novel into "a village girl in a red [calico] kerchief coming down to her eyebrows was eating an apple" and "her black shadow on a fence was eating a slightly larger apple" (*Def* 119).[128] Furthermore, Makovsky's observation that the girl stood "grinning and narrowing her eyes from the sultry light" transforms into Luzhin's similar reaction to the painting itself—"it was greasily glossed with electric light and the colors dazed him, like a sunstroke" (*Def* 119).[129]

Luzhin's joyous response to the paintings, in which Filipp Maliavin's well-known subject matter is discernible, by no means reflects Nabokov's own attitude toward the painter. It seems that the writer's opinion of Maliavin's art is expressed much later in the novel through the eyes of Luzhin's art-savvy wife who, as we recall, attended art history classes (*Def* 128), and whom Nabokov endows with his own pictorial tastes and sensibilities. It is through the eyes of Luzhin's wife that the narrator apparently expresses Nabokov's own attitude toward the art of Maliavin when he dubs his trademark motif "the falsely swaggering peasant women in the pictures" (*Def* 241).

Dobuzhinsky recognized and highly praised the artistic talents of Natalia Goncharova (1881–1962). In his Paris letter to Boris Kustodiev of November 14, 1923, he writes: "I see her [Goncharova] and Larionov. She is a mightily talented person, more so than he." And more than thirty years later, on December 28, 1954, Dobuzhinsky wrote to Sergei Makovsky from London: "The Diaghilev exhibit is closing on Jan[uary] 16, and it is a pity if you do not see it: many superb works are gathered there. Bakst, Benois, Goncharova dominate, especially the latter—in my view, the most theatrical talent."[130]

Dobuzhinsky's overt admiration of Goncharova's art is paralleled by the implicit one of Nabokov. In contrast to his apparent dislike of Maliavin's art, Nabokov pays an elegant tribute to Goncharova's artistic achievements in his "chess" novel. Among the Luzhins' guests, the narrator of the novel describes "a swarthy, brightly made-up girl who drew marvelous firebirds" ("смуглая, ярко накрашенная барышня, чудесно рисовавшая жар-птиц"; *Def* 231 and *Ssoch*, 2:449). Although the physical appearance of this fleeting character hardly matches that of Goncharova—the artist was not known for her use of heavy makeup and was in her late forties at the time of Nabokov's composing the novel—the emboldened Cyrillic letters in the original Russian passage here constitute an anagram of her first and last names. Furthermore, in mentioning firebirds, Nabokov alludes to Goncharova's stage and costume designs in Diaghilev's production of Igor Stravinsky's *Firebird* (London, 1926). This allusion, however, as so often the case with Nabokov, is also self-referential since, as I mentioned earlier, the writer recurrently published his poetry and prose in the Berlin émigré periodical so titled. Furthermore, page 2 of this magazine's seventh issue (1922) includes Nabokov's poem "Spring," signed Vlad. Sirin, side by side with a resplendent ornament, containing exotic birds by Goncharova. The opposite page contains a similar ornament by this gifted artist. And between pages 4 and 5 of that issue, there is a reproduction of Goncharova's decorative canvas with Sirin birds that certainly could not go unnoticed by Nabokov, who used the pen name Sirin in his "Russian years."[131]

Incidentally, the creative paths of Nabokov and Goncharova intersected once again in the twelfth issue of *Firebird* (1924): Nabokov was represented there by his poem "Shakespeare" (p. 32), and Goncharova by her extensive artwork that included multicolored birds (pp. 6 and 7). Finally, in paying tribute to Goncharova, Nabokov apparently recalled her Sirin birds for the Fokine staging of Nikolai Rimsky-Korsakov's *The Golden Cockerel*, better known in the West under the French title *Le Coq d'Or* (Paris, 1914). Nabokov was familiar with Goncharova's work, as her set and costume designs for this opera-ballet production met with enormous success and made her world famous.

* * *

Nabokov's references to *The World of Art* manifest his homage to the magnificent art of its painters, through whose artistic prism the writer frequently looked from great temporal and spatial distance at his native land. Accordingly, his concrete and distinctive snow imagery—"the vertically falling oversized snowflakes"—acquires a special importance, as it points to the significant mnemonic role with which Nabokov endows this metonymic formula of the *World of Art* cityscape when he re-creates the Russian past in the world of his literary works.

Nabokov's kinship with Dobuzhinsky, as expressed in multitudinous interests and sensibilities, aside from similarities in their familial background and upbringing, points to the painter's lasting impact on the world perception of his one-time pupil. Nabokov's specific allusions or references to the works of Dobuzhinsky are the writer's tribute to his drawing master, whose advice, to paint, but with words, he scrupulously followed throughout his entire creative life. Dobuzhinsky's lifelong impact is evident, too, in the affinity of Nabokov's artistic tastes with those of his former mentor and close friend. Overall, *The World of Art*'s pictorial achievements, and especially those of Dobuzhinsky, greatly enriched Nabokov's world perception and subsequently deeply permeated his fictional universe.

5. Richard Muther's *History of Painting in the XIXth Century*

> *History of Painting in the XIXth Century* was very soon trans-
> lated into many languages, and it gave rise to passionate
> talks everywhere; everywhere, old people were indignant
> about it, its harsh reevaluations, and everywhere, young
> people went into raptures over it.
>
> —Benois, *Moi vospominaniia*

> I also avidly read Muther (my father sent me a multivolume
> set of his *History of Painting*).
>
> —Dobuzhinsky, *Vospominaniia*

Richard Muther (1860–1909), a German art historian, is almost com-
pletely forgotten today.[1] At the turn of the twentieth century, however,
Muther became famous for his *History of Painting in the XIXth Century*
(*Geschichte der Malerei im XIX. Jahrhundert*). The book came out in the
original German in 1892–93 and was immediately translated into many
European languages, including Russian. The Russian translation of
Muther's book under the title *Istoriia zhivopisi v XIX veke* was published
first in ten separate issues in 1893–94 and then as a three-volume set
in 1899–1902. Curiously, the first volume had received the censor's ap-
proval for publication on April 14 (Old Style), 1899, that is, only four
days after Nabokov's birth.[2]

Muther's book exerted a considerable influence on the Russian culture of the Silver Age, and specifically on the inception of *The World of
Art* journal. Alexander Benois, one of the periodical's founders, points
out that "the editorial board of *The World of Art* began its existence six
years before the journal was initiated and saw the light of day" (that is,
in 1892, since the journal first came out at the end of 1898).[3] Benois

comments: "Our artistic desire took more definite shape owing to an external motivation. Such motivation was the book [. . .] *Geschichte der Malerei im XIX. Jahrhundert* by Richard Muther."

Furthermore, Benois underscores that this book was a "revelation" for him and his generation and that "its success was truly *worldwide*" (italics in original). Benois also points out that "with its [the book's] appearance, the very 'tone' in art criticism gradually began to change. It also gave a kind of Ariadne's thread, new criteria and new formulations, to public opinion on contemporary art issues."[4] It is not surprising, therefore, that when the Russian media attacked Muther, the journal came to his defense. Thus, Igor Grabar, a painter and art critic, who collaborated with the journal, wrote: "Muther is guilty of writing the best book in European literature on modern art."[5]

It is noteworthy that Muther's book prompted Benois, by his own admission, to embark on "historio-critical activity."[6] Feeling disappointed that Muther's book did not include any discussion of Russian art, Benois pointed out this shortcoming to the German art historian, who attributed it to his complete ignorance of the subject and suggested that Benois himself should correct this oversight and write the missing chapter. Written in 1893, the chapter was duly included in the revised 1894 edition of Muther's book. Later this chapter grew into a volume, *The History of Russian Painting in the XIXth Century*—note the Mutheresque sound of Benois' title—which came out in two parts in 1901 and 1902.[7]

Muther's book exerted no less influence on Mstislav Dobuzhinsky, another notable *World of Art* participant. Dobuzhinsky recounts in his memoirs how he was "enlightened" by "Muther's *History of Painting* [*in the XIXth Century*]," which he read "avidly" and which he "continued to study with enthusiasm."[8] In 1912–14, as we recall, Dobuzhinsky was the young Nabokov's drawing master, and even though Nabokov never mentions Muther by name, there is no doubt that Dobuzhinsky advised his charge to read the book by the German art historian which had played such an important role in the formation of his own aesthetic views. Nabokov's familiarity with the book is indirectly confirmed by its presence in his father's library.[9]

In what ways could Muther's *History of Painting in the XIXth Century* affect Nabokov? In order to answer this question, it is necessary to examine the book's reception in early twentieth-century Russia. To a great extent, Alexander Benois' retrospective assessment of Muther's legacy contributes to this understanding. In his obituary for Muther, Benois notes the timely nature of the German art historian's reevaluation of the aesthetic principles of the epoch. And even though, as Benois emphasizes, not everyone agreed with this reevaluation, the ideas that Muther put forward in his book nevertheless "became common property and permeated the society so much that even the most conservative people started using 'Muther's parlance.'"[10]

What were the essence of Muther's ideas, which, to quote Benois, "were floating in the air before Muther's book, but only it gave them solidity and harmony, absolute persuasiveness and daring exclusiveness"?[11] As Mark Etkind has maintained, "According to Muther, the historical significance of a painter depends on his role in the 'all-European spiritual concert'; the most important criterion of his estimation is a master's individual originality; and the quality of a painting, omitting sociology and demands of 'the topics of the day,' is defined, first and foremost, by artistic merits."[12]

Muther's way of thinking laid the foundation for the advent of the Silver Age, and specifically for *The World of Art*'s aesthetics, because it exerted a notable influence on the creative outlook of Benois, Dobuzhinsky, and their associates. Of course, such a creative outlook was known before Muther, already in the age of Pushkin, with its "cult of beauty and high aesthetic culture," and the artists' orientation toward Pushkin evidently contributed to their more sensitive reception of Muther's ideas.[13] Thus, Sergei Diaghilev, *The World of Art*'s editor, thought that "the great power of art namely consists in its being self-purposeful, self-sufficient, and most importantly—free" and also that "a creator should love only beauty and only with it conduct a conversation at the time of a tender, mysterious manifestation of his divine nature."[14]

It appears that Muther's approach, directly or indirectly, had an impact on Nabokov's aesthetic precepts. This is attested to by the writer's pronouncements on the aims of artistic creativity. In particular, as I mentioned earlier, Nabokov asserted: "A work of art has no importance whatever to society" and "there can be no question that what makes a work of fiction safe from larvae and rust is not its social importance but its art, only its art" (*SO* 33).

Aside from the apparent influence of Muther's book on Nabokov's

Миллэсъ: Христосъ въ домѣ родителей.

14. John Everett Millais, *Christ in the House of His Parents*

creative aims, its descriptive-illustrative material, at times quite rare, received an ingenious interpretation in the writer's oeuvre. Nabokov's familiarity with Muther's book can already be discerned in his early poetry. Thus, "The Glasses of St. Joseph" (1923) calls to mind the painting *Christ in the House of His Parents,* sometimes also known as *Christ in the Carpenter's Shop,* by the Pre-Raphaelite painter John Everett Millais (1829–96) (figure 14). The painting portrays the boy Jesus, who has wounded his hand by a nail sticking out of the joiner's bench.[15] As Muther writes,

> The Child Jesus, who is standing before the joiner's bench, has hurt Himself in the hand. St. Joseph is leaning over to look at the wound, and Mary is kneeling beside the Child, trying to console Him with her caresses, whilst the little St. John is bringing water in a wooden vessel. Upon the other side of the bench stands the aged Anna, in the act of drawing out of the wood the nail which has caused the injury. A workman is labouring busily at the join-

er's bench. The floor of the workshop is littered with shavings, and tools hang round upon the walls.[16]

The phrase "the floor [. . .] is littered with shavings" calls to mind Nabokov's earlier poem "On Golgotha," published on April 29, 1921, whose concluding line contains the phrase "shavings on the floor."[17] Of course, Nabokov could remember this imagery from Georges de La Tour's *Christ with Saint Joseph in the Carpenter's Shop* (ca. 1635–40; Musée du Louvre, Paris), in which "shavings on the floor" can be seen in the foreground. In their entirety, the two concluding lines in this latter poem: "He recalled the little house in the motley byway, / and the pigeons, and the shavings on the floor" are reminiscent of a painting by John Rogers Herbert, *Our Savior Subject to His Parents at Nazareth*, also known as *The Youth of Our Lord* (1847; Guildhall Art Gallery, London), which anticipates that of Millais.[18] (It was exhibited shortly after its composition, that same year, in the Royal Academy in London.) This painting shows the young Jesus in front of his parents' house in Nazareth bringing a basket to collect wooden chips that have been swept together on the ground. The Virgin Mary is sitting by the spinning wheel and looking concernedly at her approaching son, while Joseph is sawing a plank of wood in the shed adjacent to the house, and two pigeons are sitting near the house entrance.

Millais' painting was originally exhibited with the following words from the Old Testament, which he perceived under the influence of homiletic pronouncements by the renowned Anglican theologian Edward Bouverie Pusey as prefiguring the Crucifixion: "And one shall say unto him, What are these wounds in thine hands? Then he shall answer, Those with which I was wounded in the house of my friends" (Zechariah 13:6). And the nail wound to the hand of the boy Jesus is intended, above all, to remind the audience of his impending destiny.[19] The painting was acquired by the Tate Gallery in 1921 but has been on loan there since 1912, and consequently Nabokov could have viewed it during his forays into London while he was a student at Cambridge University (1919–22).[20] It is very likely that the original painting caused Nabokov to recall seeing its earlier reproduction in Muther's book.

Like Millais, Nabokov deliberately places the scene in his poem "The Glasses of St. Joseph" in more recent times. But while Millais achieves his effect by basing the setting on a real carpenter's shop in mid-nineteenth-century London and by dressing some of his figures in quasi-modern clothes, Nabokov does it by merely one detail, central to his poem: the spectacles—a late thirteenth-century invention that had come into common use only by the nineteenth century. Furthermore, "one sunny midday" in Nabokov's poem was presumably inspired by Millais' painting itself, with its bright sunny light flowing through the doorway into the carpenter's shop, rather than by its description and black-and-white reproduction in Muther's book:

Слезы отри и послушай: в солнечный полдень старый
плотник очки позабыл на своем верстаке. Со смехом
мальчик вбежал в мастерскую; замер; заметил; подкрался;
тронул легкие стекла, и только он тронул,—мгновенно
по миру солнечный зайчик стрельнул, заиграл по далеким
пасмурным странам, слепых согревая и радуя зрячих.
   (*Ssoch*, 1:604)

(Wipe off your teardrops and listen: One sunny midday, an aged
carpenter forgot his glasses on his workbench. Laughing,
a boy ran in; paused; espied; sneaked up;
and touched the airy lenses. Instantly
a sunny shimmer traversed the world, flashed across distant,
dreary lands, warming the blind, and cheering the sighted.)[21]

It is worth noting Nabokov's creative approach to this motif in his early poem. Unlike Millais who, despite the appearance of the setting and clothing characteristic of his time, demonstrates a rather trite approach to his subject matter, riddled with "prefigurative symbolism,"[22] Nabokov most ingeniously depicts a laughing, mischievous boy Jesus, whose playful touching of the glasses, while metaphorically alluding to his later teachings, draws the reader's attention to a joyous aspect of Christianity and its beneficial impact on humanity.

The connection between Nabokov's imagery and the descriptive-illustrative material presented in Muther's book may also be traced in the writer's later works—*Mary, Despair, Invitation to a Beheading, The Gift, Lolita,* and *Speak, Memory.* Thus, Nabokov mentions *The Isle of the Dead* (1886; Museum der Bildenden Künste, Leipzig) by the Swiss painter Arnold Böcklin (1827–1901), reproduced in Muther's book, in *Mary* (36) and *Despair* (56).[23] In *Mary*, a copy of this painting is described as hang-ing in the room of Klara, one of the Russian pension's inhabitants. The painting portrays a lone figure crossing the water in a boat toward the title island, thereby epitomizing Klara's very existence. Her life is dull and monotonous and has bleak prospects: she is hopelessly in love with Ganin (Ganin is involved with Klara's friend, Lyudmila, with whom he eventually breaks up, subsequently leaving town); and she works as a typist day after day, "watching the mauve-colored line of type as it poured onto the page with dry, staccato rattle" (*Mary* 37). Klara's exis-tence does not differ principally from that of the whole pension, "that cheerless house in which lived seven Russian lost shades" (*Mary* 22). Broader still, it demonstrates the deadening effect of exile on so many human beings, forced to flee their native country because of the bru-tal Bolshevik "experiment." And the painting, with its ominous title, strongly contributes to the atmosphere of desolation and decay that pervades the novel.[24] In *Despair*, the painting indicates the mortifying and trite character of "its neighbor" (*Des* 56)—Aradalion's portrait of Hermann Karlovich, and, by implication, the deadly and banal nature of the model's and the narrator-protagonist's verbal art, lifeless like his cheeks, "pale as death" (*Des* 56).

It is possible that Muther's book was one of the earliest sources of Nabokov's familiarity with the painting. Nevertheless one cannot as-sert this with any certainty because of the painting's extraordinary popularity, especially in Russia, at the turn of the twentieth century.[25]

Nabokov's likely familiarity with Muther's book may also be dis-cerned in *Invitation to a Beheading*. In that novel, M'sieur Pierre's speech about the various pleasures of life contains the following description: "See the butcher and his helpers dragging a pig, squealing as if it were being slaughtered" (*IB* 153). This citation calls to mind the painting (al-luded to by the telling "see" in the beginning of the passage) *Slaughter of a Pig* by Jean-François Millet (1814–75) (figure 15). (Here Nabokov once again employs a well-known ekphrastic attention-drawing device, familiar from antiquity.) In the Russian translation of Muther's study, the painting is called *Butchers*. Nabokov's familiarity with this painting in Muther's book may be suggested by the phrase "the butcher and his helpers," which corresponds to the latter title.

The painting depicts two slaughterers dragging a pig to the block where the knife is ominously glistening, while a third is pushing the

Милле: *Мясники.*

15. Jean-François Millet, *Slaughter of a Pig*

resisting animal from behind and a female helper is trying to lure it with a pail of bran. Through this allusion to Millet's painting, M'sieur Pierre sadistically reminds Cincinnatus of his impending death and hints at his own role in it as "the performer of the execution" (*IB* 176). At the same time, like the female helper in Millet's painting, M'sieur Pierre and his cohort try to dull Cincinnatus's vigilance with numerous temptations.

M'sieur Pierre and his apprentices subject Cincinnatus to endless mental tortures in order to weaken his will and force him to take a voluntary part in his own execution. Cincinnatus is well aware of this when, at a low point of confrontation with his tormentors, he admits: "I have grown so limp and soggy that they will be able to do it with a fruit knife" (*IB* 124). It is possible that this "fruit knife" is one more, oblique, reference to Millet's painting in which, as I mentioned earlier, an ominously glistening knife is depicted. In particular, the jailers are trying to dispirit Cincinnatus by mocking his hopes for liberation. For this purpose, for example, M'sieur Pierre and the prison director, Rodrig, pretending to be Cincinnatus's saviors, dig a tunnel into his cell. And Rodrig's daughter, Emmie, being egged on by the executioner, ostensibly delivers the prisoner from captivity but in the end delivers him back to prison, to her father's residence (see *IB* 158–59 and 164–66).

This mocking of Cincinnatus, whom Nabokov himself calls "a poet" (*SO* 76), brings to mind an association of the novel's protagonist with Torquato Tasso (1544–95), who was confined to a lunatic asylum and there subjected to constant derision and humiliation. More specifically, the jailers' inhuman treatment of Cincinnatus evokes a painting by Eugène Delacroix (1798–1863) that depicts this tragic period in the life of the author of *Jerusalem Delivered.* As I have mentioned elsewhere, Nabokov's novel echoes both versions of Delacroix's painting *Tasso in the Hospital of St. Anne, Ferrara* (1824 and 1839).[26] In this case, of special interest is the earlier version of the painting reproduced in Muther's book under the Baudelairean title *Tasso in Prison* (figure 16).[27]

Some of its details, such as the dominance of the black color in the garment of the Italian poet, by contrast with his light-colored shirt and the cloak on his lap, and his pensive pose, as he sits leaning on one elbow and supporting his head with his fist, suggest Nabokov's familiarity with this version of the painting. And the very fact that it was privately owned and very seldom exhibited or reproduced supports the assumption that Nabokov came across the painting for the first time in Muther's book. We recall that the novel's protagonist is garbed in "the black dressing gown [. . .], the black slippers with pompons, and the black skullcap" and that he also "sat leaning on one elbow" (*IB* 25 and 146). Furthermore, in this version of Delacroix's painting, two lunatics are boisterously laughing and mocking Tasso, who pays them no heed, remaining deeply engrossed in his thoughts. Likewise, the executioner and his myrmidons regularly deride and torment Cincinnatus, who gradually learns to disregard his persecutors.

The association with Delacroix's painting that Nabokov brings about in the novel is underscored by the similarity of Cincinnatus's jeering jailers, M'sieur Pierre first and foremost, to the madmen violating the solitude of the Italian poet. M'sieur Pierre's insanity is suggested by the reaction of Cincinnatus to the executioner's aforementioned speech about various types of pleasure, which he characterizes as "dreary, obtrusive nonsense" (*IB* 154). Already in his early play *The*

Делакруа: Тассо въ темницѣ.

16. Eugène Delacroix, *Tasso in the Hospital of St. Anne, Ferrara*

Grand-dad (1923), Nabokov portrays an executioner going mad. And in *The Gift*, the writer conveys the opinion of the protagonist's father "that innate in every man is the feeling of something insuperably abnormal about the death penalty, something like the uncanny reversal of action in a looking glass that makes everyone left-handed: not for nothing is everything reversed for the executioner" (*Gift* 203).

In their turn, the jailers attempt to insinuate, if not Cincinnatus's insanity, at least his excessive sensitivity and irritableness. Thus, reacting to Cincinnatus's fainting fit, Rodrig exclaims: "Nerves, nerves, a regular little woman" (*IB* 57). Later in the novel, however, when mulling over his naive belief that Martha will understand him one day, Cincinnatus likens *himself* to "an insane man [who] mistakes his visiting kin for galaxies, logarithms, low-haunched hyenas" (*IB* 142). With this self-comparison, Cincinnatus once again evokes an association with

Tasso in Delacroix's painting, whose melancholic demeanor points to the pernicious impact of incarceration on the poet's delicate psyche.

As I pointed out earlier (in chapter 2), the mention of a white rose that "distinctly adorned his [Cincinnatus's] place" (see *IB* 182) suggests the protagonist's martyrdom. This latter meaning is manifest in El Greco's *The Burial of the Count of Orgaz,* in which a white rose adorns the vestment of Saint Stephen, the first Christian martyr.[28] An additional pictorial source of this notion for Nabokov was possibly a painting by Gabriel von Max (1840–1915) entitled *Saint Julia* and also known as *A Female Martyr on the Cross* (figure 17). The painting depicts a Roman youth laying a wreath of roses at the base of the cross on which a young female is crucified. In the black-and-white reproduction of the painting in Muther's book, one can distinguish a large, seemingly white, rose, as its tone is identical with that of "the girl's whole figure, painted in white tones."[29] Nabokov, in all likelihood, remembered the female martyr as seen in the book by Muther, who not only reproduces the painting but also describes it in detail. Muther highlights Max's heightened interest in this subject matter throughout his artistic career. The German art historian points out that virtually every one of Max's latest canvases "depicted a scene of martyrdom whose heroes were always either a helpless woman or a pitiable child."[30] It is quite possible, therefore, that while creating Cincinnatus's character and endowing the protagonist with the characteristics of a martyr and a child, and even likening him to a woman, Nabokov recalled the artistic corpus of Max, and specifically this painting, as well as Muther's characterization of Max's late artwork.

An allusion to another painting by Max, *Light,* albeit in a somewhat whimsical manner, comes into view in *The Gift,* the composition of which overlapped with that of *Invitation to a Beheading.* The novel opens with a description of a moving van; "along its entire side" ran "the name of the moving company in yard-high blue letters" (*Gift* 3). Later in the novel, Nabokov mentions the name of the moving company—"Max Lux" (*Gift* 29)—which did in fact exist in early twentieth-century Berlin (figure 18). As often the case with Nabokov, who was fond of multifarious verbal games, the appellation also evidently suggests the artist's surname and the Latinized title of his painting. Here, once again, Nabokov follows the suit of the Old Masters. Thus, Titian in his *Portrait of Francesco Maria della Rovere, Duke of Urbino* (1536–38;

Максъ: *Мученица.*

17. Gabriel von Max, *Saint Julia*

Galleria degli Uffizi, Florence) implies the last name of his sitter by incorporating an oak branch (in Italian, *rovere* means "oak") in the painting's background; and Agnolo Bronzino in his *Portrait of Stefano IV Colonna* (1546; Galleria Nazionale d'Arte Antica, Palazzo Barberini, Rome) emblematizes his sitter's surname by positioning him next to a column.[31]

Nabokov, however, goes much further than his painterly predecessors and fully utilizes the possibilities that the verbal medium of expres-

18. An advertisement for the Max Lux moving company

sion may offer. In the Russian original of *The Gift*, immediately after the mention of the moving company's name in conspicuous Roman letters—Max Lux—Nabokov employs intricate wordplay (the sequence is omitted in the English translation) when presenting the name once more, this time in the form of a farmers' market dialogue: "What's this you've got here, a fairy-tale kitchen gardener? Mak-s [poppy]. And that? Luk-s [onion], Your Grace."[32] The apostrophe "Your Grace," but literally "Your Lightness" in the original Russian, points to the intended meaning of the preceding locution "luk-s" as *lux*, its Latin homonym, which means "light."

Max's painting *Light* depicts a blind girl garbed in a light-colored dress. In her hand she holds a lit oil lamp that she proffers to a sighted woman clad in black (figure 19).[33] It seems that Nabokov alludes to this painting in order to underline the perspicacity of blind Fate, whose "attempts" the protagonist was able to appreciate only toward the end of the novel:

> Think how fate started it three and a half odd years ago. . . . The first attempt to bring us together was crude and heavy! That moving of furniture, for example: I see something extravagant in it, a "no-holds-barred" something, for it was quite a job moving the Lorentzes and all their belongings into the house where I had just rented a room! The idea lacked subtlety: to have us meet through

Lorentz's wife. Wishing to speed things up, fate brought in Romanov, who rang me up and invited me to a party at his place. But at this point fate blundered: the medium chosen was wrong, I disliked the man and a reverse result was achieved: because of him I began to avoid an acquaintance with the Lorentzes—so that all this cumbersome construction went to the devil, fate was left with a furniture van on her hands and the expenses were not recovered [. . .] Fate made a second attempt, simpler this time but

Максъ: Свѣтъ.

19. Gabriel von Max, *Light*

promising better success, because I was in need of money and
should have grasped at the offer of work—helping an unknown
Russian girl to translate some documents; but this also failed [. . .]
Then finally, after this failure, fate decided to take no chances, to
install me directly in the place where you lived. (*Gift* 363)

It is also quite possible that by means of this whimsical allusion to
Max's painting Nabokov wishes to evoke in the reader's mind an association with his earlier novel *Laughter in the Dark,* whose protagonist
Albinus begins to "see" his terrible demise only after his physical loss
of sight.[34]

The Gift also contains an allusion to another nineteenth-century
painting reproduced in Muther's book. It appears in the mention of
a writer whom Fyodor encounters in downtown Berlin on his way to
a Russian bookshop, "a good-naturedly gloomy Muscovite whose carriage and aspect were somewhat reminiscent of the Napoleon of the
island period" (*Gift* 166). Toward the end of the novel, at the meeting
of the Society of the Russian Writers in Germany, this "novelist" (*Gift*
320) is identified: "Shahmatov immediately began to cut the sandwich,
holding his knife and fork crosswise [. . .] Shahmatov's complaisantly
Napoleonic face with its strand of steely-blue hair slanting toward the
temple appealed particularly to Fyodor at these gastronomic moments"
(*Gift* 321). Nabokov's repeated indication of Shahmatov's resemblance
to Napoleon, and specifically to "the Napoleon of the island period,"
suggests the painting *Napoleon at Fontainebleau* by a French Academic
artist best known for his depiction of historical scenes, Paul Delaroche
(1797–1856) (figure 20). The painting shows Napoleon on March 31,
1814, in the Palace of Fontainebleau, immediately after his abdication,
following his defeat at the hands of the Allied forces and the fall of
Paris, reflecting on the end of his imperial dream. He was soon exiled to the island of Elba, where he landed on May 4, 1814. Therefore,
strictly speaking, the painting depicts Napoleon shortly before "the
island period." But Shahmatov's gloomy nature corresponds to Napoleon's melancholy, contemplative figure pondering his defeat and ensuing banishment. The comparison of Shahmatov to "the Napoleon of
the island period" was apparently meant to suggest Shahmatov's failure
as a man of letters. Nabokov's allusion to this is also pointed by way of

Деларошъ: Наполеонъ 1.

20. Paul Delaroche, *Napoleon at Fontainebleau*

Pushkin's scornful epigram "There is a glum triumvirate of bards—/ Shikhmatov, Shakhovskoy, Shishkov" (1815).[35]

Curiously, there is an entangled refraction between the models and their creators that undoubtedly appealed to Nabokov's penchant for the authorial presence: in this painting, Delaroche, who was known for accentuating his physical similarities to Napoleon and for adopting the same hair style, endows the emperor with his own features and demeanor, as the painter was a man of serious, melancholic character,

particularly after the death of his wife in 1845, the year of the painting's composition.[36] Nabokov, no doubt, knew about Delaroche's con-
sciously likening himself to Napoleon. Muther's book reproduces a caricature of the painter wearing a Napoleon tricorner hat.[37] In *The Gift,*
Nabokov places the novel's protagonist Fyodor, his *alter*ish, if not *alter
ego,* between Shahmatov, reminiscent of Napoleon, whom Delaroche
endowed with his own features, and Vladimirov, whom Nabokov endows with *his* own features—an intricate self-encoding device indeed.

In his "American years," Nabokov continued to draw on the imagery
he may have first encountered in Muther's book. Thus, he mentions
The Age of Innocence (1788; Tate Gallery, London) by Sir Joshua Reynolds in *Lolita.*[38] A "sepia print" of the painting is referred to in the
episode in which Humbert is sitting next to Lolita in the classroom,
while ogling "another girl with a very naked, porcelain-white neck and
wonderful platinum hair" (*AnL* 198), and forcing his stepdaughter to
perform an act of masturbation upon him. That Humbert molests Lolita while facing the print of *The Age of Innocence* charges this gruesome
scene with distinct irony and most vividly demonstrates his depriving
the little girl of this blissful stage in the life of every human being.

Nabokov's familiarity with Reynolds's art and life via Muther's study
is suggested in "La Veneziana." As I mentioned earlier (in chapter 2),
Muther reports that Reynolds possessed great copying skill and succeeded in tricking a fellow painter into believing that his copy after
Rembrandt was a true original. This anecdote, as we recall, is at the
core of this early short story.

In the beginning of *Lolita,* in Humbert's description of his "small
squalid flat" in Paris that he shared with Valeria, his first wife, Nabokov
also invokes the assassination of Jean-Paul Marat (1743–93), the infamous bloodthirsty journalist who was stabbed to death in his bathtub by Charlotte Corday. The flat contained "a shoe-shaped bath tub"
within which, as the narrator puts it, "I felt like Marat but with no
white-necked maiden to stab me" (*AnL* 26).

Although Nabokov finds Marat's revolutionary activities abhorrent
—the writer dubs him a "celebrated headman of the French regime
of Terror" (*EO,* 3:136)—his personality apparently fascinated him for
two reasons: like Nabokov, Marat suffered from psoriasis (although his
case was much more severe than Nabokov's), and he "had been an ardent lepidopterist" (*SM* 205). Nabokov also mentions the Frenchman in

Pale Fire metaphorically—"like Marat bleed" (*PF* 66). And in *Ada,* the writer playfully conflates Marat with the Napoleonic general Joachim Murat and Leo Tolstoy's title character Hadji Murad, and transforms the surname of Marat's assassin (Corday) into Cora Day (*Ada* 171).

As a nonpictorial source of this image, Nabokov recalls seeing "Marat, who died in a shoe" (*SM* 205), at "the museum of wax figures in the Arcade off the Unter den Linden" (*SM* 204) during his three-month-long "orthodontic" stay in Berlin in the autumn of 1910. Pictorially, this *Lolita* passage, which alludes to the assassination of Marat, constitutes a composite image. Although it is the subject of the well-known painting by Jacques-Louis David, *The Death of Marat* (1793; Musées Royaux des Beaux-Arts de Belgique, Brussels), the mention of a "white-necked maiden" suggests that Humbert has instead in mind the lesser-known *Charlotte Corday* by Paul Baudry (1828–86), reproduced and described in Muther's book, rather than David's painting (figure 21). While David does not depict Corday at all, Baudry makes her the central figure of his painting, as its title clearly indicates.[39] Baudry depicts this long-necked, attractive young woman not as a murderer but rather as a martyr, a modern Judith, who exercises justice by slaying the man who used his pen to incite the executions of innocent people. (These executions, without a doubt, evoked in Nabokov's mind the Red Terror and Stalinist "purges" in his native Russia.) Since the bathtub in Baudry's painting is not distinctly "shoe-shaped," its description in Nabokov's novel suggests yet another painting not included in Muther's book: Jean-Jacques Hauer's *The Assassination of Marat* (1794; Musée Lambinet, Versailles), in which Marat is depicted in a shoe-shaped bathtub after being murdered by the "white-necked" Charlotte Corday, who stands by and holds a bloodstained knife in her right hand. Nabokov was most likely familiar with this painting, as Hauer appears to be among the very few who depicted Corday while she was still alive: he sketched her during the trial and later painted her portrait in the prison cell. The portrait became especially known thanks to the engraving after it by Étienne Larose Baudran, in which Corday's long neck is partly covered by a scarf.[40]

Humbert's allusion to this famous event in French history seems to receive a peculiar twist in the novel. Humbert the pedophile is unhappy in his marriage to Valeria, whom he wedded only because of "the imitation she gave of a little girl" but who turned out to be "a

Бодри: Шарлотта Кордэ.

21. Paul Baudry, *Charlotte Corday*

large, puffy, short-legged, big-breasted and practically brainless *baba*"
(*AnL* 25 and 26). Humbert is longing for any interaction with a "white-
necked maiden"—the key phrase in the above-quoted sentence. A
"maiden" implies innocence and purity that attract Humbert the pervert (it is not clear whether Humbert was aware that Corday had been
twenty-five years old at the time of her assassination of Marat), and
"white-necked," aside from alluding to Corday's tragic end—for her
assassination of Marat she was guillotined—foreshadows his obsession

with girlish necks that finds its expression later in the novel.[41] We recall the "davenport episode" at the end of which, in the paroxysm of orgasm, Humbert's "moaning mouth" "almost reached her [Lolita's] bare neck" (*AnL* 61). This is also illustrated in the last name of one of Lolita's classmates—"pretty Rosaline" (*AnL* 53) Honeck (a portmanteau locution that combines "honey" and "neck" or "hot" and "neck"), as well as by the earlier quoted *Age of Innocence* passage describing "another girl with a very naked, porcelain-white neck" (*AnL* 198). The peculiar twist does not stop here. After divorcing Valeria, Humbert marries Charlotte Corday's namesake (Charlotte Haze) and entertains plans of murdering her, and specifically drowning her in the lake (the "Marat situation" somewhat in reverse) in order to pursue "a white-necked maiden" in his stepdaughter. Furthermore, since Humbert, as we recall, is writing his memoir in prison after fully realizing that his "fatherhood" had the most adverse effect on Lolita's life, he may be yearning in retrospect to be stabbed to death by a "white-necked maiden." The stabbing, on the one hand, would provide him with a sexual thrill and, on the other, with the coup de grâce that would put him out of his misery.

In *Lolita*, Nabokov also mentions James Abbott McNeill Whistler's *Arrangement in Gray and Black: Portrait of the Painter's Mother* (1871; Musée d'Orsay, Paris), which is described in Muther's book.[42] In the novel's episode, Lolita uses "a hole in the wall behind Whistler's Mother" (*AnL* 184) to hide the money she has been saving, as Humbert rightly fears, so that "she might accumulate sufficient cash to run away" (*AnL* 185). It is telling that Nabokov titles the painting merely *Mother*. It looks as if Lolita uses maternal "protection" to hide cash as the basis for liberation from her pervert stepfather. This maternal "protection" from the grave is reminiscent of that in *The Enchanter*, the precursor to *Lolita*.[43] The episode constitutes a poignant comment on Humbert's "parenting": instead of nurturing and protecting Lolita, he sexually exploits the child and abuses her trust, making her life utterly unbearable. So much so that Lolita prefers working in "the foul kitchen of a diner (Help Wanted) in a dismal ex-prairie state, with the wind blowing, and the stars blinking, and the cars, and the bars, and the barmen, and everything soiled, torn, dead" (*AnL* 185) rather than living with her "dream dad" and "guardian" (*AnL* 149).

Finally, Nabokov mentions *The Flute Concert of Frederick the Great at*

Менцель: Концертъ въ Санъ-Суси.

22. Adolph von Menzel, *The Flute Concert of Frederick the Great at Sans Souci*

Sans Souci by the German painter Adolph von Menzel (1815–1905), reproduced in Muther's book (figure 22). The painting is initially referred to in the earlier story "The Doorbell" (ca. 1927; *Stories* 195) to demonstrate the philistine taste of the protagonist's aging mother, but it perhaps also suggests the authorial presence by way of Nabokov's ancestor, Carl Heinrich Graun. This may be gleaned from a passage in Nabokov's memoir that contains the writer's account of Graun, an eighteenth-century German composer best known for his religious music, and especially for his oratorio *The Death of Jesus* (1755). Nabokov believed that Carl Heinrich Graun "is shown (posthumously) standing somewhat aloof, with folded arms, in Menzel's picture of Frederick the Great playing Graun's composition on the flute," adding that "the reproductions of this kept following me through all the German lodgings I stayed in during my years of exile" (*SM* 55). Menzel experts assert, however, that Carl Heinrich Graun is portrayed in the earlier, smaller version of the painting (1848), and that the widely known painting in question depicts his younger brother, also a composer, Johann

Gottlieb, standing behind the sofa on the right.[44] Once again, it is possible that Muther's book was one of the earliest sources of Nabokov's familiarity with the painting, although one cannot allege this with any certainty because of its extraordinary popularity in the second half of the nineteenth and the early twentieth centuries, especially in Germany.[45] It is clear, however, that Nabokov was thoroughly familiar with Menzel's works. Thus "*Carl Lorentz, Geschichtsmaler*," "who had spent his whole life painting parades, battles, the imperial phantom with his star and ribbon, haunting the Sans-Souci park" (*Gift* 57 and 58), looks very much like an epigone of his famous fellow countryman, who was especially memorable for depicting Frederick the Great and his epoch.

* * *

The examples from Nabokov's works discussed in this chapter allow us to surmise that Muther's *History of Painting in the XIXth Century* was one of the earliest sources of the writer's familiarity with the western European art of the time. As can be seen, Nabokov, by and large, employs paintings with historical subjects—Millais' *Christ in the House of His Parents* or Delaroche's *Napoleon at Fontainebleau*. At times, the writer makes use of artwork with symbolic meaning, such as Böcklin's *The Isle of the Dead*, or utilizes a genre composition (Millet's *Slaughter of a Pig*) or a portrait (Whistler's *Mother*), endowing them, too, with figurative undertones. And in each case, the descriptive-illustrative material contained in the book of the German art historian receives its unique imaginative refraction in the works of the Russian-born writer.

Muther's influential study provided the gifted boy with a very informative survey of nineteenth-century Western art and also allowed him to see his native Russian art in the context of European art at large. Furthermore, Muther's aesthetic precepts as expressed in the book were instrumental in shaping the literary tenets of Nabokov, that last classic of Russian literature, who above all valued unconstrained freedom of creation and artistic merit. Finally, Nabokov's indebtedness to Muther, whose survey of nineteenth-century European art was most likely introduced to him by Dobuzhinsky, serves as an additional example of that mentor's impact on his pupil's aesthetic values and, what is more, points to the further importance of *The World of Art* in Nabokov's creative universe.

6. GERMAN EXPRESSIONISTS: PORTRAYAL OF METROPOLIS

> The tiled roofs of Berlin were visible through the window's broad span, their outlines varying with the iridescent inner irregularities of the glass; in their midst, a distant cupola rose like a bronze watermelon. The clouds were scudding, rupturing, fleetingly revealing an astonished, gossamer autumnal blue [. . .] I realized that the world does not represent a struggle at all, or a predaceous sequence of chance events, but shimmering bliss, beneficent trepidation, a gift bestowed on us and unappreciated.
>
> —Nabokov, "Beneficence"

> But our wanderings are not always doleful, and courageous nostalgia does not always preclude us from enjoying a foreign country, refined solitude on a foreign electric night, on a bridge, in a square, at a railway station.
>
> —Nabokov, "The Jubilee"

Nabokov's works demonstrate his divergent attitude toward *The World of Art* and the German Expressionists—two artistic groups that distinguished themselves in cityscape, St. Petersburg and Berlin respectively. As we saw earlier (in chapter 4), Nabokov understandably displays a nostalgic fondness for and emotional attachment to St. Petersburg in the habitually retrospective depiction of his birthplace. In doing so, the writer shows, among other things, his deep appreciation of and aesthetic affinity with *The World of Art*'s chief participants. While Nabokov's approach to St. Petersburg could be expected, his outlook on Berlin is quite surprising: although the city was his place of exile, Nabokov nonetheless finds himself fascinated with it and draws artistic inspiration in depicting its various facets of life. In this regard,

Nabokov's depiction of Berlin reveals principal dissimilarities between his world perception and those of his German counterparts.

Both Nabokov and many German Expressionist artists lived in Berlin in the interwar years, and that city served as a major, if not central, setting for their works. In this chapter, I intend to compare and contrast the portrayal of various manifestations of metropolitan life in the German capital as reflected in the artists' paintings and in Nabokov's writings. I shall attempt to provide an explanation for their distinctly disparate, frequently opposite, visions of the European Metropolis.

German Expressionism had emerged at the time of the country's rapid industrialization and economic modernization, between the unification of Germany in 1871 and World War I (1914–18), which resulted in vast urban expansion, especially in Berlin. At the turn of the twentieth century, Berliners grew accustomed to well-developed railroads, distant and suburban (S-Bahn) trains, streetcars, automobiles, and subways (U-Bahn) as means of surface and underground transportation; good sewage and electric lighting systems; large department stores with enticing shop windows, such as Wertheim (1896) and KaDeWe (1907); luxurious hotels, such as the Adlon (1907), with hot running water, baths, and telephones in every room; and night life and entertainment in cafés, cabarets, music halls, and movie theaters. The city also boasted world-class museums: the Alte Nationalgalerie (1876), the Pergamon Museum (1901), and the Kaiser Friedrich Museum (1904), as well as the voluminous State Library (1910). "By the late nineteenth century, Berlin had eclipsed Paris as the political, economic, and military capital of continental Europe. Culturally it was emerging as a cosmopolitan city of world significance."[1] On the other hand, the rapid increase in the city's population gave rise to overcrowded conditions in working-class districts of the northwest and southeast (Wedding and Neukölln), contrasted with luxurious upper-middle-class environs to the west and southwest (Charlottenburg and Grunewald). The steep upsurge in the city population led to the hazards of metropolitan life—air pollution and insufficient hygiene, as well as crime and prostitution. World War I brought about additional painful predicaments—a huge gender imbalance and a depleted labor force due to the large number of combat fatalities and war cripples. The terms of the Treaty of Versailles (1919)—enormous reparations, the loss of over 10 percent of Germany's home territory and population, as well as all of its colonies—inevitably led to the country's economic downfall, with staggering inflation and unemployment, adding more afflictions and disparities to life in the *Weltstadt*. At the same time, the fall of the stifling imperial regime and its institutions at the end of World War I infused the arts with new vitality. Modernism took hold, and avant-garde culture flourished even as democracy struggled and the economy became fragile.

German Expressionism, which constituted a major avant-garde movement in the early twentieth century and became the dominant artistic style during the war and its aftermath, reflected the contradictory, and at times disconcerting, experiences of metropolitan life as well as the postwar atmosphere of cynicism, alienation, and disillusionment. Following in the footsteps of Vincent van Gogh, James Ensor, and Edvard Munch, German Expressionists developed a manner notable for its harshness and visual intensity. During World War I, some German Expressionists, such as Ernst Ludwig Kirchner (1880–1935) and George Grosz (1893–1958), became part of the anti-aesthetic, nihilistic Dada movement, which surfaced to express the confusion felt by artists as the war turned their world upside down. Some Expressionists, such as Hermann Max Pechstein (1881–1955), founded the politically radical Novembergruppe, and others—Max Beckmann (1884–1950), Otto Dix (1891–1969), and the same Grosz—created a more pointed, socially critical blend of Expressionism known as New Objectivity (Neue Sachlichkeit), or German Verism.[2]

We find manifestations of modern self-reflection and circumspection with regard to a large city in such works, to name only a few, as Nikolai Gogol's "Nevsky Prospect" (1835), Edgar Allan Poe's "The Man of the Crowd" (1840), Charles Baudelaire's *Le Spleen de Paris* and Gustave Flaubert's *L'Éducation Sentimentale* (both 1869), Andrei Bely's *Petersburg* (1913–14), James Joyce's *Ulysses* (1922), John Dos Passos's *Manhattan Transfer* (1925), and Alfred Döblin's *Berlin Alexanderplatz* (1929), referring, respectively, to St. Petersburg, London, Paris, Dublin, New York City, and Berlin. Further, the works of Georg Simmel (1858–1918), the renowned German social and political theorist, were crucial to the modern understanding of urbanity, specifically in Berlin. In their turn, Simmel's works exerted considerable influence on such philosophers, more contemporaneous with Nabokov, as Siegfried Kracauer and Walter Benjamin.[3]

Nabokov's perceptions of Berlin over his fifteen-year residence in the city find expression in his numerous short stories, novels, and even poems set and written in the German capital. Dieter E. Zimmer has astutely observed that Nabokov "has left us the most vivid and even endearing literary picture of Berlin in the twenties and early thirties— more exactly of its western parts, not the proletarian northeastern quarters of Döblin's *Berlin Alexanderplatz*, of its streets, its gray apartment houses and bourgeois villas, its skies, its light, its parks and gardens, the pines and lakes of the Grunewald, its shops, *pissoirs*, streetcars and subways."[4]

To this I might add that Nabokov's verbal images of Berlin also complement those in Walther Ruttmann's documentary film *Berlin: Symphony of a Great City* (1927), which Nabokov evidently had a chance to watch. It should be noted, however, that the "literary picture" of the German capital by Nabokov and its pictorial representation by the German Expressionist painters reveal essential differences that stem from the writer's and the painters' dissimilar backgrounds and life experiences.

Nabokov was born into a highly refined aristocratic family. He was at home in many languages and cultures from his very birth, was well traveled from his childhood, and received a diverse and splendid education. As a foreigner, Nabokov came to the German capital from St. Petersburg, where he was born and where he spent his formative years. In spite of all their understandable unique attributes, however, St. Petersburg and Berlin shared their status and role as the capitals of two empires that collapsed in the aftermath of World War I.[5] We recall that Nabokov also visited Berlin as a boy prior to the war (1910). He stayed in the German capital for three months to have his teeth fixed, and he enjoyed a festive atmosphere there: he lodged at the luxurious Adlon Hotel (although his tutor Filipp Zelensky, known as Lenski in *Speak, Memory,* moved him to a pension for "a more democratic form of life"), visited a roller-skating rink on the Kurfürstendamm, and a dancing show in the Wintergarten (*SM* 159–62 and 204–7). Albeit a stranger, Nabokov to some extent observed life in postwar Berlin through the prism of his prewar boyhood experience, as well as through the comparative lens of his pre-revolutionary life in St. Petersburg. Thus, for example, when watching Berlin streetcars, Nabokov's narrator of the short story "A Guide to Berlin" (1925) is "reminded of how, some eighteen years ago in Petersburg, the horses used to be unhitched and led around the pot-bellied blue tram" (*Stories* 157). And Martin, the protagonist of *Glory*, recalls the difference between the two cities in the layout and crossing of their railways when returning to Berlin years later:

> It was night by the time he [Martin] neared Berlin. Looking from the train onto the wet lighted streets he relived his childhood impression of Berlin, whose fortunate inhabitants could enjoy daily, if they wished, the sight of trains with fabulous destinations, gliding across a black bridge over a humdrum thoroughfare; in this respect Berlin differed from St. Petersburg, where railroad operations were concealed like a secret rite. (*Glory* 133)

Unlike Nabokov, the Expressionist painters were born into the families of commoners, and their education and cultural exposure were in no way comparable to those of the writer. Although native Germans, the painters grew up in the provinces and were outsiders to Berlin. (Grosz's case is somewhat complicated: although born in Berlin, he moved to the small Pomeranian town of Stolp [now Słupsk, Poland] at the age of five, came back to Berlin for two years, and left the German capital once again, only to return at the age of nineteen [1912] and to remain there until his emigration to the United States in 1933.)[6] With the exception of Dix, who moved to Berlin as late as 1925, the artists settled in the German capital prior to World War I and were overwhelmed by the glamour and turmoil of the Metropolis.

The painters, born between the early 1880s (Beckmann, Kirchner, Pechstein) and the early 1890s (Dix and Grosz), were older than Nabokov and, with the outbreak of World War I, were all drafted into the army. This military experience deeply traumatized them. Thus Grosz writes in 1917 that while stationed with the home troops, he "saw the war more clearly by then and could observe the widespread change of mood among the majority of the soldiers, with whom I had shared the initial enthusiasm of 1914. This oppressed me very much, and slowly, within me, somber pictures began to take shape. My faith in men in general had received a severe blow. I began to draw small satirical drawings to express my inner turmoil."[7]

This traumatic war experience also found its graphic manifestation in Kirchner's haunting *Self-Portrait as a Soldier* (1915; Allen Memorial Art Museum, Oberlin College, Oberlin, Ohio). The painting depicts the artist in a military uniform, with an illusorily amputated right hand, thereby presenting a striking metaphor for his perception of the war as both an individual and national tragedy.[8]

Nabokov, on the other hand, did not acquire any personal warfare experience: he was too young to be drafted into the Russian army in the war's earlier years. Toward the end of the war, the Bolshevik coup d'état of November 1917 forced him and his family to depart from St. Petersburg for the Crimea, a stronghold of the Whites at the time. While there, as Nabokov recalls in his Russian memoir, he considered joining General Denikin's army in the winter of 1918–19 (*Ssoch,* 5:299), but in the end he did not enlist, and in April 1919, a week before his twentieth birthday, he left his native country never to return there again.[9]

Despite his lack of military experience, Nabokov was deeply affected by the events that abruptly put an end to his happy life and forced him to flee his familiar milieu amidst the collapse of the Russian Empire. For example, he describes how from the oriel window of his mother's boudoir "at the outbreak of the Revolution, I watched various engagements and saw my first dead man: he was being carried away on a stretcher, and from one dangling leg an ill-shod comrade kept trying to pull off the boot despite pushes and punches from the stretchermen" (*SM* 89). Brian Boyd quotes Nabokov as recalling that at this fatal, ominous period after the Bolshevik takeover, while he was composing poetry as usual, "fierce rifle fire and the foul crackle of a machine gun could be heard from the street."[10] In retrospect, in his memoir, Nabokov describes the upheaval in his native country in a somewhat detached and dry manner as follows: "When, at the end of the year [1917], Lenin took over, the Bolsheviks immediately subordinated everything to the retention of power, and a regime of bloodshed, concentration camps, and hostages entered upon its stupendous career" (*SM* 241). Naturally, Nabokov conveys an immediate, impassioned response to this grievous experience, hot on the heels of these shocking events, in his poem "Revolution" (1917), in which his lyrical "I," with remarkable candor and emotional force, reveals his feelings of horror and disgust over the violence and destruction he witnessed:

Я слово длинное с нерусским оконча́ньем
нашел нечаянно в рассказе для детей;
и отверну́лся я со странным содрога́ньем.

В том слове был извив неведомых страстей,
рычанье, вопли, свист, нелепые виденья:
стеклянные глаза убитых лошадей,

кривые улицы, зловещие строенья,
кровавый человек, лежащий на спине,
и чьих-то жадных рук звериные движенья!

А, некогда, читать так сладко было мне
о зайчиках смешных со свинками морскими,
танцующих на пнях, весною при луне!

Но слово грозное над сказками моими,
как буря пронеслось! Нет прежней простоты,
и мысли страшные ночами роковыми

шуршат, как серые, газетные листы!

(I found a lengthy word with a non-Russian ending,
unwittingly, inside a children's storybook,
and turned away from it with a strange kind of shudder.

That word contained the writhing of mysterious passions:
The growls, the howls, the whistles, and the senseless visions,
assassinated horses' vitreous eyes,

the sinuous streets, the evil-auguring constructions,
a man, incarnadine, prostrate upon his back,
the bestial motions of somebody's avid hands!

And, once upon a time, how sweet I used to find it
to read of funny rabbits who would dance in spring
with guinea pigs on stumps beneath the moon.

But now the fateful word above my childhood tales,
stormlike, has rushed! Gone is their old simplicity;
and terrifying thoughts, during the doomful nights,

now crepitate like gray newspaper sheets.)[11]

The cataclysmic changes that the Bolshevik takeover brought in its wake were understandably a source of deep distress for this highly sensitive and perceptive young man. Nabokov's pain was deepened by the loss of his first cousin and the best friend of his youth, Yuri Rausch von Traubenberg (1898–1919), who was "a cavalry officer in Denikin's army" and who "was killed fighting the Reds in northern Crimea" (*SM* 200), and immeasurably so by the loss of his father in 1922 at the hands of Russian ultra-monarchist thugs in Berlin. In spite of these wide-ranging ordeals and overwhelming personal tragedies, Nabokov's blissful, felicitous years in Russia stood him in good stead as the rock-solid base, the fountainhead, for his resilient personality. Even in the most arduous years of his life in Europe, full of hardship and uncertainty, he never succumbed to despondency—his works radiate hope and happiness. Nabokov most certainly would not share Grosz's sentiments of "inner turmoil," of "a severe blow" to his "faith in men in general," and Kirchner's programmatic painting would definitely not be to his liking. Moreover, it is very telling that Nabokov dubs Erich Maria Remarque's *All Quiet on the Western Front* (*Im Westen nichts Neues,* 1929), a disturbing account of the horrors of World War I that is, to an extent, a verbal counterpart of Kirchner's *Self-Portrait,* "some cloyingly rhetorical, pseudobrutal tale about war [which] is considered the crown of literature" (*Gift* 350).[12]

Nabokov fundamentally differed from the German Expressionist painters in his political outlook: he belonged to a family of traditional liberals and espoused the political views of his father, who envisioned the Western democracies, and specifically Great Britain, as models for Russia's prospective political system. Needless to say, Nabokov vehemently rejected the totalitarian doctrine of the Bolsheviks and their usurpation of power. Many of the German painters, on the other hand, embraced and championed markedly leftist political views and greeted the Bolshevik coup d'état fervently (Grosz for some time was even a card-carrying member of the German Communist Party and was its most prominent artist).[13] The painters enthusiastically welcomed the Communists' short-lived Spartacist revolt (1919) and mourned its suppression and the assassination of its leaders, Karl Liebknecht and Rosa Luxemburg. These sentiments are evident in Pechstein's *Don't Strangle Our Newborn Freedom* (ca. 1919), Beckmann's *Martyrdom* (1919), and Grosz's *In Memory of Rosa Luxemburg and Karl Liebknecht* (ca. 1919).[14]

Finally, for the painters Berlin was the center of their native country, defeated and humiliated. They lamented their homeland's disgrace and were disgusted and shocked by the capital's disturbing socioeconomic divides. Nabokov in Germany, on the other hand, was "a stranger in a strange land," and this enabled him to describe its main city with emotional detachment and keen foresight. All of these substantial dissimilarities between the background, life experience, and world outlook of Nabokov and the painters find expression in their different portrayals of the city.[15]

When and how could Nabokov have become familiar with the art of the German Expressionists? Prior to World War I, he could have heard about it from Dobuzhinsky, his drawing master, who was very familiar with artistic trends in western Europe and "approved the Expressionist art of some German painters in the beginning of the twentieth century."[16] Years later, however, Dobuzhinsky considerably modified his assessment of German Expressionist art. Thus, in 1926, although admitting that Dix's works were captivating and splendidly drawn, Dobuzhinsky expressed revulsion at his "intestines turned inside out of syphilitic women and other filths" and astutely remarked that the artist "was a man bruised by the war, and apparently hopelessly."[17]

Nabokov's closer familiarity with German Expressionist art, however, presumably occurred only after his emigration to western Europe, first during his vacation visits (1919–22) from Cambridge University to Berlin, where his family resided at the time, and later when upon graduation he himself settled in the German capital (1922–37). He could certainly see it in German periodicals, such as *Der Sturm* (1910–32), which reproduced a great deal of German Expressionist art as well as the artwork of many Russian-born painters—Marc Chagall, Natalia Goncharova, and Vasily Kandinsky. More specifically, Nabokov could have come upon Grosz's artwork by way of the Malik Press's "hit-and-run" distribution of his illustrated pamphlets at Berlin street corners, as well as in his albums.[18] The latter supposition is all the more plausible because the tenth issue of the Berlin-based Russian periodical *Firebird* (1923) contained an advertisement for George Grosz's portfolio *Ecce Homo,* and Nabokov, an avid reader of and frequent contributor to the journal, could have caught sight of it there. Furthermore, Nabokov could see Expressionist artists' works at the Crown Prince Palace (Kronprinzenpalais), which housed the Museum of Contemporary Art (Museum der Gegenwart) as a division of the Nationalgalerie in the interwar years (1919–37).[19] (The Nazi "degenerate art" campaign, accompanied by looting and burning of contemporary avant-garde art, led to the dissolution of the museum.) The writer could also see their works displayed in private galleries. Thus, Grosz's artwork was exhibited in the 1920s and early 1930s at the Alfred Flechtheim and Bruno Cassirer Galleries.[20]

Although Nabokov nowhere directly voiced an opinion on German Expressionist art, he undoubtedly had an aversion to its world perception because of its focus on the sociopolitical. As a true aesthete, Nabokov strongly believed that a work of art should carry no "message" and "has no importance whatever to society" (*SO* 33). By contrast, the Marxist-minded Grosz contested in *My Life* (1928): "The task of art is to help the worker understand his exploitation and his suffering, to compel him to acknowledge openly his wretchedness and enslavement, to awaken his self-consciousness in him and to inspire him to engage in class warfare. My art is dedicated to these aims."[21]

In light of all these disparities, it is worth considering Nabokov's depiction of Berlin life in its various manifestations—sports, brawls, crime, prostitution, mannequins, war cripples, and resort activities—as well as his overall perception of the city as contrasted to those of the German painters.

Not merely a cultured, artistic intellectual, Nabokov was also highly athletic and was fond of playing and watching sports. Soccer, hockey, and boxing, along with tennis, were among his favorites. Nabokov had played soccer as a boy at the Tenishev School, as a student at Cambridge, and as an adult in Berlin, and enjoyed watching soccer games throughout his life. Thus, in a postcard to Véra on April 4, 1937, from Paris, Nabokov writes: "Today I am going with the Kiandzhuntsevs to a soccer match."[22] In his early poem "Football" (1920), in "The University Poem" (stanzas 20 and 21), and in the novel *Glory* (chapter 26), the writer conveys his great appreciation for the sport and reflects his own experience as a goalkeeper.

While Nabokov himself did not play hockey, he much enjoyed the game, and in later years would even rent a TV to watch its high-level matches.[23] His attraction to the sport is evident in the description of the hockey match in *Laughter in the Dark:* "The crowd was roaring with excitement as nimble sticks pursued the puck on the ice, and knocked it, and hooked it, and passed it on, and missed it, and clashed together in rapid collision" (*Laugh* 151), a passage in which he superbly conveys the powerful dynamism of the game.

Boxing was another of Nabokov's passions. He was a competent boxer himself and, while in Berlin, reportedly considered giving boxing lessons.[24] In the poem "A Boxer's Girl" (1924; *Ssoch,* 1:622), Nabokov describes a boxing match ostensibly through the eyes of the boxer's girlfriend, although the exactitude of the account betrays the authorial point of view. He also expertly depicts the boxing bout between Martin and Darwin in *Glory* (chapter 28). Nabokov's fascination with and vast knowledge of this sport are particularly evident in his account of the 1925 boxing match between the German Hans Breitensträter and the Basque Paolino Uzcudun.[25] In this essay, Nabokov professes his great love for the sport: he speaks of the beauty of the art of boxing, illustrates it with examples from literature, briefly discusses the history of the sport and its most prominent representatives, describes the match itself, and does all this with tremendous competence and gusto. In his essay, Nabokov specifically quotes from Mikhail Lermontov's "Song About the Merchant Kalashnikov" (1837; *Ssoch,* 1:750 and 814–15). More than thirty years later, in *Pnin,* while lecturing Victor on the manifestations of sport in Russian literature, the novel's title character, referring to that same poem, points out, in his quaint Pninian English, that "the first description of box in Russian literature we find in a poem by Mihail Lermontov" (*Pnin* 105). Altogether, in his depictions of athletic activities, Nabokov tends to poeticize them, focusing on their vibrant, competitive, and entertaining attributes. Thus, in his essay "On Generalities" (ca. 1926), Nabokov writes:

> The Greeks played hockey and hit the punching ball. Sports, be it hunting, or a knights' tournament, or a cockfight, or good old Russian *lapta* [a game reminiscent of cricket], always gladdened

and captivated mankind. It is senseless to search for signs of bar-
barity in it [sport] because a true barbarian is always a very poor
sportsman.[26]

Nabokov also emphasizes the heroic and virtuous nature of sports,
which originated in the Olympic Games in ancient Greece and continued down to the modern world through ancient Rome and Renaissance Italy. To him, athletic activities are, above all, a test of resolve
and courage.[27]

The German painters, on the other hand, occasionally politicized
sports and saw in them a means for creating a "new" man. For example,
in *The New Man* and *Cycling and Weightlifting* (both 1920), Grosz envisions a utopian man who is training both his body and mind.[28] By and
large, however, the painters depicted athletic activities, such as soccer,
hockey, and boxing, as they were, because as artists, in spite of their sociopolitical agenda, they were apparently captivated by the dynamism
of these sports' fierce physical encounters as well as by the competitive
spirit and vying nature of the events. This is evident in Beckmann's
Soccer Players (1929), which looks, however, more like rugby, Kirchner's
watercolor series *Hockey Players* (1934), Pechstein's *Boxer in the Ring*
(1910), and Grosz's 1926 portrait of the heavyweight champion Max
Schmeling.[29] Be that as it may, it is doubtful that the painters saw any
manifestation of valor and virtue in athletics, as did Nabokov.

Somewhat concomitant to boxing is brawling, which both Nabokov
and the Expressionist painters present as part of metropolitan life. In
the story "The Fight," Nabokov's narrator describes a fistfight between
Krause, an elderly tavern keeper, and Otto, a young electrician and
his daughter's lover. Being "enthralled" by their quarrel, prompted by
Otto's not paying twenty pfennigs for a shot of brandy, the narrator
recalls "a splendid scuffle" he himself once had "in a seaport dive" (*Stories* 145). A verbal painter, he is further captivated "by the reflections
of the streetlamp on the distorted faces, the strained sinew in Krause's
naked neck" (ibid.). He skillfully conveys the "muffled thumping of
fists" in the ensuing "hand-to-hand combat" between Otto and Krause
(ibid.). He perceptively notes that each combatant possessed his own
style: while Otto struck in silence, Krause, who ultimately prevailed in
the brawl, "emitted a short grunt with every blow" (ibid.). One may only
guess whether the twenty-pfennig shot of brandy was merely a pretext

for the fight, which was most likely about jealousy, control, and domination. It is noteworthy, however, that Nabokov's narrator concludes the story by declaring that he does not wish to know "who was wrong and who was right in this affair" (*Stories* 146). He manifestly states his unwillingness to pass judgment or draw any foregone conclusions from the incident and programmatically asserts that "what matters is not the human pain or joy at all but, rather, the play of shadow and light on a live body" (ibid.). Here, once again, attention to the visual, Nabokov's hallmark, reigns supreme.[30]

Although at times the Expressionist painters apparently saw the depiction of brawls as a unique artistic opportunity to convey the dynamism of line in the graphic confrontation of human bodies, as is evident, for example, in Grosz's *Brawl* (1913; Galerie Pels-Leusden, Berlin), scholars argue that some of them, and specifically Grosz, "may have depicted violence to sublimate his boiling resentment at the claustrophobic atmosphere of militaristic, authoritarian Germany."[31] In addition to venting his political frustrations, the artist apparently saw the depiction of brawls as an opportunity for social commentary. Thus, in his drawing *The Attack* (1915; Joseph H. Hirshhorn Museum, Smithsonian Institution, Washington, D.C.), Grosz depicts three assailants striking a man and apparently murdering him either in a burglary attempt or in an underworld score settling, as yet another man watches the scene from his balcony.

While the depiction of athletic activities and of brawling shows some distant similarities between Nabokov and the painters, their respective portrayals of life in Berlin for the most part display a total contrast. This contrast is manifested, for example, in their disparate treatment of crime. Oddly, the artists exhibited a morbid fascination with criminal acts, specifically with sex offenses and murders. Scholars believe that this fascination reflects the painters' "inner rebellion against the Prussian mentality of law and order." They further suggest that by identifying with the criminal, the artists revolt "against the society's status quo."[32] Such, for example, are Grosz's *Sex Murder on Acker Street* (1916–17; Leopold Museum, Vienna) and Dix's *Self-Portrait as Sex Murderer* (1920; present whereabouts are unknown), which depict the crime in gory detail, betraying the artists' penchant for perversion and grisly fantasies.[33] Moreover, Grosz had no qualms in playfully assuming the identity of a sex offender and murderer. The photograph shown in

23. George Grosz, "Self-Portrait as Jack the Ripper"

figure 23 presents the artist, in the guise of Jack the Ripper, mockingly clenching a knife in his hand as he approaches his fiancée Eva Peter, who is posing as an unsuspecting victim.

Nabokov by no means shared this perverse attraction with the German artists and de facto polemicized with them. In *King, Queen, Knave,*

Kurt Dreyer voices an opinion, apparently close to that of his creator, that crime exposes banality and lack of imagination on the part of its perpetrator. Thus, upon visiting a crime exhibit, Dreyer muses:

> What a talentless person one must be, what a poor thinker or hysterical fool, to murder one's neighbor. The deathly gray of the exhibits, the banality of crime, pieces of bourgeois furniture, a frightened little console on which a bloody imprint had been found, hazel nuts injected with strychnine, buttons, a tin basin, again photographs—all this trash expressed the very essence of crime. How much those simpletons were missing! Missing not only the wonders of everyday life, the simple pleasure of existence, but even such instants as this, the ability to look with curiosity upon what was essentially boring. (*KQK* 207)

This supposition seems to be accurate, since in his Cornell lectures Nabokov expressed sentiments very similar to those of his character:

> Criminals are usually people lacking imagination [. . .] Lacking real imagination, they content themselves with such half-witted banalities as seeing themselves gloriously driving into Los Angeles in that swell stolen car with that swell golden girl who had helped to butcher its owner [. . .] [C]rime is the very triumph of triteness, and the more successful it is, the more idiotic it looks. (*LL* 376)

The painters', and specifically Grosz's, attraction to crime and its "creativity" finds an intriguing parallel in Hermann Karlovich, the deranged protagonist of *Despair,* who equates art with crime, compares "the breaker of the law which makes such a fuss over a little spilled blood, with a poet or a stage performer," and speaks of "the genius of a perfect crime" (*Des* 3 and 123).[34] Incidentally, like Grosz and many other Expressionists, this Russian-born German character in Nabokov's novel dreams of uniting people "in the classless society of the future" (*Des* 158) and maintains that a work of art—in this case "his" novel—should contain "the social message" (*Des* 159). It is very likely, therefore, that by way of the novel's protagonist, Nabokov derides this bizarre twofold fascination with crime and leftist sociopolitical ideas on the part of some German Expressionists.

In his depiction of prostitution, Nabokov manifestly avoids any social commentary and emphasizes instead, first and foremost, its deplorable human aspect. In *King, Queen, Knave*, while endowing a prostitute with the recognizable attributes of her profession—"bright-eyed" (*KQK* 68) and "bleached" ("belenaia"; *Ssoch,* 2:174)—the writer shows her conducting a conversation with an old watchman "about rheumatism and its cures" (*KQK* 68). In describing the prostitute, Nabokov demonstrates a remarkably unconventional point of view by focusing not on the ill repute of her occupation but on the fact that both she and the watchman have similar "professional hazards" related to their outdoor nocturnal activities, which can lead to the chronic disease of rheumatism. While exposing the human side of this member of the "oldest profession," Nabokov at the same time shows in a later passage how Franz foolishly idealizes these "ladies of the night" when perceiving the emergence of "a sleek-hosed harlot" "at every corner" as an "emblem of ineffable happiness" (*KQK* 74). This latter passage, permeated with irony, suggests that the young man remains "quite blind" (*KQK* 30) in spite of his regaining physical sight after replacing his broken glasses. (In this regard, Franz is akin to Albinus, the protagonist of Nabokov's later novel *Laughter in the Dark:* while sighted, he remains "sightless," and only upon becoming physically blind does he gradually envision and comprehend the true nature of the people around him.)

Another example of Nabokov's depiction of prostitutes comes into view in his early story "A Letter That Never Reached Russia" (1925), in which the narrator matter-of-factly observes and reports the seen: "Farther on, at the corner of a square, a stout prostitute in black furs slowly walks to and fro, stopping occasionally in front of a harshly lighted shop window where a rouged woman of wax shows off to night wanderers her streamy, emerald gown and the shiny silk of her peach-colored stockings" (*Stories* 138). He then proceeds to relay the whole mercenary process in markedly detached and nonjudgmental fashion: the prostitute, approached by a client, leads him to "a nearby building," and walks past "a polite and impassive old porter" and "an equally impassive old woman" who "will unlock with sage unconcern an unoccupied room and receive payment for it" (*Stories* 138–39). The singularly bizarre detail in this account that adds a touch of caricature to the whole episode is the description of how "this placid middle-aged whore," while waiting for a client, is ogling the fully clad mannequin that the narrator dubs "a rouged woman of wax" (*Stories* 138). The latter phrase seems to imply that the whore and the "rouged woman of wax" are on a similar footing: while one advertises and sells her body, the other advertises the "streamy, emerald gown" and "peach-colored stockings" (ibid.). This juxtaposition also evokes a scathing contrast: while the mannequin "makes a living" by "putting" the clothes on, the prostitute makes her living by taking them off. It also suggests that the prostitute mimics an ordinary woman by wistfully eyeing the clothes in a shop window.

A similar caricaturish depiction of prostitutes pretending to look at shop windows can be found in Nabokov's last Russian novel: "At the next corner his approach automatically triggered off the doll-like mechanism of the prostitutes who always patrolled there. One of them even tried to look like somebody lingering by a shop window, and it was sad to think that these pink corsets on their golden dummies were known to her by heart, by heart. . . ." (*Gift* 325). The writer, once again, shows the prostitutes' resemblance to mannequins: their automaton-like response to the appearance of a potential client "triggered off the doll-like mechanism." An accomplished lepidopterist, Nabokov offers here, as in the earlier story, another excellent example of mimicry when demonstrating how a streetwalker poses for an ordinary window-shopping woman. Furthermore, in these descriptions Nabokov displays his penchant for the comic and his predilection for caricature.[35]

Dix's portrayal of prostitutes in *Three Prostitutes on the Street* (figure 24) stands in stark contrast to Nabokov's descriptions. The artist depicts "ladies of pleasure" positioning themselves by a lavish shop window. The predatory expressions on their faces indicate that they are "hunting" for a wealthy client. Their ominous facial features are also reminiscent of skull-heads and perhaps are designed to hint at the deadly diseases they may carry. In addition, as an overall social commentary, their depiction is apparently meant to suggest that altogether they are a menace to society.[36] Grosz's approach to the subject, like that of Dix, is also fraught with public commentary, as exemplified in his *Married Couple: Man and Woman* (1926; private collection). In spite of its

24. Otto Dix, *Three Prostitutes on the Street*

primary title,[37] the painting depicts a well-dressed older man tying his shoelaces, evidently after a casual sexual encounter with a prostitute: this is indicated by the chance décor of the boudoir and the worn-out, vulgar-looking woman in a transparent negligee, who is gazing in the mirror at the necklace which the man apparently presented to her for her "services."

An analogous dissimilarity is perceptible in Nabokov's and the painters' approach to the subject of mannequins.[38] In his description of mannequins, Nabokov was perhaps prompted by the dummies displayed in the shop windows of various department stores, including KaDeWe near which, on Passauer Straße, Nabokov had resided in 1926–29, at the time of composing *King, Queen, Knave* and *The Defense.*

175

Brian Boyd has perceptively suggested that the initials of the novel's Russian title—*Korol', dama, valet*—are phonetically reminiscent of the name of the store.[39]

The Defense contains three distinct mannequin images. Two of them appear as wax dummies in barbershop windows: one, in St. Petersburg, at the time when Luzhin begins to learn the art of chess playing (*Def* 50); the other, in Berlin, shortly before his death (*Def* 243–44). Nora Buhks has astutely pointed out that these barbershop dummies evoke Dobuzhinsky's images from his *Barbershop Window* (1906) and *Night in St. Petersburg* (1924). Buhks has also aptly suggested that the three female dummies in the St. Petersburg episode of the novel represent the Parcae (the three Roman goddesses of Fate), implying that Luzhin is destined to become a chess player. The single female dummy at the end of the novel, which evokes in Luzhin's memory the triad from his St. Petersburg childhood, is apparently Morta, the counterpart of the Greek Atropos, the deity known to cut the thread of life, that foreshadows Luzhin's death.[40] Nabokov presumably links Luzhin's St. Petersburg and Berlin experiences through his own successive familiarity with two of Dobuzhinsky's paintings. Both paintings depict St. Petersburg scenery, but the second one, composed in 1924, Nabokov apparently saw for the first time at the 1926 Dobuzhinsky exhibit in Berlin.

An additional wax dummy image that figures in the novel can be linked to Nabokov's Berlin experience. It is described as "the wax dummy of a man with two faces, one sad and the other joyful," that Luzhin comes across in "a stationery store" (*Def* 204). The dummy "was throwing open his jacket alternately to left and right: the fountain pen clipped into the left pocket of his white waistcoat had sprinkled the whiteness with ink, while on the right was the pen that never ran" (ibid.). As Dieter E. Zimmer has convincingly demonstrated, Nabokov based this image on a Montblanc German advertisement that depicted a smiling man pointing to the pen clipped into the pocket of his white waistcoat. The caption reads: "Montblanc, the elegant safe fountain-pen for white waistcoats" ("Montblanc, der elegante Sicherheitsfüllhalter für weisse Westen").[41] As in the later case of the Berlin barbershop dummy, Luzhin entertains the thought of buying this fountain-pen advertising mannequin. In this episode his thoughts are interrupted by his wife's inquiries about his father's death, whereas in the barbershop episode the shop proprietor tells Luzhin that the dummy is "not for sale" (*Def* 243). It is noteworthy that the two mannequins are linked to Death and all of them with Fate.

The mannequin motif is of great import in *King, Queen, Knave*.[42] Franz as a salesman at Dreyer's Dandy department store resembles "those figures of fashion with waxen or wooden faces in suits pressed by the iron of perfection, arrested in a state of colorful putrefaction on their temporary pedestals and platforms, their arms half-bent and half-extended in a parody of pastoral appeal" (*KQK* 81). In fact, his entire existence is automaton-like: "But there still existed the store, where he bowed and turned like a jolly doll, and there still were the nights when like a dead doll he lay supine on his bed not knowing whether he was asleep or awake" (*KQK* 152–53), so much so that he does not significantly differ from the "automannequins" (*KQK* 263) that Dreyer considers using in his clothing business. The young man is also a puppet in the hands of Martha. She willfully casts him in the role of her dutiful lover and accomplice to the contemplated murder of Dreyer, whom she mentally transforms into a "kind of subhuman dummy."[43]

It is worth considering the protagonists' surnames inasmuch as they shed some light on their characters. Bubendorf, Franz's last name in the English version of the novel (it is absent in the original Russian), stands in German for "knave's village." "Knave," of course, connotes both the playing card as well as a "scoundrel." There is also an old German expression, *huren und buben,* which means "to whore and to fornicate"—very fitting here indeed. In Russian "knave" signifies "valet," which also means "a male servant attending to his master's needs." We recall that Franz works in Dreyer's department store and pretends to be loyal and grateful to his "Uncle" (*KQK* 50). At the same time, he is unquestioningly obedient to Martha in her libidinous and murderous pursuits. Also in French, of which Nabokov had an excellent command, the word *valet* appears as part of the expression *âme de valet* ("an obsequious soul"), which once again tallies well with Franz's personality. The name Dreyer, on the other hand, suggests "three"—*dreier* is a genitive case of *drei*, that is, unbeknownst to himself, Dreyer is part of a ménage à trois. The surname also implies that its bearer's business is moneymaking: *Dreier* is a small coin of three pfennigs and is used generically as a word for "money," as, for example, in the German expression *spar deine Dreier,* that is "save (spare) your money." But, of course, all three main personages of the novel, whom Nabokov deliberately endows with stock characters' traits, are nothing but marionettes in the hands of their creator, the "puppeteer"—Nabokov preferred to use the German word *puppenmeister* (*Gift* 10; *Ssoch*, 4:198; *Stories* 559)—who makes a cameo appearance in the last two chapters, together with his wife, for "visits of inspection" (*KQK* viii).

Curiously, the Russian original of the novel (1928) contains only male mannequins (*Ssoch*, 2:271 and 295–96)—their female counterpart first emerges in the English translation. The latter is described as "a stiff-looking, bronze-wigged lady" characterized by "high cheekbones and a masculine chin" (*KQK* 261), with "angular hips" and a "profile like that of a skull" (*KQK* 262)—a "Scandinavian type," in the words of the Inventor—that in Dreyer's opinion required "a little more bosom" (*KQK* 261). In the 1967 translation of the novel, Nabokov accurately conveys women's fashions of the late 1920s in which straight-as-a-board figures and angular lines were dominant, as may be seen in the 1927 female mannequin—blonde, heavy-chinned, angular-faced, and small-breasted (figure 25).[44] Furthermore, Nabokov's own attitude toward mannequins is evidently reflected in the negative overtones of the female mannequin's description, as substantiated by her "profile like that of a skull." As in *The Defense,* the connection of the mannequin with death is discernible.

Earlier in the novel, Dreyer is fascinated by the dummies and finds the idea of making them quite appealing. Toward the end of the novel, however, Dreyer is totally disillusioned with this idea: "Dreyer wondered what aberration of the mind had ever made him accept, let alone admire, those tipsy dummies" (*KQK* 262–63). When further reflecting upon the matter later that evening, Dreyer realizes: "The automannequins had given all they could give. Alas, they had been pushed too far. Bluebeard had squandered his hypnotic force, and now they had lost all significance, all life and charm. He was grateful to them, in a vague sort of way, for the magical task they had performed, the excitement, the expectations. But they only disgusted him now" (*KQK* 263). For Dreyer, it seems, this was a briefly amusing but on the whole utterly distasteful, unappealingly boring, poor emulation of the boundless human potential, of individual abilities. Dreyer's ultimate perception of the "automannequins" presumably reflects that of Nabokov himself.

25. Mannequin, 1927

Insightful in this regard are the astute comments of Iosif Gessen, a close friend of Nabokov's father and of Nabokov himself, on the young writer's émigré experience:

> Thrown out of Russia via the Crimea, where he had to endure one of the most severe episodes of the fratricidal sedition, Sirin [Nabokov's pen name of the "Russian years"] has been to Greece, London, Paris, Switzerland, and Germany. What, then, could his keen eye see over these years except for the persistent distortion of human nature, extinction of the meaning of life, efforts to create a robot, and such symptomatic accomplishments in this direction?[45]

Nabokov's humanistic approach to the mannequin theme contrasts with that of the German artists who tend, once again, to endow it with a sociopolitical meaning. For example, in his *Republican Automatons* (1920; Museum of Modern Art, New York), Grosz depicts a couple of faceless, flag-waving and hurray-patriotic robots, embodying the brainless jingoistic nationalism that indeed became so prevalent in Germany in the 1930s. Occasionally, Grosz even goes so far as to employ a robot for self-representation, as exemplified in *Daum Marries Her Pedantic Automaton "George" in May 1920: John Heartfield Is Very Glad of It* (1920; Berlinische Galerie, Landesmuseum für Moderne Kunst, Fotografie und Architektur, Berlin). While Wieland Herzfelde, John Heartfield's brother and Grosz's friend, explained the watercolor in general and the robot in particular as "an attack on the bourgeois institution of marriage," one should keep in mind that the robot "is an image central to Berlin Dadaism, which proposed among other things that the artist should suppress every sign of subjectivity or individualism in his work and become like a machine."[46] Nabokov, who above all cherished individuality and artistic freedom, would find the latter sentiment rather bizarre and totally abhorrent. To him, mannequins and robots are the handiwork and epitome of the phenomenon he wittily dubbed "a Communazist state" (*CE* 217). In *Speak, Memory,* long after his departure from Russia-turned-Soviet and after the collapse of Germany-turned-Nazi, Nabokov sarcastically speaks of "those ruthless, paste-faced automatons in opulent John Held trousers and high-shouldered jackets, those *Sitzriesen* looming at all our conference tables, whom—or shall I say which?—the Soviet State began to export around 1945 after more than two decades of selective breeding and tailoring" (*SM* 264–65).[47]

The distinction between Nabokov and the Expressionist painters is also evident in their handling of the blind match-seller motif. Nabokov broaches this subject poetically when presenting the action by means of an antithetic metaphor. His is "the blind man, who sold sight and light, kept thrusting a box of matches into eternal darkness" (*Glory* 192). In this description, Nabokov does not specify the cause of the man's blindness but rather unravels and underscores the peculiar essence of a phenomenon full of contradictions. A similarly antithetic description can be found in *The Gift* in which "an elderly, rosy-faced beggar woman with legs cut off at the pelvis was set down like a bust at the foot of a wall and was selling paradoxical shoelaces" (*Gift* 163). In this regard, Nabokov follows in the footsteps of Dobuzhinsky, who depicted a legless man on a St. Petersburg street corner against the backdrop of a shoe store signboard in his *City Types: Legless* (1908; until 2005 in the collection of R. M. Dobuzhinsky, Paris; present whereabouts are unknown).[48]

Conversely, in his 1920 *Match Vendor I* (figure 26), Dix portrays a blind man with amputated limbs, apparently a war veteran (compare his *War Cripples* of the same year).[49] The painter emphasizes that the cripple, ignored by society (he contrastingly and pointedly depicts the legs of well-dressed passersby) and without any support from the state, is relegated to the pitiful role of a beggar, thinly disguised as a match-seller. As Grosz recalls in his autobiography: "War cripples, real or sham, hung around every street corner. Some would doze away until a passer-by came, when they would start to twist their heads and jerk their bodies. They were known as 'shakers,' and children would jeer at them: 'Look, Mummy, there's another funny man!' People quickly got used to dreadful and disgusting sights."[50] Grosz conveys this latter sentiment in his drawing *Ecce Homo* (1919–20; Galerie Nierendorf, Berlin). The artist portrays a blind war veteran who holds a matchbox in one hand (the other hand is but an empty sleeve) among several passersby: a policeman, representing the state, and three men and a woman, all paying no attention to him whatsoever.[51]

Although strictly speaking not located in the metropolis, resort set-

26. Otto Dix, *The Match Vendor I*

tings attract crowds that customarily arrive there from big cities, specifically from Berlin. Nabokov depicts resort activities, and particularly
evening dancing, in *King, Queen, Knave* and *Laughter in the Dark*. In
the former, feverish Martha is becoming gravely ill while dancing in
the Tanz Salon with various partners, other than her husband, and all
the time suffering from both a real and a presumably metaphorical
chill (*KQK* 252–53). In the latter, Magda is shown dancing in the Solfi
resort casino with Albinus, her "protector," and other dance partners.
She tries "her utmost to remain quite faithful" (*Laugh* 117) to Albinus
(note this sarcastic "quite"), not because she loves him, but because
she is afraid to lose the comforts that the life with the well-to-do benefactor offers her.

While Nabokov's respective descriptions of resort nightlife in these
two novels provide additional brushstrokes for the portraits of his

main female characters, the depiction of nightlife by the painters is more generalized and is fraught, yet again, with social commentary. Such, for example, is Beckmann's *Dance in Baden-Baden* (figure 27). The painting shows a nouveau riche crowd, in which Kurt and Martha as well as Albinus and Magda would have felt very much at home, in a dancing salon of the famous resort: the men are garbed in tuxedoes and the women are clad in luxuriant dresses. The partners, although dancing together, completely ignore each other. The couple in the foreground, portrayed at shoulder length, do not seem to connect at all: while he is casting his eyes down to the point of almost closing them, she is looking past him. The dancers on the front right, depicted in full length, are each gazing in a different direction. The pair on the front left looks more like part of a ménage à trois: the woman, although holding hands with her partner, is dancing with her eyes shut; the man is intensely staring at her; whereas another woman, who stands nearby, is intensely staring at him. In the right background, there is a lonely woman with a detached glance, whereas on the left, there is a grotesquely mismatched couple: a large woman, with big hands and a thick neck, and a diminutive man who barely reaches her shoulder. The latter duo, although embracing, pay no attention to each other. This painting, which contains eerie images of marionette-like dancers, unaware of the state of the world around them, may be perceived as a biting comment on people's disconnectedness and miscommunication.

In their depictions of the Metropolis, the painters hardly if ever presented any of its attractive aspects. In this regard, Dix's triptych *Metropolis* illustrates this tendency well (figure 28). The canvas depicts the city as the modern Babylon. The central part of the triptych, similarly to Beckmann's *Dance in Baden-Baden,* displays a fashionably dressed crowd in a dance hall, with a jazz band playing. People are shown in different poses: dancing, sitting, or merely standing, but all looking like melancholy strangers to one another. The side panels, not unlike previously discussed paintings by the same Dix and by Grosz, show war cripples, one of them lying dead drunk, being totally ignored by provocatively dressed fury-like prostitutes, brothel inhabitants on the left, and streetwalkers on the right. Here Dix renders his social commentary in grotesque fashion by using the form of an altar triptych to depict the degradation of contemporary society and its lack of spirituality.[52]

27. Max Beckmann, *Dance in Baden-Baden*

28. Otto Dix, *Metropolis* (triptych)

* * *

While it is evident that the German Expressionist painters could find no redeeming features in their metropolitan surroundings, Nabokov always discovered enchantment everywhere, including the life of the German capital.[53] For example, the narrator of the short story "Beneficence" (1924) sees "the profound beneficence" "in the speeding street sounds, in the hem of a comically lifted skirt, in the metallic yet tender drone of the wind, in the autumn clouds bloated with rain" (*Stories* 77). Another early short story, "A Guide to Berlin," suggests that keen poetic observation and creative imagination find charm in the most trivial of activities. Thus, the narrator observes "a young white-capped baker" and notices "something angelic about a lad dusted with flour" (*Stories* 157). Similarly, in *The Gift,* set in Berlin, its protagonist-narrator likens the sun that "played on various objects along the right side of the street" to "a magpie picking out the tiny things that glittered," and he alliteratively dubs "a water-sprayer" that "crawled slowly by with a wet hissing sound" "a whale on wheels" (*Gift* 328 and 329). Here Nabokov discerns and unravels mesmerizing magic in the most mundane manifestations of metropolitan life. By doing so Nabokov fully realizes the approach to cityscape which is manifest in the art of Dobuzhinsky, his drawing master, who tended to portray and poeticize the city's odd, incongruous, and at times fanciful aspects, or, in his own words, "the inner seamy side of the city."

Unlike Dobuzhinsky, however, who had a great affection for St. Petersburg—a trait he shared with his one-time pupil—Nabokov depicts life in Berlin, the capital of the other, foreign, vanquished and vanished empire, with the keen eye of an emotionally detached outsider. In this regard, Nabokov follows the dictum of Georg Simmel concerning "the currents of life" in the Metropolis: "It is not our task either to accuse or to pardon, but only to understand."[54] To be sure, Simmel exerted considerable influence on German Expressionists in their portrayal of the big city.[55] In many ways, however, Nabokov appears closer to him in spirit than were his painter-compatriots. Nabokov's portrayal of the city, vividly descriptive and with careful attention to detail, is largely nonjudgmental. It is precisely Nabokov's position of a stranger which enables him to manifest such dispassionate objectivity in his portrayal of life in the Metropolis.[56]

Furthermore, unlike the German Expressionists, who charged their art with sociopolitical commentary, Nabokov refused to sociopoliticize *his* art. Instead, in keeping with a pledge given in his early poem dedicated to Ivan Bunin, Nabokov remained faithful to his chosen path of a true aesthete and independent genius.[57]

CONCLUSION

If the mind were constructed on optional lines and if a book could be read in the same way as a painting is taken in by the eye, that is without the bother of working from left to right and without the absurdity of beginnings and ends, this would be the ideal way of appreciating a novel, for thus the author saw it at the moment of its conception.

—Nabokov, *Lectures on Literature*

The book, by virtue of its being at the intersection of the history of literature and the history of art, contributes to the tradition of *ut pictura poesis,* to the history of art criticism, and the history of taste, as well as to the better comprehension of reception aesthetics. The book also allows for a more nuanced perspective on the customary practices of writers with training in the visual arts. It specifically deepens our understanding of the creative processes of one of the greatest novelists of the modern era by providing a historical context for his visual imagination.

In the preceding pages, I have attempted to demonstrate the exceptional importance of the pictorial to Nabokov's poetics. How to account for this importance? What are the contributing factors? First of all, Nabokov was exposed to the most refined atmosphere that reigned in the home of his parents, who were great connoisseurs and passionate lovers of all the arts, including literature and painting. Furthermore, the future writer's immersion in the rich culture prevalent in St. Petersburg at the time, his education at the Tenishev School, one of the best and most progressive learning institutions in imperial Russia, his frequent travels to western Europe—all contributed greatly to Nabokov's outstanding cultural development.

More specifically, Nabokov's predilection for the pictorial originated in his unique personal traits—grapheme-color synesthesia, enhanced by an extraordinarily nuanced sense of color, and attention to the minutiae of details. Nabokov's experience of grapheme-color synesthesia suggests that the writer, in his own words, had "this rather freakish gift of seeing letters in color" (*SO* 17). This means that Nabokov viewed the world around him as intensely colorized, and especially so because to him, the writer, the letters (both Cyrillic and Roman) were literally his palette of colors. Nabokov's casting of "this precise beam of light upon a precious detail" (*SO* 215) stemmed, first and foremost, from his intense and in-depth studies of entomology, and particularly lepidoptery. Nabokov's scrupulous examination under the microscope of butterflies, those exquisite, often brightly colored creatures, no doubt highly contributed to his paying close attention to the finest of details. These attributes were amplified by Nabokov's inborn keen sense of vision, his exceptional memory, his studies of the fine arts under the tutelage of private drawing masters, especially the distinguished Dobuzhinsky, and by his own brilliant verbal gifts.

Nabokov's turning to the works of the Old Masters in his own writings enabled him to view himself as part and parcel of European cultural continuity and to rightly claim his rich cultural ancestry. Furthermore, by employing, for the sake of the authorial presence, chefs d'oeuvre of the Old Masters in which the painters set their own images or alluded to their presence "in a dark corner" of their canvases, Nabokov placed himself on a par with these great artists and engaged himself in a creative discourse and competition of sorts with his painterly predecessors.

By encoding his own, his wife's, and his son's presence in the text, Nabokov pays tribute to his "best audience." First of all, it is "the person he sees in his shaving mirror every morning" (*SO* 18). Nabokov was well aware that in shaping his fictional universe, an artist draws on his own experience, his innermost feelings, on the world within himself, and models his creative process after that of the Creator (see *SO* 32). The other members of his most sophisticated, knowledgeable, and receptive reading audience were his wife Véra and his son Dmitri, both of whom were also his primary collaborators, either by way of literary critique and linguistic advice (Véra was Nabokov's first reader at all times) or by way of translation.

Landscape, the most colorful pictorial form, whose subject matter is the portrayal of nature, fascinated Nabokov, an accomplished entomologist, who aspired to become a landscape artist in his early youth.

Upon turning to the literary medium of expression, Nabokov frequently resorted to the description of landscape. Of course, literature has such a long history of depicting nature that this trope no longer necessarily calls to mind a painting. Nabokov apparently viewed this as a challenge and, by virtue of his verbal pictorial magic, succeeded in overcoming this automatism of perception. He did so by portraying landscape in such strikingly unique and unforgettable terms and by endowing it with such indispensable and diverse functions that it forced the reading audience to pay undivided attention to the genre and to see it afresh. The writer achieves this, for example, in *Glory* by describing the landscape both as an oil painting and as its occurrence in real nature and by demonstrating the protagonist's adamant determination either to step over into the painting or to dissolve into the respective landscape as the pictogram for his path of life. Most often, however, Nabokov employs an elaborate description of scenery highly fraught with ironic connotations. A character and, most importantly, the reader learn not to perceive the described scenery as merely a depiction of nature but rather to view it functioning as a meaningful learning experience. For example, in *Invitation to a Beheading*, Cincinnatus's perception of the Tamara Gardens as captivating turns out to be fallacious: this perception gradually transforms into his and the reader's understanding that the gardens are as deceptive as the rest of the surrounding world, which eventually disintegrates by the power of the protagonist's resistance, or rather by the will of his creator who liberates his hero from the dystopian nightmare. Similarly, albeit in the opposite fashion, in *Pnin*, the scenery that initially appears as a delightfully unremarkable, wintry landscape of the American northeastern countryside, all of a sudden becomes the *locus amoenus* of an epiphanic message to both the unsuspecting and unobservant character and to the reader when the author liberates the title hero from his predicaments in deus ex machina fashion.[1] All this highlights the larger issue, namely the concept of pattern in Nabokov: his most perceptible characters may discern the underside weave of the world around them, but only the creator of that fictional universe and his "good readers" are capable of comprehending its actual outside configuration.

Nabokov grew up in the Russian imperial capital at the time when the Silver Age, that spectacular convergence of cultural abundance, diversity, and spirituality, reigned supreme. *The World of Art*, perhaps the most important contemporary artistic association in Russia, had appealed strongly to Nabokov's refined Westernized taste and to his predilection for and remembrance of things past. Dobuzhinsky, Nabokov's highly acclaimed and influential drawing master, without a doubt quickly recognized that the young Nabokov had all the necessary makings of a great painter, some of which the preeminent artist and talented pedagogue helped to nurture. At the same time, Dobuzhinsky apparently sensed that his charge, when facilitating scenery on canvas, did not do entire justice to his exceptional artistic gifts. This may be discerned in retrospect in Dobuzhinsky's jocular and no doubt teasingly exaggerated remark, "*you* were the most hopeless student I ever had" (*SM* 94).[2] Upon familiarizing himself with Nabokov's early poetic experiments, however, Dobuzhinsky evidently understood that his protégé had found a congenial avenue of expression, highly suitable for his enormous painterly talents. Hence his prophetic advice to Nabokov: "You have a talent for painting, but you must write!"

Richard Muther's *History of Painting in the XIXth Century*, which according to Igor Grabar was "the best book in European literature on modern art," provided the gifted, budding painter-turned-writer with a broad, informative survey of nineteenth-century Western art and allowed him to see his native Russian art in a much broader context. Furthermore, Muther's aesthetic precepts expressed in the book, such as unconstrained freedom of creation and the supremacy of artistic merit, were, in all likelihood, instrumental in shaping Nabokov's literary tenets. Of course, this does not mean that Muther's seminal study was the youth's only inspiration: after all, Nabokov could absorb these principles from purely literary sources. Other sources notwithstanding, it is important, however, to consider the role that this highly important work of art history at the time presumably played in Nabokov's aesthetic development. Finally, Nabokov's apparent indebtedness to Muther, whose survey of nineteenth-century Western art was most likely introduced to him by Dobuzhinsky, serves as an additional example of that mentor's impact on his pupil's aesthetic values and, what is more, points to the further importance of *The World of Art* in Nabokov's creative universe.

The World of Art's and specifically Dobuzhinsky's influence is also palpable in Nabokov's fascination with the portrayal of the metropolis. Already early in his career, Nabokov demonstrated his enchantment with the city when ekphrastically conveying the image of his beloved native St. Petersburg, depicted by Dobuzhinsky, but looked at through his own nostalgic lenses. Nabokov, however, turns to the depiction of Berlin, the capital of another vanished empire—that of Germany—in which he resided and created the vast majority of his Russian works and which served as their primary setting.

Nabokov's portrayal of this European metropolis drastically departs from those of the German Expressionist artists and stems from the writer's and the painters' dissimilar backgrounds and life experiences, which resulted in very different world outlooks. Most importantly, these differences are manifest in their respective aesthetics: while the German Expressionist painters imbued their canvases with sociopolitical commentary, Nabokov, by and large, refused to sociopoliticize his art, including the portrayal of various manifestations of urban life in Berlin.[3]

Nabokov's sharp criticism of the German artists' aesthetics finds its most distinct expression in *Despair*. In this novel, in the opinions of its protagonist and narrator, Hermann Karlovich, a deranged Russian-born German, Nabokov derides the German artists' leftist, pro-Soviet political leanings, their orientation toward a social message, their fascination with robots and collectivism that echo Joseph Stalin's infamous pronouncement about humans viewed as merely cogs in the gigantic administrative-economic machine of Socialism, and their glorification of crime as a creative artistic venue.[4]

The deeply traumatized German Expressionist artists seldom saw beyond their ideological agenda and could rarely find any charm or beauty in the world around them. In this they are a world apart from Nabokov, who has taught several generations of his innumerable readers to recognize and appreciate the sunny sense of Creation, the joy and happiness of imaginative magic. Therein lies Nabokov's main exploit: in spite of his deep personal traumas and tragedies (the loss of his close friend and cousin, loss of his father, and forced exile from his native Russia), he found solace and happiness in everything he did—writing, butterfly collecting, scholarship, college-teaching, marriage, fatherhood—and this happiness, as the leitmotif and the light motif, traverses and shines throughout his entire life.[5]

Nabokov's writings contain numerous references and allusions to painters and their works, from Old Masters to modern Russian and

Western artists.[6] In addition, Nabokov's works are densely populated with references to imaginary artists and their works. Among these are, to name only a few, Axel Rex and his cartoons (*Laughter in the Dark*), Ardalion and his portrait of Hermann (*Despair*), Romanov and his "Coincidence" (*The Gift*), Roy Carswell and his portrait of Sebastian Knight (*The Real Life of Sebastian Knight*), Cynthia Vane and her "Seen Through a Windshield" ("The Vane Sisters"), Jean Farlow and her "lakescapes" (*Lolita*), Ivan Gramineev and his "April Glade" (*Pnin*), Maud Shade, "a poet and a painter" (*Pale Fire*), and the *Ada* title heroine and her botanical illustrations (*Ada*). Most importantly, throughout his oeuvre Nabokov creates a myriad of verbal pictures in various forms, be it a "portrait," "landscape," "cityscape," or "genre."

Furthermore, throughout his literary career, Nabokov describes the process of drawing or painting in a variety of works, from poetry ("Ut pictura poesis" and "The Painter" as part of the cycle tellingly titled *Paint Drops*) to dramaturgy (*The Event*) to prose (*The Gift, Pnin*). Most significantly, when dealing with a work of literature, Nabokov habitually treats it as and compares it to artwork. The writer reveals:

> There comes a moment when I am informed from within that the entire structure is finished. All I have to do now is take it down in pencil or pen. Since this entire structure, dimly illumined in one's mind, can be compared to a painting, and since you do not have to work gradually from left to right for its proper perception, I may direct my flashlight at any part or particle of the picture when setting it down in writing. (*SO* 31–32)

It is hardly surprising, therefore, that Nabokov also frequently describes both the act of literary composition and its end result in painterly terms. Thus, Nabokov remarks, elegantly linking memory, attention to detail, and the processes of writing and painting: "The good memoirist [. . .] does his best to preserve the utmost truth of the detail. One of the ways he achieves his intent is to find the right spot on his canvas for placing the right patch of remembered color" (*SO* 186).

To overcome the mechanical page-leafing process, Nabokov recommends multiple rereadings of a literary work so that the reader can see in his mind's eye the whole work in its entirety very much like a spectator would view a work of art. Thus, Nabokov maintains:

When we look at a painting we do not have to move our eyes in a special way even if, as in a book, the picture contains the elements of depth and development. The element of time does not really enter in a first contact with a painting. In reading a book, we must have time to acquaint ourselves with it. We have no physical organ (as we have the eye in regard to a painting) that takes in the whole picture and then can enjoy its details. But at a second, or third, or fourth reading we do, in a sense, behave towards a book as we do towards a painting. (*LL* 3)[7]

Moreover, Nabokov himself habitually worked on his novelistic prose out of sequence, much like an artist would paint a large panoramic canvas. Thus Nabokov admits: "I don't write consecutively from the beginning to the next chapter and so on to the end. I just fill in the gaps of the picture, of this jigsaw puzzle which is quite clear in my mind, picking out a piece here and a piece there and filling out part of the sky and part of the landscape" (*SO* 16–17).

Painting in its various manifestations lies at the very core of Nabokov's creation, and in fact of his entire creative process. We observe this in the countless occurrences of various forms of the fine arts in Nabokov's oeuvre, coupled with his treatment of the letters like a canvas. By following Dobuzhinsky's pithy dictum to paint, but with words, Nabokov channeled his superb pictorial abilities into the congruous, literary, medium of expression and became the most incomparable and brilliant verbal painter that belles lettres has ever known.

Notes

The original Russian for this book's epigraph reads: «примечательно еще одно свойство гоголевского письма: его редкая картинность, искусная красочность [. . .] Эпитет «цветное» так и просится на уста, когда стараешься определить гоголевское творчество. Сочиняя «Мертвые души», автор как бы превращал каждую каплю чернил, дрожавшую на конце его пера, в живую каплю краски. Такой дивно окрашенной прозы русская муза еще не знала. И при этом Гоголь-живописец чрезвычайно разнообразен: то он сочный акварелист, то тщательный график, то неожиданной миниатюрой, картинкой на табакерке он мимоходом очарует меня [. . .] Кажется, что можно взять карандаш и кисть и иллюстрировать каждую фразу «Мертвых душ», по две, по три картинки на страницу. Но подчеркиваю: *кажется*, ибо на самом деле никакому художнику не удалось бы так запечатлеть красками, как Гоголь запечатлел свой мир словами»; Vladimir Nabokov, "Gogol´," *Zvezda* 4 (1999): 16–17.

INTRODUCTION

1. For a discussion of *ut pictura poesis,* see, for example, Rensselaer Wright Lee, *Ut Pictura Poesis: The Humanistic Theory of Painting* (New York: W. W. Norton, 1967); Mario Praz, "'Ut Pictura Poesis,'" in his *Mnemosyne: The Parallel Between Literature and the Visual Arts* (Princeton, N.J.: Princeton University Press, 1970), 3–28; and Niklaus R. Schweizer, *The Ut Pictura Poesis Controversy in Eighteenth-Century England and Germany* (Bern: Herbert Lang, 1972). For a more recent and illuminating survey of the *ut pictura poesis* relation, from Leonardo da Vinci to W. J. T. Mitchell, see Simon Alderson, "*Ut Pictura Poesis* and Its Discontents in Late Seventeenth- and Early Eighteenth-Century England and France," *Word and Image* 11, no. 3 (July–September 1995): 256–63. For a discussion of poetry and painting

as sister arts, see Jean H. Hagstrum, *The Sister Arts: The Tradition of Literary Pictorialism and English Poetry from Dryden to Gray* (Chicago: University of Chicago Press, 1958); and Ann Hurley and Kate Greenspan, eds., *So Rich a Tapestry: The Sister Arts and Cultural Studies* (Cranbury, N.J.: Associated University Presses, 1995).

2. For Ruskin's views on the relationship between literature and painting, see George P. Landow, *The Aesthetic and Critical Theories of John Ruskin* (Princeton, N.J.: Princeton University Press, 1971). For the influence of Ruskin's aesthetic views on Russian culture at the turn of the twentieth century, see Rachel Polonsky, *English Literature and the Russian Aesthetic Renaissance* (New York: Cambridge University Press, 1998), 141–51; and Virginia Bennett, "The Russian Symbolists and John Ruskin's Aesthetics," paper presented at the annual meeting of the American Association of Teachers of Slavic and East European Languages (AATSEEL), Philadelphia, December 28, 2004.

3. For Nabokov in his relation to lepidoptera, see Kurt Johnson and Steve Coates, *Nabokov's Blues: The Scientific Odyssey of a Literary Genius* (Cambridge, Mass.: Zoland Books, 1999); Brian Boyd and Robert Michael Pyle, eds., *Nabokov's Butterflies: Unpublished and Uncollected Writings* (Boston: Beacon, 2000); Dieter E. Zimmer, *A Guide to Nabokov's Butterflies and Moths* (Hamburg: n.p., 2001); and Robert Dirig, "Theme in Blue: Vladimir Nabokov's Endangered Butterfly," in *Nabokov at Cornell,* ed. Gavriel Shapiro (Ithaca, N.Y., and London: Cornell University Press, 2003), 205–18.

4. See, for example, Ralph A. Ciancio, "Nabokov's Painted Parchments," 235–69; and Christine Raguet-Bouvart, "European Art: A Framing Device?" 183–212—both chapters in *Nabokov at the Limits: Redrawing Critical Boundaries,* ed. Lisa Zunshine (New York and London: Garland, 1999); Gavriel Shapiro, "Nabokov and *The World of Art,*" *Slavic Almanac* 6, no. 9 (2000): 35–52; Susan Elizabeth Sweeney, "Looking at Harlequins: Nabokov, the *World of Art* and the Ballets Russes," 2:73–95; and Neil Cornwell, "Paintings, Governesses and 'Publishing Scoundrels': Nabokov and Henry James," 2:96–116—both chapters in *Nabokov's World,* ed. Jane Grayson, Arnold McMillin, and Priscilla Meyer, 2 vols. (New York: Palgrave, 2002); and Gavriel Shapiro, "Nabokov and Early Netherlandish Art," in Shapiro, *Nabokov at Cornell,* 241–50.

5. Gerard de Vries and D. Barton Johnson, with an essay by Liana Ashenden, *Vladimir Nabokov and the Art of Painting* (Amsterdam: Amsterdam University Press, 2006).

6. For example, Jürgen Bodenstein has registered numerous shades of blue in Nabokov's English prose, and Gennady Barabtarlo has recorded 237 occurrences of various colors and hues in *Pnin* alone. See, respectively, Jürgen Bodenstein, "'The Excitement of Verbal Adventure': A Study of Vladimir Nabokov's English Prose" (Ph.D. diss., Ruprecht-Karl University at Heidelberg, 1977), 234–35; and Gennady Barabtarlo, *Phantom of Fact: A Guide to Vladimir Nabokov's "Pnin"* (Ann Arbor, Mich.: Ardis, 1989), 303–8.

7. See Paul Barolsky, *Walter Pater's Renaissance* (University Park and London: Pennsylvania State University Press, 1987), esp. 71–74 and 77–89; and his "Leonardo, Satan, and the Mystery of Modern Art," *Virginia Quarterly Review* 74, no. 3 (Summer 1998): 401.

8. Nabokov knew, of course, that the 1812 War Gallery in the Winter Palace (St. Petersburg) contains Dawe's portrait of his ancestor, Major General Ivan Nabokov (1787–1852), a hero of the Napoleonic Wars. By translating and discussing Pushkin's poem about Dawe, who portrayed his ancestor, Nabokov subtly linked himself to his most revered poet.

9. For a mention of ancient and medieval as well as Asian and American art and artists, see the "Index of Artists" in de Vries and Johnson, *Vladimir Nabokov and the Art of Painting*, 219–23.

10. For earlier analogous studies, see, for example, Maurice E. Chernowitz, *Proust and Painting* (New York: International University Press, 1945); Simone Kadi, *La Peinture chez Proust et Baudelaire* (Paris: La Pensée Universelle, 1973); Archie K. Loss, *Joyce's Visible Art: The Work of Joyce and the Visual Arts, 1904–1922* (Ann Arbor, Mich.: UMI Research, 1984); Adeline R. Tintner, *Henry James and the Lust of the Eyes: Thirteen Artists in His Work* (Baton Rouge: Louisiana State University Press, 1993); Roger Anderson and Paul Debreczeny, eds., *Russian Narrative and Visual Art: Varieties of Seeing* (Gainesville: University Press of Florida, 1994); and Daniel R. Schwarz, *Reconfiguring Modernism: Explorations in the Relationship Between Modern Art and Modern Literature* (New York: St. Martin's, 1997).

CHAPTER 1

1. Andrew Field, *Nabokov: His Life in Part* (New York: Viking, 1977), 86.

2. M. V. Ledkovskaia, "Zabytyi poet: Kirill Vladimirovich Nabokov," *Nabokovskii vestnik* 2 (1998): 130–38; L. N. Beloshevskaia and V. P. Nechaev, "Kirill Nabokov," in *"Skit": Praga, 1922–1940: Antologiia, biografii, doku-*

menty, comp. L. N. Beloshevskaia and V. P. Nechaev (Moscow: Russkii put´, 2006), 553–64.

3. See Field, *Nabokov: His Life in Part,* 86.

4. Nicolas Nabokov, *Bagazh: Memoirs of a Russian Cosmopolitan* (New York: Atheneum, 1975), 102.

5. Ibid.

6. See *Sistematicheskii katalog biblioteki Vladimira Dmitrievicha Nabokova* (St. Petersburg: "Tovarishchestvo Khudozhestvennoi Pechati," 1904); *Sistematicheskii katalog biblioteki Vladimira Dmitrievicha Nabokova: Pervoe prodolzhenie* (St. Petersburg: "Tovarishchestvo Khudozhestvennoi Pechati," 1911). See also L. F. Klimenko, "Biblioteka doma Nabokovykh," *Nabokovskii vestnik* 1 (1998): 193–200.

7. «Литературу он знал назубок, особенно иностранную; в газете «Речь» так были уверены в его всезнайстве, что обращались к нему за справками [. . .]: откуда эта цитата? В каком веке жил такой-то германский поэт? И Набоков отвечал»; Kornei Chukovsky, *Dnevnik 1901–1929,* 2nd ed. (Moscow: Sovremennyi pisatel´, 1997), 206. Here and henceforth, all translations, unless otherwise indicated, are mine.

8. As secretary of the Literary Fund, V. D. Nabokov took part in its 1909 jubilee celebrations at which he delivered a speech entitled "Piatidesiatiletie Literaturnogo Fonda." See S. A. Vengerov, ed., *Iubileinyi sbornik Literaturnogo Fonda, 1859–1909* (St. Petersburg: "Obshchestvennaia Pol´za," ca. 1910), 80 and 474–87. For V. D. Nabokov's occupying the positions of secretary, deputy president, and then president of the Literary Fund, see, respectively, the yearbooks *Ves´ Peterburg na 1910 god,* 586; *Ves´ Peterburg na 1911 god,* 615; *Ves´ Peterburg na 1913 god,* 437 and col. 921; *Ves´ Peterburg na 1914 god,* 455 and col. 986; and *Ves´ Petrograd na 1915 god,* 454 and col. 903 (see columns under the Mutual Aid Societies [Общества взаимопомощи] rubric).

9. See Manfred S(c)hruba, *Literaturnye ob˝edineniia Moskvy i Peterburga 1890—1917 godov* (Moscow: Novoe literaturnoe obozrenie, 2004), 40.

10. For V. D. Nabokov's essay "Fet (K stoletiiu so dnia rozhdeniia)," see *Rul´,* December 5, 1920, 6. See also Nabokov's recollection of a disagreement he had with his father about the authorship of the poem "The Night Was Shining" («Сияла ночь», 1877): the young Nabokov erroneously asserted that the poem was composed by Alexei Apukhtin, whereas V. D. Nabokov, who "amazingly knew Fet's poetry" («изумительно знал Фета»), correctly attributed it to Fet (see *Perepiska* 58).

Chukovsky confirms V. D. Nabokov's expert knowledge of Dickens. He recalls that Nabokov senior "had a special game: to enumerate all the names of Dickens's characters—nearly three hundred in all. He competed with me. I was exhausted after the first hundred" (Klimenko, "Biblioteka doma Nabokovykh," 198). V. D. Nabokov wrote articles on the occasion of Dickens's centenary and later contributed a chapter on the English writer to a multivolume history of western European literature. See, respectively, V. D. Nabokov, "Charl´z Dikkens (K 100-letiiu so dnia ego rozhdeniia)," *Rech´,* January 25 (February 7), 1912, 3; V. D. Nabokov, "Charl´z Dikkens, kak kriminalist," *Pravo,* January 29, 1912, 188–95; and V. D. Nabokov, "Charl´z Dikkens" [chapter 2], in *Istoriia zapadnoi literatury,* ed. F. D. Batiushkov, 4 vols. (Moscow: "Mir," 1912–17), 4:52–70.

11. For a discussion of some of Nabokov's novels in their relation to *Bleak House,* see Leona Toker, "Between Allusion and Coincidence: Nabokov, Dickens and Others," *Hebrew University Studies in Literature and the Arts* 12, no. 2 (Autumn 1984): 180–96.

12. «кудесник», «захватывающий рассказчик», «неправдоподобность фабулы, и деланность многих положений, и вычурность чувств, и частые излишества стиля»; see V. D. Nabokov, "Charl´z Dikkens (K 100-letiiu so dnia ego rozhdeniia)," 3.

13. See *Rul´,* August 14, 1921, 4.

14. «чудесные пейзажи Клода Лоррена», «фантастические световые симфонии Тэрнера»; see V. D. Nabokov, *Iz voiuiushchei Anglii: Putevye ocherki* (Petrograd: "Union," 1916), 119.

15. «в отдельной, недавно открытой, зале голландской школы можно любоваться четырьмя Рембрандтами первоклассного достоинства, отличными картинами Метсю, Остаде, двумя Гоббема и недавно приобретенным "Концертом" (другое название "La Collation"—ужин) Питера де-Гооха—этого восхитительного, единственного в своем роде мастера (моего любимого)»; ibid. V. D. Nabokov apparently refers here to de Hooch's *Musical Party in a Courtyard* (1677; National Gallery, London). De Hooch's painting entitled *Concert* (1680) is at the Hermitage Museum.

16. Klimenko, "Biblioteka doma Nabokovykh," 194.

17. See the Hermitage website at http://www.hermitagemuseum.org (Digital Collection, Quick Search: Nabokov). Nabokov mentions Palma the Elder, also known as Palma Vecchio, in *Ada* (141).

18. P. I. Miagkov, "Zapadnoevropeiskaia zhivopis´ v sobranii sem´i

Nabokovykh," *Nabokovskii vestnik* 1 (1998): 213–15. It appears that Kozlov amassed one of the best Russian private art collections of Old Masters. It is telling that Gustav Friedrich Waagen, one of the foremost nineteenth-century experts on the art of Old Masters, who was commissioned to catalogue the Hermitage and private collections in Russia, considered it necessary to inspect and to include the register of N. I. Kozlov's collection in his catalogue. See G. F. Waagen, *Die Gemäldesammlung in der Kaiserliche Ermitage zu St. Petersburg nebst Bemerkungen über andere dortige Kunstsammlungen*, 2nd ed. (St. Petersburg: Verlag der Kaiserlichen Hofbuchhandlung H. Schmitzdorff [C. Röttger], 1870), 437–38.

19. Translated by Gavriel Shapiro with Dmitri Nabokov. The original Russian reads: «действительно прелестные, дождем набухшая «Бретань» и рыже-зеленый «Версаль» соседствовали с «вкусными», как тогда говорилось, «Турками» Бакста и сомовской акварельной «Радугой» среди мокрых берез» (*Ssoch*, 5:172).

20. See *Sistematicheskii katalog biblioteki Vladimira Dmitrievicha Nabokova*, 45–49; and *Sistematicheskii katalog biblioteki Vladimira Dmitrievicha Nabokova: Pervoe prodolzhenie*, 28–29.

21. Translated by Gavriel Shapiro with Dmitri Nabokov. «Я сделался страстным театралом с четырнадцатилетнего возраста. Гимназистом 6-го класса я бредил русской оперой, увлекался русской драмой, французским театром. Эту страсть я пронес через всю свою жизнь»; V. D. Nabokov, "Iz vospominanii o teatre (za 35 let)," *Teatr i Zhizn´* (*Theater und Leben*), nos. 1–2 (September 1921): 4.

22. Brian Boyd, *Vladimir Nabokov: The Russian Years* (Princeton, N.J.: Princeton University Press, 1990), 103.

23. Boyd, *Vladimir Nabokov: The Russian Years,* 148, 261, and 273. For Nabokov's and Evreinov's genealogical kinship, see Jacques Ferrand, *Les Nabokov: Essai généalogique* (Montreuil, France: J. Ferrand, 1982), 13. For more on Nabokov and Evreinov, see Vladimir E. Alexandrov, "Nabokov and Evreinov," in *The Garland Companion to Vladimir Nabokov,* ed. Vladimir E. Alexandrov (New York: Garland, 1995), 402–5; and Savely Senderovich and Yelena Shvarts, "Starichok iz evreev (kommentarii k *Priglasheniiu na kazn´* Vladimira Nabokova)," *Russian Literature* 43, no. 3 (April 1, 1998): 297–327.

24. For the most recent discussion of Nabokov's dramaturgy, see Siggy Frank, "Exile in Theatre / Theatre in Exile—Nabokov's Early Plays, *Tra-*

gediia gospodina Morna and *Chelovek iz SSSR,*" *Slavonic and East European Review* 85, no. 4 (October 2007): 629–57; Andrei Babikov, "Izobretenie teatra," and Dmitri Nabokov, "Nabokov i teatr," in Vladimir Nabokov, *Tragediia gospodina Morna. P´esy. Lektsii o drame* (St. Petersburg: "Azbuka-klassika," 2008), 5–42 and 519–38 respectively.

25. For an informative discussion on the subject, see Charles Nicol, "Music in the Theater of the Mind: Opera and Vladimir Nabokov," in *Nabokov at the Limits,* ed. Lisa Zunshine (New York and London: Garland, 1999), 21–41. See also Julian W. Connolly, "The Quest for a Natural Melody in the Fiction of Vladimir Nabokov," in Zunshine, *Nabokov at the Limits,* 69–85; and Nora Buhks, "Sur la structure du roman de Vl. Nabokov 'Roi, dame, valet,'" *Revue des Études Slaves* 59 (1988): 799–810; as well as her "Les fantômes de l'opéra dans les romans de Nabokov," *Revue des Études Slaves* 72, nos. 3–4 (2000): 453–66.

26. For illuminating surveys of St. Petersburg's cultural life during Nabokov's adolescence and youth, see *Ezhegodnik gazety "Rech´"* for the years 1912 to 1914; and V. P. Lapshin, *Khudozhestvennaia zhizn´ Moskvy i Petrograda v 1917 godu* (Moscow: "Sovetskii khudozhnik," 1983).

27. See also Stephanie Merkel's assumption that "Nabokov likely participated in Meierkhol´d's 'demonstration of studio exercises . . . given in the school auditorium [of the Tenishev School] . . . on the evening of February 12, 1915.'" See Stephanie L. Merkel, "Vladimir Nabokov's *King, Queen, Knave* and the *Commedia Dell'Arte,*" *Nabokov Studies* 1 (1994): 85. The portion in the single quotation marks is a citation from Marjorie L. Hoover, *Meyerhold: The Art of Conscious Theater* (Amherst: University of Massachusetts Press, 1974), 84–85.

28. Boyd, *Vladimir Nabokov: The Russian Years,* 103.

29. A. G. Mets, "Tenishevskoe uchilishche: Vzgliad na arkhiv skvoz´ stekla 'Shuma vremeni,'" in his *Osip Mandel´shtam i ego vremia* (St. Petersburg: "Giperion," 2005), 11.

30. See, respectively, T. F. Verizhnikova, "Vladimir Nabokov i iskusstvo knigi Anglii rubezha vekov: 'Khram Shekspira' v biblioteke V. D. Nabokova," *Nabokovskii vestnik* 1 (1998): 207; Boyd, *Vladimir Nabokov: The Russian Years,* 117–18; and Field, *Nabokov: His Life in Part,* 116–17.

31. «один из самых выдающихся петербургских преподавателей русской словесности»; S. A. Vengerov, ed., *Russkaia literatura XX veka (1890–1910),* 3 vols. (Moscow: "Mir," 1914–16), 1:270–71.

32. See, respectively, Field, *Nabokov: His Life in Part,* 121; and Boyd, *Vladimir Nabokov: The Russian Years,* 115. Curiously, a Russian scholar points to some parallels between Nabokov's poem "Being in Love" («Влюбленность»), included in *Look at the Harlequins!* (*LATH* 25), and Gippius's eponymous poem of 1916. See Iu. I. Glebov, "'Vliublennost'' Vladimira Nabokova: Potainoi istochnik," *Russian Studies* 1, no. 3 (1995): 273–77.

33. For a brief discussion of Nabokov's drawing masters, see Vadim Stark, "Ut pictura poesis: Nabokov-risoval´shchik," *Vyshgorod* 3 (1999): 118–20.

34. On Nabokov's synesthesia, see D. Barton Johnson, "Nabokov as Man of Letters," in his *Worlds in Regression: Some Novels of Vladimir Nabokov* (Ann Arbor, Mich.: Ardis, 1985), 7–46; and Kevin T. Dann, "*The Gift:* Vladimir Nabokov's Eidetic Technique," in his *Bright Colors Falsely Seen: Synaesthesia and the Search for Transcendental Knowledge* (New Haven, Conn.: Yale University Press, 1998), 120–64.

35. For the information on Cumming's birthplace and about his parents, I am greatly indebted to Marie-Louise Karttunen of the University of Helsinki. For Cumming's art education, see S. N. Kondakov, comp., *Spisok russkikh khudozhnikov k iubileinomu spravochniku Imperatorskoi Akademii Khudozhestv* (1914; reprint, Moscow: "Antik-Biznes-tsentr," 2002), 121 and 587. I am indebted to Tat´iana Filippovna Verizhnikova, professor of art history at the Russian Academy of the Fine Arts (St. Petersburg), for drawing my attention to this source.

36. See http://petersburgcity.com/news/city/2003/09/02/painting/ and "Ceremony of Transfer of Historical and Artistic Values," http://www .hermitagemuseum.org/html_En/11/2003/hm11_2_117.html.

37. ««*Graphic*»'а в мраморных переплетах» (*Ssoch,* 5:222).

38. *The Graphic,* October 17, 1908, 447.

39. See, respectively, *Ves´ Peterburg na 1894 god,* 125; *Ves´ Peterburg na 1903 god,* 357; *Ves´ Peterburg na 1904 god,* 352; and *Ves´ Petrograd na 1917 god,* 308.

40. In 1881, Evgeny Ivanovich Miussar (Mussard) (1814–96) initiated a society that was named posthumously after him—Miussar Mondays. The purpose of the society was to assist the families of painters in need. The society, comprised of professional artists, art collectors, and philanthropists, met on Mondays at Miussar's mansion on the English Quay, 6. The weekly events included group painting, concerts, and suppers. In lieu of membership dues, painters contributed their artwork. This artwork and

the works painted during the Miussar Monday meetings were sold at auctions or exhibitions, and the proceeds were donated to charity. See D. Ia. Severiukhin and O. L. Leikind, *Zolotoi vek khudozhestvennykh ob´´edinenii v Rossii i SSSR (1820–1932)* (St. Petersburg: Izdatel´stvo Chernysheva, 1992), 139–41.

41. See *Ves´ Peterburg na 1902 god,* 342; and *Ves´ Peterburg na 1903 god,* 357 and col. 832.

42. See, respectively, Boyd, *Vladimir Nabokov: The Russian Years,* 28; *Ves´ Peterburg na 1909 god,* 427; and *Ves´ Peterburg na 1912 god,* 486. The Levitsky school, named after Elena Sergeevna Levitsky (1868–1915), its initiator and owner, was the first coed school in Russia. It was founded in Tsarskoe Selo, near St. Petersburg, in 1900.

43. «Рисование при толковом объяснении, приносит положительную пользу всякому зрячему ребенку и взрослому, при желании изучать это интересное занятие» (Cumming's style and punctuation are preserved); Aleksandr Gavrilovich and Maria Konstantinovna Maximovy, "Sobranie avtografov raznykh lits," St. Petersburg, Russian National Library, Department of Manuscripts, f. 459. I am indebted once again to Professor Verizhnikova, who provided me with this inscription.

44. Translated by Gavriel Shapiro with Dmitri Nabokov. The original reads: «при стирании резинкой не превращать с треском бумагу в гармонику» (*Ssoch,* 5:199).

45. Boyd, *Vladimir Nabokov: The Russian Years,* 75.

46. «Ты в Выре рисуешь закат, оранжевые верхушки деревьев из окон правого балкона» (*Perepiska* 56).

47. See, respectively, S. P. Iaremich, *Mikhail Aleksandrovich Vrubel´: Zhizn´ i tvorchestvo* (Moscow: Izdanie I. Knebel´, 1911); Ol´ga Forsh and S. P. Iaremich, *Pavel Petrovich Chistiakov* (Leningrad: Izdanie komiteta populiarizatsii khudozhestvennykh izdanii pri gosudarstvennoi akademii istorii material´noi kul´tury, 1928); and *Russkaia akademicheskaia shkola zhivopisi v XVIII veke* (Moscow and Leningrad: OGIZ, 1934). The anonymous author of the preface to the latter book calls Iaremich's contribution to the volume "central and fundamental" («центральной и основной»; p. 12).

48. See V. F. Levinson-Lessing, "S. P. Iaremich (1869–1939)," *Soobshcheniia Gosudarstvennogo Érmitazha* 2 (1940): 26–27. For additional biographical information about Iaremich, see also M. V. Dobuzhinsky, *Vospominaniia* (Moscow: Nauka, 1987), 416; I. S. Zil´bershtein and V. A. Samkov, comps.,

Sergei Diagilev i russkoe iskusstvo, 2 vols. (Moscow: Izobrazitel´noe iskusstvo, 1982), 2:404; and, most recently, I. I. Vydrin and V. P. Tret´iakov, comps., *Stepan Petrovich Iaremich* (St. Petersburg: Izdatel´stvo "Sad iskusstv," 2005).

49. «едва уловимым»; Alexander Benois [Aleksandr Benua], *Moi vospominaniia,* 2 vols. (Moscow: Nauka, 1990), 2:276.

50. «Он мог быть очень ехидным, но при этом он сам был полон милейшего добродушия. Я только часто не знал, говорит он всерьез или шутит»; Dobuzhinsky, *Vospominaniia,* 209–10.

51. «бесподобным, чисто украинским юмором «Стипа» Яремича»; Benois, *Moi vospominaniia,* 2:376.

52. «Серость колорита Яремича была чем-то ему органически присущим (яркие колеры, и особенно зеленые, он ненавидел), и в зависимости от этого он выработал целое учение, будто живописец может вполне обходиться всего тремя красками: «костью» (черной краской), желтой охрой и белилами»; Benois, *Moi vospominaniia,* 2:432.

53. V. L. Mel´nikov, "N. K. Rerikh i izdatel´stvo 'Svobodnoe Iskusstvo' (1916–1917)," *Peterburgskii Rerikhovskii sbornik* 1 (1998): 305–6.

54. For an account of Dobuzhinsky's life, aside from the artist's own memoirs (*Vospominaniia*), see G. I. Chugunov, *Mstislav Valerianovich Dobuzhinsky* (Leningrad: "Khudozhnik RSFSR," 1984).

55. «У тебя есть талант к живописи, но—пиши»; Dmitri Nabokov, "Zapis´ vystupleniia v Natsional´noi Rossiiskoi biblioteke. S.-Peterburg, 12 iiunia 1995 g.," *Zvezda* 11 (1996): 7.

56. Boyd, *Vladimir Nabokov: The Russian Years,* 103.

57. See, respectively, Prince Sergei Shcherbatov, *Khudozhnik v ushedshei Rossii* (New York: Izdatel´stvo imeni Chekhova, 1955); and N. M. Gershenzon-Chegodaeva, *Pervye shagi zhiznennogo puti (vospominaniia docheri Mikhaila Gershenzona)* (Moscow: Zakharov, 2000). For a discussion of the distinctive features of Nabokov's generation, and specifically its acute visual memory, see Leona Toker, "Lichnoe i chastnoe v avtobiografii Vladimira Nabokova: 'mirazh prinimaemyi za landshaft,'" *Revue des Études Slaves* 72, nos. 3–4 (2000): 415–21.

CHAPTER 2

For a detailed discussion of the concept of *ogni pittore dipinge sé* (each painter paints himself) quoted in the first epigraph to this chapter, see

Frank Zöllner, "'Ogni Pittore Dipinge Sé': Leonardo da Vinci and 'Automimesis,'" in *Der Künstler über sich in seinem Werk,* ed. Matthias Winner (Weinheim, Ger.: VCH, Acta Humaniora, 1992), 137–60.

The passage quoted in the second epigraph for this chapter calls to mind Lorenzo Lotto's portrait of *Giovanni Agostino della Torre and His Son Niccolò* (1515; National Gallery, London). in which a trompe l'oeil fly is painted on the white cloth that Giovanni, who died the following year, holds in his right hand. The description may also suggest Sebastiano del Piombo's *Group Portrait of Cardinal Bandinello Sauli and Three Companions* (1516; National Gallery of Art, Washington, D.C.), in which a fly appears on the alb of the cardinal, who died less than two years later; see Michael Hirst, *Sebastiano del Piombo* (Oxford: Oxford University Press, 1981), 99. Some scholars suggest, however, much in accordance with this epigraph quotation from Nabokov, that the flies were added after the sitters' deaths. See Josephine Jungić, "Prophecies of the Angelic Pastor in Sebastiano del Piombo's *Portrait of Cardinal Bandinello Sauli and Three Companions,*" in *Prophetic Rome in the High Renaissance Period,* ed. Marjorie Reeves (Oxford: Clarendon, 1992), 367–68. These and other occurrences of a trompe l'oeil fly in art apparently originated, according to an anecdote related by Giorgio Vasari, in Giotto's painting a fly on a portrait by his mentor Cimabue. See Giorgio Vasari, *Lives of the Most Eminent Painters, Sculptors and Architects,* trans. Gaston du C. de Vere, 10 vols. (London: Macmillan and Medici Society, 1912–15), 1:94. For Nabokov's attitude toward trompe l'oeil, see Ciancio, "Nabokov's Painted Parchments," 263–64; and de Vries and Johnson, *Vladimir Nabokov and the Art of Painting,* 68.

1. It appears that the text of this talk has not survived. The talk, entitled "Leonardo the Great," sponsored by the Italian Department and by the so-called Circolo Italiano, which Nabokov gave on February 23, 1942, was briefly featured in the Wellesley College newspaper. For the announcement and a concise account of the talk, see, respectively, *Wellesley College News,* February 19, 1942, 3 and February 26, 1942, 5.

2. For more on Nabokov and Leonardo, see Ciancio, "Nabokov's Painted Parchments," 247–49; de Vries and Johnson, *Vladimir Nabokov and the Art of Painting,* 87–97.

3. Nikolai Gogol, *The Complete Tales of Nikolai Gogol,* ed. Leonard J. Kent, 2 vols. (Chicago and London: University of Chicago Press, 1985), 2:258 and 260.

4. Chernowitz, *Proust and Painting,* 4.

5. Gogol, *Complete Tales of Nikolai Gogol,* 2:260.

6. Ibid., 2:67.

7. We recall that "gentle chiaroscuro, offspring of veiled values and translucent undertones," is mentioned in *Pnin* (98). For a discussion of the perception of chiaroscuro in Nabokov's works, see Lara Delage-Toriel, "Brushing Through 'Veiled Values and Translucent Undertones': Nabokov's Pictorial Approach to Women," *Transatlantica* 1 (2006), http://www .transatlantica.revues.org/document760.html.

8. For a detailed discussion of this episode, see Gavriel Shapiro, *Nikolai Gogol and the Baroque Cultural Heritage* (University Park: Pennsylvania State University Press, 1993), 211–13.

9. Chernowitz, *Proust and Painting,* 60.

10. See Marcel Proust, *Remembrance of Things Past,* trans. C. K. Scott Moncrieff and Terence Kilmartin, 3 vols. (New York: Vintage Books, 1982), 1:244–45 and 665. For additional studies discussing Proust's oeuvre in relation to painting, see, for example, Helen Osterman Borowitz, *The Impact of Art on French Literature: From de Scudéry to Proust* (Newark: University of Delaware Press, 1985); Peter Collier, *Proust and Venice* (Cambridge: Cambridge University Press, 1989); and Jonathan Paul Murphy, *Proust's Art: Painting, Sculpture and Writing in "À la recherche du temps perdu"* (New York: Peter Lang, 2001).

11. For other allusions to Proust in Nabokov's works, see John Burt Foster Jr., "Nabokov and Proust," in *Garland Companion to Vladimir Nabokov,* 472–81.

12. To the best of my knowledge, it was Pekka Tammi who first noted and discussed this passage; see his *Problems of Nabokov's Poetics: A Narratological Analysis* (Helsinki: Suomalainen Tiedeakatemia, 1985), 317.

13. See Joanna Woods-Marsden, *Renaissance Self-Portraiture: The Visual Construction of Identity and the Social Status of the Artist* (New Haven, Conn., and London: Yale University Press, 1998).

14. On the authorial presence in literature, see Bruce E. Chaddock, "Authorial Presence and the Novel" (Ph.D. diss., Cornell University, 1974); and G. R. Thompson, *The Art of Authorial Presence: Hawthorne's Provincial Tales* (Durham, N.C., and London: Duke University Press, 1993). The most extensive discussion of Nabokov's self-encoding is in Tammi, *Problems of Nabokov's Poetics,* esp. 314–59.

15. Ross Wetzsteon, "Nabokov as Teacher," *TriQuarterly* 17 (Winter 1970): 245. Nabokov's "divine details" brings to mind the motto "God is in the de-

tails" by the renowned art historian Aby Warburg, who, incidentally, loved butterflies. See Philippe-Alain Michaud, *Aby Warburg and the Image in Motion*, trans. Sophie Hawkes (New York: Zone Books, 2004), 80, and 171, 173–74. For some parallels between Nabokov and Warburg, see Antonella Sbrilli, "Le mani fiorentine di Lolita: Coincidenze warburghiane in Nabokov (e viceversa)," *La Rivista di Engramma* 43 (September 2005): 1–21, www .engramma.it/engramma_v4/rivista/saggio/43/043_sbrilli_nabokov.html.

16. For a detailed lepidopteral analysis of the poem, see Robert Dirig, "Theme in Blue: Vladimir Nabokov's Endangered Butterfly," in Shapiro, *Nabokov at Cornell,* 212–15. Nabokov could use a microscope as early as the 1910s, at home and in the Tenishev School. He undoubtedly used it at Cambridge University where he was initially majoring in, or, using the British term, reading Zoology. This is suggested in Nabokov's early poem "Biology," written at Cambridge (ca. 1921), and in "The University Poem" (1927), composed on the heels of his Cambridge experiences. In each poem, the lyrical "I" recalls his delight in working with a microscope; see *Ssoch,* 1:549 and 2:564.

17. For painters' fascination with mirrors, and in particular the convex mirror, see G. F. Hartlaub, *Zauber des Spiegels: Geschichte und Bedeutung des Spiegels in der Kunst* (Munich: R. Piper, 1951); Heinrich Schwarz, "The Mirror in Art," *Art Quarterly* 15 (1952): 97–118; and Jan Białostocki, "Man and Mirror in Painting: Reality and Transience," in his *The Message of Images: Study in the History of Art* (Vienna: Istituto per le Ricerche di Storia dell'Arte, 1988), 93–107. A comparison between the eye and man-made convex surfaces inevitably suggests itself. Thus, Meyer Schapiro characteristically calls the convex mirror in the *Arnolfini Wedding Portrait* "the beautiful, luminous, polished eye." See Meyer Schapiro, "'Muscipula Diaboli,' The Symbolism of the Mérode Altarpiece (1945)," in his *Late Antique, Early Christian and Mediaeval Art* (New York: George Braziller, 1979), 10.

18. See David M. Levin, *The Philosopher's Gaze* (Berkeley: University of California Press, 1999), 15.

19. Pauline Moffitt Watts, *Nicolaus Cusanus: A Fifteenth-Century Vision of Man* (Leiden: E. J. Brill, 1982), 163.

20. Nicholas of Cusa, *The Vision of God,* trans. Emma Gurney Salter (New York: E. P. Dutton, 1928), 3. For the supposition that Nicholas of Cusa had van der Weyden's self-portrait in mind, see Ernst Cassirer, *The Individual and the Cosmos in Renaissance Philosophy,* trans. Mario Domandi (New York: Harper and Row, 1963), 31.

21. On Nabokov the entomologist and the correspondence between his lepidopteral and literary pursuits, see Daniil Aleksandrov, "Nabokov—naturalist i entomolog," in *V. V. Nabokov: Pro et contra*, comp. B. V. Averin, M. E. Malikova, and A. A. Dolinin, 2 vols. (St. Petersburg: Russkii Khristianskii gumanitarnyi institut, 1997–2001), 1:429–38. On the wide-ranging meaning of optical surfaces in Nabokov's oeuvre, see L. N. Riaguzova, "'Prizma' kak universal´naia kategoriia v khudozhestvennoi sisteme V. V. Nabokova," in *Nabokovskii sbornik: Iskusstvo kak priem*, ed. M. A. Dmitrovskaia (Kaliningrad: Izdatel´stvo Kaliningradskogo gosudarstvennogo universiteta, 2001), 19–29.

22. «раскрываюсь, как глаз, посреди города на крутой улице, сразу вбирая все: и прилавок с открытками, и витрину с распятиями, и объявление заезжего цирка, с углом, слизанным со стены, и совсем еще желтую апельсинную корку на старой, сизой панели, сохранившей там и сям, как сквозь сон, странные следы мозаики» (*Ssoch*, 4:563). I have slightly modified the English translation of this passage. In the standard translation, the eye metaphor is substituted for "all my senses wide open" (*Stories* 413).

23. К одному исполинскому оку
    без лица, без чела и без век
    без телесного марева сбоку,
    наконец-то сведен человек. (*PP* 100–101)

24. See Carl R. Proffer, ed., *A Book of Things About Vladimir Nabokov* (Ann Arbor, Mich.: Ardis, 1974). For a reproduction of the relevant portion of this book's dust jacket, see also Shapiro, *Nabokov at Cornell*, 248.

25. For a discussion of authorial self-representation in a convex mirror, see Victor I. Stoichita, *The Self-Aware Image: An Insight into Early Modern Meta-Painting* (Cambridge: Cambridge University Press, 1997), 215–21.

26. See the discussion in Alfred Appel Jr., *Nabokov's Dark Cinema* (New York: Oxford University Press, 1974), 246 and 249.

27. Erwin Panofsky, *Early Netherlandish Painting*, 2 vols. (Cambridge, Mass.: Harvard University Press, 1953).

28. William S. Heckscher, "Erwin Panofsky: A Curriculum Vitae," in Erwin Panofsky, *Three Essays on Style*, ed. Irving Lavin (Cambridge, Mass.: MIT Press, 1995), 182.

29. The precise title of Panofsky's essay in question is "*Et in Arcadia*

Ego: Poussin and the Elegiac Tradition," which is part of the collection *Meaning in the Visual Arts.* Although in this letter Nabokov provides Wilson with the most recent publication information on this essay by Panofsky, he could have read it almost twenty years earlier, upon the publication of its earlier version. See Erwin Panofsky, "*Et in Arcadia Ego:* On the Conception of Transience in Poussin and Watteau," in *Philosophy and History: Essays Presented to Ernst Kassirer,* ed. Raymond Klibansky and Herbert James Paton (Oxford: Clarendon, 1936), 223–54.

30. Panofsky, *Early Netherlandish Painting,* 1:2.

31. Ibid., 1:181.

32. Compare Nabokov's dubbing Visible Nature "that other V. N." (*SO* 153).

33. Compare Alfred Appel's remarks in *AnL* 360–61. Almost thirty years earlier, Nabokov employs a metallic convex surface in *The Defense:* "He [Luzhin] looked about him and saw the table and the faces of people sitting there, their reflection in the samovar—in a special samovarian perspective" (*Def* 133).

34. It appears that G. A. Levinton was the first to note the Van Bock–Van Eyck connection; see his "The Importance of Being Russian ili Les allusions perdues," in *V. V. Nabokov: Pro et contra,* 1:314.

35. For this supposition see, respectively, Erwin Panofsky, "Jan van Eyck's *Arnolfini Portrait,*" *Burlington Magazine* 64 (1934): 117–28; David G. Carter, "Reflections in Armor in the *Canon van der Paele Madonna,*" *Art Bulletin* 36 (1954): 50–52; and John L. Ward, "Disguised Symbolism as Enactive Symbolism in Van Eyck's Paintings," *Artibus et Historiae* 29 (1994): 9–53.

36. Gennady Barabtarlo was the first to identify Van Eyck's *Arnolfini Wedding Portrait* and Christus's *Saint Eligius as a Goldsmith* in this *Pnin* passage. See Barabtarlo, *Phantom of Fact,* 173.

37. For a discussion of these sculptures and capital reliefs and their meaning in the painting, see Lawrence Naftulin, "A Note on the Iconography of the van der Paele Madonna," *Oud Holland* 86, no. 1 (1971): 3–8.

38. For a detailed discussion of various manifestations of the authorial presence in Nabokov's works, see my chapter "Setting His Myriad Faces in His Text: Nabokov's Authorial Presence Revisited" in *Nabokov and His Fiction: New Perspectives,* ed. Julian W. Connolly (Cambridge: Cambridge University Press, 1999), 15–35.

39. On Nabokov's chromesthetic system, see *SM* 34–35.

40. Barabtarlo, *Phantom of Fact,* 246. Compare Nabokov's response to

Clarence F. Brown's assertion that he is "extremely repetitious": "I do not think I have seen Clarence Brown's essay, but he may have something there. Derivative writers seem versatile because they imitate many others, past and present. Artistic originality has only its own self to copy" (*SO* 95).

41. As some art historians suggest, Early Netherlandish artists depicted themselves reflectedly, and not directly, out of humility. For the most recent discussion, see Justus Müller Hofstede, "Der Künstler in Humilitas-Gestus: Altniederländische Selbstporträts und ihre Signifikanz im Bildkontext: Jan van Eyck—Dieric Bouts—Hans Memling—Joos van Cleve," in *Autobiographie und Selbstportrait* [sic] *in der Renaissance,* ed. Gunter Schweikhart (Cologne: Walther König, 1998), 39–69.

42. See Abraham Bredius, ed., *The Paintings of Rembrandt* (Vienna: Phaidon Verlag, 1936), illus. 128, 480, and 479. While working on *The Gift,* Nabokov could consult this English edition as well as the original Dutch or the German editions, published in 1935.

43. For a more detailed discussion on the subject, see Gavriel Shapiro, *Delicate Markers: Subtexts in Vladimir Nabokov's "Invitation to a Beheading"* (New York: Peter Lang, 1998), 91–92.

44. We recall that Rembrandt's corpus contains a painting entitled *The Betrayal of Peter* (1660), which was part of the Hermitage Collection until 1933, when it was sold to the Rijksmuseum in Amsterdam. See Nikolas Il´in and Natal´ia Semenova, *Prodannye sokrovishcha Rossii* (Moscow: Trilistnik, 2000), 162–63. It is likely that at the time of writing chapter 4 of the novel (mid-1934 to mid-1935), Nabokov learned about the fate of this painting, which to him apparently epitomized the Soviet betrayal of true art. For Nabokov's time frame of composing chapter 4 of *The Gift,* see Boyd, *Vladimir Nabokov: The Russian Years,* 416 and 419.

45. Some scholars believe, however, that the Munich painting includes a figure whose face "has something of Rembrandt's own younger features." See Simon Schama, *Rembrandt's Eyes* (New York: Alfred A. Knopf, 1999), 293.

46. See Fritz Erpel, *Die Selbstbildnisse Rembrandts* (Berlin: Henschelverlag, 1969), 22, pl. 21, and 35 (illus. 24); and Mariët Westermann, *Rembrandt* (London: Phaidon, 2000), 107.

47. For a discussion of these two biblical paintings by Rembrandt, separately and in juxtaposition, see Jakob Rosenberg, Seymour Slive, and E. H. ter Kuile, *Dutch Art and Architecture: 1600 to 1800* (Harmondsworth, Eng.:

Penguin Books, 1966), 56; Schama, *Rembrandt's Eyes,* 291–94; and John I. Durham, *The Biblical Rembrandt: Human Painter in a Landscape of Faith* (Macon, Ga.: Mercer University Press, 2004), 113–19.

48. Omry Ronen has astutely linked this passage to Pushkin's diary account of his chance meeting at the Luga station with his close Lyceum friend, the Decembrist Wilhelm Küchelbecker, in a group of convicts being transferred from the Shlisselburg fortress. Pushkin first mistook Küchelbecker for a Jew, with the "inseparable notions of a Jew and a spy," before realizing the convict's true identity. See Omry Ronen, "Emulation, Anti-Parody, Intertextuality, and Annotation," *Facta Universitatis,* series Linguistics and Literature, 3, no. 2 (2005): 164.

49. Nabokov's grandfather, Dmitri Nikolaevich Nabokov (1826–1904), state minister of justice (1878–85) and a protector of the liberal reforms of the 1860s, was instrumental in releasing Chernyshevsky from his Siberian exile (see *SM* 57 and *Gift* 292), and Nabokov's father, Vladimir Nabokov Sr., a prominent jurist, was a resolute opponent of capital punishment.

50. On the link between Botticelli's *Birth of Venus* and *Primavera* and Nabokov's wreathed mermaids, see Gerard de Vries, "Sandro Botticelli and Hazel Shade," *The Nabokovian* 49 (Fall 2002): 12–23.

51. See Michael Levey, "Botticelli and Nineteenth-Century England," *Journal of the Warburg and Courtauld Institutes* 23, nos. 3–4 (1960): 291–306.

52. For a discussion of ekphrasis in the context of Nabokov's works, especially with regard to young females, see Marie C. Bouchet, "Crossbreeding Word and Image: Nabokov's Subversive Use of Ekphrasis," www.ucl .ac.uk/english/graduate/issue/2/marie.htm.

53. Translated by Dmitri Nabokov. The translation is quoted by permission of the Estate of Vladimir Nabokov. All rights reserved. The original reads:

> Оставил я один узо**р** слове**сн**ый
> **мг**но**в**енно **ра**скружи**вш**ийся цв**е**ток . . .
> **И** за**в**тра снег бесшумн**ы**й и **отв**е**сн**ый
> запо**рош**ит исче**рч**енн**ы**й кат**ок**. (*Ssoch,* 1:635)

54. See Shapiro, "Setting His Myriad Faces in His Text," 23; see also Mikhail Golubovsky, "Anagrammnye variatsii: Sostukivanie slov," *Vestnik Online* 24 (335), November 26, 2003, http://www.vestnik.com/issues/ 2003/1126/koi/golubovsky.htm.

55. Brian Boyd, *Vladimir Nabokov: The American Years* (Princeton, N.J.: Princeton University Press, 1991), 642.

56. Ibid., 253.

57. Brian Boyd, "The Nabokov Biography and the Nabokov Archive," *Biblion* 1, no. 1 (Fall 1992): 36.

58. Compare Nabokov's poem "The Encounter" («Встреча», 1923) dedicated to this auspicious, fatidic, event; see *Ssoch*, 1:610–11.

59. Boyd, "The Nabokov Biography and the Nabokov Archive," 30 and 32.

60. For a comprehensive discussion of wordplay in Nabokov's works, see A. M. Liuksemburg and G. F. Rakhimkulova, *Magistr igry Vivian van Bok: Igra slov v proze Vladimira Nabokova v svete teorii kalambura* (Rostov-on-Don: Izdatel´stvo instituta massovykh kommunikatsii, 1996).

61. This meaning of the word *vera* is recorded as early as 1814; see Manlio Cortelazzo and Paolo Zolli, *Dizionario etimologico della lingua italiana*, 5 vols. (Bologna: Zanichelli, 1988), 5:1425.

Italy always meant a great deal to Nabokov. According to his son Dmitri, Nabokov possessed an "innate love for the country and its language." He shared with Véra "her love for the Italian poets perhaps more intensely than before the move to Europe." His interest in the Italian language and culture evidently intensified in the 1960s after Dmitri, a professional opera singer, settled in Italy, where Vladimir and Véra visited him from Montreux. They also "did love and frequent Italy, especially for her art." We recall that at the time Nabokov visited Italy, and specifically Italian museums, due to his work on the *Butterflies in Art* project, as well as because of his contacts with "Mondadori and other Italian publishers." Even though Nabokov "did not really know the language," "the refinement of his understanding was nonetheless amazing" (Dmitri Nabokov's electronic communications of February 13 and November 28, 2005).

The novel came out only months before their golden wedding anniversary: the first standard edition was published on August 27, 1974, and the book club edition appeared in December of that year. See Michael Juliar, *Vladimir Nabokov: A Descriptive Bibliography* (New York: Garland, 1986), 348–49.

62. Stacy Schiff, *Véra (Mrs. Vladimir Nabokov)* (New York: Modern Library, 2000), 53 and 18.

63. Nabokov evidently knew that the two main festivals of Venus, the central figure in the painting, were celebrated in spring: Veneralia on April 1, and Vinalia Priora on April 23, his own birthday. Nabokov's most

probable source of this information was Ovid's *Fasti*. See Ovid, *Fasti* (London: Penguin Books, 2000), 86–87 and 109–10, respectively.

64. See Ronald W. Lightbown, *Sandro Botticelli: His Life and Work,* 2 vols. (Berkeley: University of California Press, 1978), 1:80–81; Joseph Archer Crowe and Giovanni Battista Cavalcaselle, *A History of Painting in Italy,* 6 vols. (New York: Charles Scribner's Sons, 1903–14), 4:253n1; and Herbert Percy Horne, *Alessandro Filipepi, Commonly Called Sandro Botticelli, Painter of Florence* (London: George Bell and Sons, 1908), 50.

65. For a detailed discussion of Dmitri as the intended subject of the story, see Charles Nicol, "Nabokov and Science Fiction: 'Lance,'" *Science-Fiction Studies* 14, no. 1 (March 1987): 13–14. Compare Dmitri Nabokov's own recent assertion that "'crossing through a notch between two stars' and 'attempting a traverse on a cliff face so sheer, and with such delicate holds' (*Stories* 638) are a giveaway that, while the story may be read on more than one level, including the medieval, its inspiration was the anguish and the empathy my parents experienced when I began climbing seriously and would depart, sometimes alone, sometimes into uncharted territory." See "Miscellaneous Comments from Dmitri Nabokov on Nov. 2004 Postings," Vladimir Nabokov Forum (Nabokv-L), November 23, 2004.

66. Alfred Appel maintains that Humbert describes the farmer in this passage "as though he were 'El Greco'—his elongated 'mummy neck' is optically distorted in the manner of this artist" (*AnL* 388). The mention of the fan at the end of this passage is designed to evoke El Greco's adopted country—Spain.

67. «Как характерны для Греко эти грозовые сизые облака, что встречаются почти на всех его картинах, изображающих открытый воздух»; «так хорош ее сизый, грозовой тон, так красив вид Толедо в глубине позади фигур»; Alexander Benois, *Istoriia zhivopisi,* 4 vols. (St. Petersburg: Shipovnik, 1912), 3:76 and 74n93. In addition to El Greco's famous *Laocoön* (ca. 1610–14; National Gallery of Art, Washington, D.C.), with its "stormy dove-gray clouds" in the background, both Benois and Nabokov could have had in mind El Greco's other well-known canvas, *View of Toledo* (ca. 1597; Metropolitan Museum of Art, New York), with its "dove-gray, stormy tone." For the latter suggestion, I am indebted to Paul Barolsky; see also Raguet-Bouvart, "European Art: A Framing Device?" 205–6.

68. See, respectively, T. F. Thiselton Dyer, *The Folk-Lore of Plants* (London: Chatto and Windus, Piccadilly, 1889), 106 and 158; and Wolfgang

Menzel, *Christliche Symbolik,* 2 vols. (Regensburg, Ger.: G. Joseph Manz Verlag, 1854), 2:284.

69. Dante Alighieri, *The Divine Comedy,* trans. John D. Sinclair, 3 vols. (New York: Oxford University Press, 1979), 3:447. See Barbara Steward, *The Symbolic Rose* (New York: Columbia University Press, 1960), 44.

70. Benois, *Istoriia zhivopisi,* 3:71.

71. Manuel Bartolomé Cossio appears to have been the first scholar to make this conjecture. See his *El Greco,* 2 vols. (Madrid: Victoriano Suárez, 1908), 1:284. I am indebted for this reference to Dr. Xavier Bray, the assistant curator of the National Gallery in London. Nabokov could also have come across this supposition shortly before composing the novel; see August L. Mayer, *El Greco* (Berlin: Klinkhardt und Biermann, 1931), 12 and 77.

72. For a detailed discussion of the authorial presence in *Invitation to a Beheading,* see Shapiro, *Delicate Markers,* 26–29. Nabokov later employed a similar device for rescuing his protagonist in such works as "Cloud, Castle, Lake," *Bend Sinister,* and *Pnin.*

73. The boy was identified as El Greco's son as early as 1914; see Manuel Bartolomé Cossio, *El Entierro del Conde de Orgaz* (Madrid: Victoriano Suárez, 1914), 102–3; and Mayer, *El Greco,* 77.

74. Providence would have it that twenty-five years later Dmitri Nabokov translated this novel, in which the occasion of his birth is commemorated, into English.

75. For a detailed analysis of the painting, see Sarah Schroth, *"Burial of the Count of Orgaz," Studies in the History of Art* 11 (1982): 1–17.

76. Christine Raguet-Bouvart, who was the first to notice this reference to del Piombo in the novel, seems to be mistaken when she further maintains that the "description of Albinus, 'pale as Lazarus, his blue eyes swollen and wet, his clothes worn to shreds, his arms wide open'—(*Laugh* 109) [. . .] happens to evoke a picture by Sebastiano del Piombo, kept in the National Gallery in London" (Raguet-Bouvart, "European Art: A Framing Device?" 196). The iconography of del Piombo's *Raising of Lazarus* does not correspond to Nabokov's above-quoted description of Albinus; it is rather Caravaggio's canvas (1608–9; Museo Regionale, Messina) on the same subject that tallies well with it. Furthermore, the city location of the painting alludes, by contrast, to Albinus's upcoming obliteration, as Messina, in the year of the painting's tercentenary, was the site of a devastating earthquake (December 28, 1908) that Nabokov mentions in his memoirs

(see *SM* 142), thereby charging the whole passage about Elizabeth's hopes of her husband's return with narrative irony and already portending his final doom earlier in the novel.

77. See Vasari, *Lives of the Most Eminent Painters*, 6:184.

78. See Cesare Guasti, *Le rime di Michelangelo Buonarroti, pittore, scultore e architetto* (Florence: F. Le Monnier, 1863), 287n2.

79. With regard to sonnets, the Colonel, like Albinus and Rex after him, confuses Sebastiano del Piombo with Raphael, who indeed composed several mediocre love-sonnets. Nabokov could have familiarized himself with Raphael's sonnets, for example, in François Anatole Gruyer, *Raphaël, peintre de portraits, fragments d'histoire et d'iconographie sur les personnages représentés dans les portraits de Raphael*, 2 vols. (Paris: Librairie Renouard, 1881), 1:82–84; and in Louis Alexander Fagan, *Raffaello Sanzio, His Sonnet in the British Museum* (London: Fine Art Society, 1884).

80. According to Dmitri Nabokov, "it is almost certainly the same artist's [del Piombo's] *Ritratto di donna*, which is in the Earl of Rador's [Radnor's] collection at Longford Castle, to which Nabokov alludes in his brief mention of 'Lord Northwick from London, the owner . . . of another painting by the same del Piombo'" (*Stories* 646). Indeed, the Earl of Radnor's collection catalogue lists del Piombo's *Portrait of a Lady*, presumably of Giulia Gonzaga; see Helen Matilda, Countess of Radnor, and William Barclay Squire, with a preface by Jacob Pleydell-Bouverie, 6th Earl of Radnor, *Catalogue of the Pictures in the Collection of the Earl of Radnor*, 2 vols. (London: Chiswick, 1909), 1: fig. 83 and pp. 49–51. Del Piombo's additional female portrait is part of the collection of another English aristocrat, the Earl of Harewood. See Carlo Volpe and Mauro Lucco, *L'opera completa di Sebastiano del Piombo* (Milan: Rizzoli, 1980), tab. LIX and p. 119 (fig. 83).

81. Leopold D. Ettlinger and Helen S. Ettlinger, *Raphael* (Oxford: Phaidon, 1987), 12.

82. See Hans Posse, *Die Gemäldegalerie des Kaiser-Friedrich-Museums*, 2 vols. (Berlin: Julius Bard Verlag, 1909), 1:174.

83. Richard Muther, *The History of Modern Painting*, 4 vols. (London: J. M. Dent, 1907), 1:21; for this passage in the Russian translation, which was more readily available to Nabokov at his father's library, see Richard Muther, *Istoriia zhivopisi v XIX veke*, trans. Zinaida Vengerova, 3 vols. (St. Petersburg: "Znanie," 1899–1902), 1:14. This motif in its numerous variations—the artist who possesses superb skills that enable him to deceive his fellow artists—has been known from antiquity; see Ernst Kris

and Otto Kurz, *Legend, Myth, and Magic in the Image of the Artist* (New Haven, Conn., and London: Yale University Press, 1979), 8 and 62.

84. See, respectively, Raguet-Bouvart, "European Art: A Framing Device?" 192–95; Michel Niqueux, "*Ekphrasis* et fantastique dans *la Vénitienne* de Nabokov ou l'Art comme envoûtement," *Revue des Études Slaves* 72, nos. 3–4 (2000): 475–84; and Maxim D. Shrayer, *The World of Nabokov's Stories* (Austin: University of Texas Press, 1999), 28–32.

85. Niqueux, "*Ekphrasis* et fantastique," 484.

86. This explicit V-shaped gesture can be also found in *Portrait of a Woman,* attributed to Sebastiano del Piombo, especially in one of its versions located in the Szépművészeti Múzeum, Budapest; see Volpe and Lucco, *L'opera completa di Sebastiano del Piombo,* 135 (fig. 193b). A similarly contrived V-shaped gesture also appears in the painter's alleged portrait of Christopher Columbus (1519; Metropolitan Museum of Art, New York). On the meaning of the "V" configuration in early sixteenth-century Venetian-school painting, see Nancy Thomson de Grummond, "VV and Related Inscriptions in Giorgione, Titian, and Dürer," *Art Bulletin* 57, no. 3 (September 1975): 346–56. I have intentionally refrained from using the term "V-sign" because of its contemporary, irrelevant connotations.

87. Nabokov was mindful of Raphael's *Portrait of a Lady* (*La Donna Velata,* 1512–13; Galleria Palatina, Palazzo Pitti, Florence) in which, by contrast, the sitter holds her right hand on her heart, with the index and middle fingers spread in the most natural way, without any visible tension.

88. See Sarah Funke, *Véra's Butterflies: First Editions by Vladimir Nabokov Inscribed to His Wife* (New York: Glenn Horowitz, 1999).

89. For a discussion of quinces as a nuptial symbol in *The Feast of the Gods* by Giovanni Bellini, Sebastiano del Piombo's teacher, see Virginia Woods Callahan, "Alciato's Quince-Eating Bride, and the Figure at the Center of Bellini's *Feast of the Gods,*" *Artibus et Historiae* 35 (1997): 73–79.

90. Roberto Contini, "Portrait of a Young Roman Woman (Dorothea)," in *Sebastiano del Piombo 1485–1547,* ed. Giuseppe Scandiani (Rome: Federico Motta Editore, 2008), 144.

91. For a discussion of anamorphosis in relation to Nabokov's literary art, see Ciancio, "Nabokov's Painted Parchments," 252–64.

92. On the importance of *mise-en-abîme* in Nabokov's oeuvre, see Gregory Khasin, "The Theatre of Privacy: Vision, Self, and Narrative in Nabokov's Russian Language Novels" (Ph.D. diss., University of Chicago, 1999), 157 and 172.

CHAPTER 3

1. See, respectively, David Rosand, "Giorgione, Venice, and the Pastoral Vision," and Lawrence Gowing, "The Modern Vision," in *Places of Delight: The Pastoral Landscape,* by Robert C. Cafritz, Lawrence Gowing, and David Rosand (Washington, D.C.: Phillips Collection in association with National Gallery of Art, 1988), 41 and 196.

2. Philostratus, *Imagines;* Callistratus, *Descriptions,* trans. Arthur Fairbanks (Cambridge, Mass.: Harvard University Press, 1931), 3.

3. It is worth noting that one of Elena Ivanovna's landscapes has survived and is among the holdings of the Nabokov Museum in St. Petersburg. See the museum's website at www.nabokovmuseum.org under the rubric Museum Collection.

4. Richard Rand, with contributions by Antony Griffiths and Colleen M. Terry, *Claude Lorrain—The Painter as Draftsman: Drawings from the British Museum* (New Haven, Conn., and London and Williamstown, Mass.: Yale University Press and Sterling and Francine Clark Art Institute, 2006), 22.

5. H. Diane Russell, *Claude Lorrain, 1600–1682* (Washington, D.C.: National Gallery of Art, 1982), 47.

6. «Закатные люблю я облака» (*Ssoch,* 1:551). For a discussion of sunsets in Nabokov's works, see Nassim Winnie Berdjis, *Imagery in Vladimir Nabokov's Last Russian Novel (Дар), Its English Translation (The Gift), and Other Prose Works of the 1930s* (Frankfurt am Main: Peter Lang, 1995), 311–12.

7. See Sergei Daniel, "The Art of Claude Lorrain as a Cultural Phenomenon," in *Claude Lorrain: Painter of Light,* by Sergei Daniel and Natalia Serebriannaya (Bournemouth, Eng., and St. Petersburg: Parkstone Press and Aurora, 1995), 27. I adjusted for accuracy the poem's translation given in this book. The stanza in the original Russian reads:

Уж вечер . . . облаков померкнули края,
Последний луч зари на башнях умирает;
Последняя в реке блестящая струя
С потухшим небом угасает.

See V. A. Zhukovsky, *Sobranie sochinenii v chetyrekh tomakh* (Moscow and Leningrad: Gosudarstvennoe izdatel´stvo khudozhestvennoi literatury, 1959–60), 1:47.

8. The mention of Rembrandt playfully alludes to the fixtures, with

their metallic gleam so characteristic of the artist's work. The mention of Lorrain, on the other hand, suggests the faucet's obvious function as a conduit of running water. Nabokov, a composer of charades, plays here upon the phonetic likeness of the painter's surname to "lo" + "rain." This passage is absent in the Russian original.

9. Nabokov was familiar with William Hazlitt's essay "On a Landscape of Nicholas Poussin" included in his *Table-Talk: Essays on Men and Manners* (1822), the book which Nabokov mentions in his commentary to Pushkin's *Eugene Onegin* (*EO*, 2:56). For Hazlitt's essay, see his *Complete Works*, ed. P. P. Howe, 21 vols. (London and Toronto: J. M. Dent and Sons, 1930–34), 8:168–74. On Poussin's landscapes, see Sheila McTighe, *Nicolas Poussin's Landscape Allegories* (Cambridge: Cambridge University Press, 1996).

10. For an illuminating discussion of Panofsky's article, see Louis Martin, "Panofsky and Poussin in Arcadia," in his *Sublime Poussin* (Stanford, Calif.: Stanford University Press, 1999), 104–19.

11. For a detailed discussion of the Arcadian motif in Nabokov's oeuvre, see Michael Long, *Marvell, Nabokov: Childhood and Arcadia* (Oxford: Clarendon, 1984). For a discussion of the Arcadian motif in *Ada*, see Brian Boyd, *Ada*online, www.libraries.psu.edu/nabokov/ada, Index of Motifs: Arcady. For a comprehensive survey of the Arcadian motif in the fine arts, see Luba Freedman, "Arcadia in Visual Arts," in her *The Classical Pastoral in the Visual Arts* (New York: Peter Lang, 1989), 103–52.

Penny McCarthy establishes a valuable Arcadian motif link between Nabokov's novel *Ada* and Sir Philip Sidney's posthumously published prose romance *The Countess of Pembroke's Arcadia* (1590). At the same time, however, McCarthy comes up with an utterly preposterous and slanderous idea, unbecoming of a serious scholar, that Nabokov and his sister Elena had been intimately involved, which she "substantiates" on the basis of the Van–Ada incestuous relationship. See Penny McCarthy, "Nabokov's *Ada* and Sidney's *Arcadia*," *Modern Language Review* 99, no. 1 (January 2004): 17–31.

12. «гобеленовые купы деревьев, а с боков, оттененные сиреневой гуашью, таинственные небоскребы под пуссеновым небом» (*Perepiska* 104).

13. On Nabokov's indebtedness to the French Impressionists, see Ciancio, "Nabokov's Painted Parchments," 240–47.

14. Translated by Gavriel Shapiro with Dmitri Nabokov. «Дирекция Западных и Восточных Небес угостила нас чудовищно-прекрасным закатом. Наверху небо было глубоко-голубое, и только на западе

стояло громадное облако в виде лилового крыла, раскинувшего оранжевые ребра. Река была розовая словно в воду капнули портвейна,—и вдоль нее летел экспресс из Праги в Париж. А на самом горизонте, под тем фиолетовым облаком, отороченным оранжевым пухом, полоса неба сияла легкой зеленоватой бирюзой, и в нем таяли огненные островки»; Vladimir Nabokov Archives, Montreux. Quoted by permission of the Estate of Vladimir Nabokov. All rights reserved.

15. «своеобразны», «одна маленькая его акварель,—поистине чудесная вещица: темный пляж в Альбеке, серое набухшее небо, охряный парус и красно-черные силуэты рыбаков, стоящих у тусклой воды» (*Ssoch,* 3:700).

16. James A. W. Heffernan, *Museum of Words: The Poetics of Ekphrasis from Homer to Ashbery* (Chicago and London: University of Chicago Press, 1993), 3. For an illuminating discussion on ekphrasis, see Valerie Robillard and Els Jongeneel, eds., *Pictures into Words: Theoretical and Descriptive Approaches to Ekphrasis* (Amsterdam: VU University Press, 1998). For discussions of ekphrasis in Russian literature, see Maria Rubins, *Crossroad of Arts, Crossroad of Cultures: Ecphrasis in Russian and French Poetry* (New York: Palgrave, 2000); and Leonid Geller, ed., *Ekfrasis v russkoi literature: Trudy Lozannskogo simpoziuma* (Moscow: "MIK," 2002).

17. It is noteworthy that the Russian verb "to write" (*pisat´*) may be applied to both writing and painting. See Christoph Henry-Thommes, *Recollection, Memory and Imagination: Selected Autobiographical Novels of Vladimir Nabokov* (Heidelberg: Universitätsverlag Winter, 2006), 263–64.

18. On the watercolor's reverse, Nabokov inscribed in Russian for his son and wife: "For Miten´ka and Véra from V." and dated it "12. VIII. 42. Vermont." The description of the watercolor is based on a Xerox copy I made, pro memoria, in the fall of 2001. Regrettably, when several years later the Vladimir Nabokov Archives was moved to its present location in Dmitri Nabokov's Montreux residence, the watercolor was apparently misplaced and thus far has not been found.

19. See, respectively, Boyd, *Vladimir Nabokov: The American Years,* 15; Barabtarlo, *Phantom of Fact,* 195 and 197; and Galya Diment, *Pniniad: Vladimir Nabokov and Marc Szeftel* (Seattle and London: University of Washington Press, 1997), 50–51.

20. I am greatly indebted to Dmitri Nabokov for his explanation of the inscriptions. One wonders whether Monsieur Séchaud is a descendant of the renowned Swiss chocolatier Jules Séchaud of Montreux, who intro-

duced a process of manufacturing filled chocolates in 1913. For the date of the Nabokovs' arrival in Montreux and their taking up a temporary residence in the Hotel Belmont, see Boyd, *Vladimir Nabokov: The American Years,* 421.

21. For a good reproduction of the drawing, see Ellendea Proffer, comp. and ed., *Vladimir Nabokov: A Pictorial Biography* (Ann Arbor, Mich.: Ardis, 1991), 128. For a discussion of the drawing, albeit mistitled as Le Don du Midi, see Stark, "Ut pictura poesis: Nabokov-risoval´shchik," 120–21.

I take strong exception to Gerard de Vries's dubbing Nabokov's illustrations for his *Lectures* and his Dents du Midi drawing "poor" (de Vries and Johnson, *Vladimir Nabokov and the Art of Painting,* 16). On the contrary, I find these and many other of Nabokov's drawings, which I have had numerous opportunities to examine, to be skillful and elegant. In this I perfectly agree with Alfred Appel, who calls Nabokov "an accomplished draftsman"; see Appel, *Nabokov's Dark Cinema,* 308n3.

22. Maria Malikova has noted the connection between the watercolor imagery in the novel and the corresponding imagery in *Other Shores* (see *Ssoch,* 5:692).

23. Translated by Gavriel Shapiro with Dmitri Nabokov.

> Смотри: зеленый луг,
> а там, за ним, чернеет маслянисто
> еловый бор, – и золотом косым
> пронизаны два облака . . . а время
> уж к вечеру . . . и в воздухе, пожалуй,
> церковный звон . . . толчется мошкара . . .
> Уйти бы – а? – туда, в картину эту,
> в задумчивые краски травяные,
> воздушные . . .

See Nabokov, *Tragediia gospodina Morna. P´esy. Lektsii o drame,* 196.

24. Philostratus, *Imagines;* Callistratus, *Descriptions,* 21, 39, 47.

25. See H. C. Andersen, *The Complete Andersen,* trans. Jean Hersholt, 6 vols. (New York: Limited Editions Club, 1949), 5:153.

Curiously, Isak Dinesen (Baroness Karen Blixen, 1885–1962), Nabokov's older contemporary and Andersen's younger fellow countrywoman, employs a similar imagery in her posthumously published novel *Ehrengard* (1963): "You ask me for a description of Schloss Rosenbad. Imagine to yourself that you be quietly stepping into a painting by Claude Lorrain, and that the landscape around you becomes alive, balsamic breezes wafting and violets turning the mountain sides into long gentle waves of blue!" See Isak Dinesen, *Ehrengard* (New York: Random House, 1963), 31. It appears that Dinesen arrived at the employment of the stepping-into-a-painting device independently of Nabokov, since "La Veneziana" was first published in the French, Italian, and English translations in the 1990s (see *Stories* 646).

26. On the importance of this periodical in Nabokov's works, see Savely Senderovich and Yelena Shvarts, "Tropinka podviga (Kommentarii k romanu V. V. Nabokova 'Podvig')," *Nabokovskii vestnik* 4 (1999): 140–53.

27. On the "path" motif and its main variants in the novel, see, for example, Edythe C. Haber, "Nabokov's *Glory* and the Fairy Tale," *Slavic and East European Journal* 21, no. 2 (Summer 1977): 215–16; Leona Toker, *Nabokov: The Mystery of Literary Structures* (Ithaca, N.Y., and London: Cornell University Press, 1989), 88–106, esp. 100–102; Pekka Tammi, "*Glory*," in *Garland Companion to Vladimir Nabokov,* 175; Maxim D. Shrayer, "The Perfect Glory of Nabokov's Exploit," *Russian Studies in Literature* 35, no. 4 (Fall 2000): 29–41; and Aleksandr Dolinin, *Istinnaia zhizn' pisatelia Sirina: Raboty o Nabokove* (St. Petersburg: "Akademicheskii proekt," 2004), 82–90.

28. In Russian, the adjective in the italicized phrase reads «нужную» (*Ssoch*, 3:222), that is, "the needed one."

29. In Russian the beginning of the passage reads, «упруго идя по тропе» (*Ssoch*, 3:221), that is, "walking with a buoyant gait along the path," thereby containing once again the phrase-ending, emphatic keyword "path"; translated by Gavriel Shapiro with Dmitri Nabokov.

30. Translated by Gavriel Shapiro with Dmitri Nabokov.

> Среди цветущих огненных дерев
> грустит березка на лугу,
> как дева пленная в блистательном кругу
> иноплеменных дев.
>
> И только я дружу с березкой одинокой,
> тоскую с ней весеннею порой: —
> она мне кажется сестрой
> возлюбленной далекой. (*Ssoch*, 1:474)

For a more detailed discussion of the lonely birch image in Nabokov's earlier poetry, see Gavriel Shapiro, "Nabokov and the 'Other Shores,'" in *The*

Russian Emigration: Literature, History, Chronicle of Films, ed. V. Khazan, I. Belobrovtseva, and S. Dotsenko (Jerusalem, Israel: The Hebrew University of Jerusalem; Tallinn, Estonia: Tallinn Pedagogical University, 2004), 110–11. Compare the lone birch image, "the slender white birch that stands on tiptoe in the wind," in Nabokov's later poem, "An Evening of Russian Poetry"; see *PP* 160.

31. In the Russian original, Nabokov employed the names of the two settlements that indeed exist along the Russian-Latvian border—Rezhitsa, which stems from *rezat´* ("to cut" or "to kill with a sharp instrument"), and Pytalovo, which stems from *pytat´* ("to torture"); see *Ssoch*, 3:228 and 739.

32. In the original, Nabokov entitled the novel *Podvig,* that is, "gallant feat," "high deed" (*Glory* x). Initially, the novel's working title was *Romanticheskiy vek,* that is, "romantic times," by which Nabokov, at least in part, wanted to refute the notion of his era being "'materialistic,' 'practical,' 'utilitarian'" (ibid.).

33. Shapiro, *Delicate Markers,* 183–207.

34. «обаятельно» (*Ssoch*, 4:68); translated by Dmitri Nabokov.

35. Translated by Gavriel Shapiro with Dmitri Nabokov. «До сих пор, я не могу побороть волнения при взгляде на Таврический дворец. И конечно, в данной обстановке иметь его перед глазами—значит видеть перед собою как бы воплощенным то короткое и недавнее, но кажущееся так бесконечно далеким прошлое, которое ни нами, ни историей забыто не будет»; see V. D. Nabokov, *Tiuremnye dosugi* (St. Petersburg: "Obshchestvennaia Pol´za," 1908), 12.

36. For a more detailed discussion of the passages, see Gavriel Shapiro, "Otgoloski *Tiuremnykh dosugov* V. D. Nabokova v *Priglashenii na kazn´,*" *Cahiers de l'Émigration Russe* 5 (1999): 71–72.

37. See Igor´ Grabar´, ed., *Istoriia russkogo iskusstva,* 6 vols. (Moscow: Izdanie I. Knebel´, 1909–16), 3:154–55. Incidentally, the surname Starov appears in both *The Real Life of Sebastian Knight* and *Look at the Harlequins!*

38. The Tauride Garden is mentioned in *The Defense:* "to pass time" before returning home at an opportune hour, the skipping-classes schoolboy Luzhin "wandered into Tavricheski Park" («Таврический сад»; *Def* 51–52 and *Ssoch*, 2:332). Here the Tauride Garden, as part of the palace, is also associated with the motif of deceit.

39. In Russian, the respective phrases read: «тупое «тут»» and «тупик тутошней жизни», that is, "the obtuse 'here'" and "the dead end of the here-being" (*Ssoch*, 4:101 and 174).

40. For a discussion of the prison-house of language, see Johnson, *Worlds in Regression*, 34–42.

41. See Sergej Davydov, *"Teksty-matreški" Vladimira Nabokova* (Munich: Otto Sagner, 1982), 152–53 and 156. See also Julian W. Connolly, *"Invitation to a Beheading:* Nabokov's 'Violin in a Void,'" in *Nabokov's "Invitation to a Beheading": A Critical Companion,* ed. Julian W. Connolly (Evanston, Ill.: Northwestern University Press, 1997), 19–22; and Véra Nabokov's letter of July 2, 1960, to Gilbert and Patricia Millstein, as cited by Brian Boyd in his "'Welcome to the Block': *Priglashenie na kazn´ / Invitation to a Beheading,* A Documentary Record," in Connolly, *Nabokov's "Invitation to a Beheading,"* 167.
Marthe may be linked to the Tamara Gardens through a partial anagram. The anagram is most distinct in the original Russian—Марфинька/Тамарины—especially if we recall that the former is a diminutive of Марθа and the latter is a derivative of the biblical Θамарь, both spelled in the old orthography to which Nabokov had adhered throughout his "Russian years."

42. See Shrayer, *World of Nabokov's Stories,* 143–52.

43. The earliest, most celebrated example of a spiritualized "cloud, castle, lake" landscape can be found in Annibale Carracci's *The Flight into Egypt* (ca. 1604; Galleria Doria-Pamphili, Rome); see Rudolf Wittkower, *Art and Architecture in Italy, 1600 to 1750* (Harmondsworth, Eng.: Penguin Books, 1958; reprint, 1985), 70.

44. As cited in Boyd, *Vladimir Nabokov: The Russian Years,* 245. In this letter, Nabokov demonstrates his close familiarity with the following topoi: artist as *alter deus* as well as *ars simia naturae* and artist as *simius dei.* See, respectively, Leon Battista Alberti, *On Painting,* trans. John R. Spencer (New Haven, Conn.: Yale University Press, 1956), 64; Kris and Kurz, *Legend, Myth, and Magic,* 58–61; H. W. Janson, *"Ars Simia Naturae,"* in his *Apes and Ape Lore in the Middle Ages and the Renaissance* (London: Warburg Institute, University of London, 1952), 287–325; and Kris and Kurz, *Legend, Myth, and Magic,* 86. On Nabokov's creative universe in its relation to Alberti and his system, see Ciancio, "Nabokov's Painted Parchments," 250–64.

45. Vladimir Nabokov, "Tolstoy," trans. Dmitri Nabokov, *New York Review of Books* 35, no. 3 (March 3, 1988): 6.

46. See Robert Rosenblum, "Friedrichs from Russia: An Introduction," in *The Romantic Vision of Caspar David Friedrich,* ed. Sabine Rewald (New York: Metropolitan Museum of Art, 1990), 3.

47. See Boris I. Asvarishch, "Friedrich's Russian Patrons," and Rosenblum, "Friedrichs from Russia: An Introduction," both in Rewald, *The Romantic Vision of Caspar David Friedrich*, 19 and 4, respectively.

48. See, for example, Willi Wolfradt, *Caspar David Friedrich und die Landschaft der Romantik* (Berlin: Mauritius Verlag, 1924).

49. The poem is neither identified nor cited in the English translation, where the reader is merely told that the protagonist opens "a little volume of Tyutchev" (*Stories* 431).

50. «Мысль изреченная есть ложь», «Мы слизь. Реченная есть ложь» (*Ssoch*, 4:583). We recall that Nabokov himself translated "Silentium!" into English. In his translation of the poem, Nabokov has rendered this programmatic line as "A thought once uttered is untrue" (*TRP* 34).

On Tiutchev's poem as part and parcel of the Romantic notion of the inexpressible, see Sofya Khagi, "Silence and the Rest: The Inexpressible from Batiushkov to Tiutchev," *Slavic and East European Journal* 48, no. 1 (Spring 2004): 41–61. On the essential role of Tiutchev's poetry in Nabokov's oeuvre, see Christine A. Rydel, "Nabokov and Tiutchev," in Shapiro, *Nabokov at Cornell*, 123–35. Rydel makes a very valid point that the "Tiutchevian landscape" is especially pertinent to the story because the "most beautiful nature lyrics" of the Russian poet, who spent a great deal of his adult life in Germany, "describe not Russian scenes—which he found barren and hostile—but German scenes, many of which feature clouds, castles, lakes, and even towers." The scholar has observed that "in Tiutchev's poetry, towers appear twice, castles seven times, clouds twenty-one times, and lakes eleven times" (ibid., 133).

51. See Nora Buhks, *Eshafot v khrustal'nom dvortse: O russkikh romanakh Vladimira Nabokova* (Moscow: Novoe literaturnoe obozrenie, 1998), 58.

52. See Shapiro, *Delicate Markers*, 139.

53. Andrew Field, *Nabokov: His Life in Art* (Boston and Toronto: Little, Brown, 1967), 197.

54. As concomitant with this motif, one may perceive the suicide pact episode in *The Gift*. To carry out their plan, the three characters, Yasha Chernyshevski, Rudolf, and Olya, choose the Berlin Grunewald, where they intend "to find a lonely spot and shoot themselves one after the other" (*Gift* 46). Their act may be viewed as a crime, as every suicide is, against God and nature. Additionally, it may be viewed, at least partially, as a crime manqué, since after Yasha's successful suicide, Rudolf "lost all desire to kill himself" and "had immediately hidden the revolver" from Olya (*Gift* 48).

55. Here Nabokov's narrator, of course, exhibits a great deal of sarcasm: obviously, there is nothing "natural" or "pure" about murder.

56. For a detailed discussion of landscape in *Lolita* and its important role in the novel, see Roy C. Flannagan III, "'Beauty of Distance': The Centrality of Landscape Description in Vladimir Nabokov's *Lolita*" (Ph.D. diss., Southern Illinois University at Carbondale, 1996).

57. For N—'s disdainful treatment of Pnin, see Paul Grams, "*Pnin:* The Biographer as Meddler," in Proffer, *A Book of Things About Vladimir Nabokov,* 193–202.

58. Compare Barabtarlo's comment: "Pnin's car squeezed between two trucks makes a nice pictograph of his imprisonment in this thick-walled, well-guarded fortress of his life-story" (Barabtarlo, *Phantom of Fact,* 289).

59. See G. M. Hyde, *Vladimir Nabokov: America's Russian Novelist* (London: Marion Boyars, 1977), 156. For a different treatment of the relationship among Pnin, the narrator, and the author, see, for example, Toker, *Nabokov,* 21–35; Barabtarlo, *Phantom of Fact;* and Levinton, "The Importance of Being Russian," esp. 316–19.

60. W. J. T. Mitchell, "Introduction," in *Landscape and Power,* ed. W. J. T. Mitchell (Chicago and London: University of Chicago Press, 1994), 2.

CHAPTER 4

1. For a depiction of *The World of Art*'s typical meeting, see Boris Kustodiev, *A Group Portrait of "The World of Art" Painters* (1916–20; State Russian Museum, St. Petersburg).

2. For a detailed discussion of *The World of Art,* see, for example, Alla Gusarova, *"Mir iskusstva"* (Leningrad: "Khudozhnik RSFSR," 1972); Janet Kennedy, *The "Mir iskusstva" Group and Russian Art* (New York: Garland, 1977); Natalia Lapshina, *"Mir iskusstva"* (Moscow: "Iskusstvo," 1977); John E. Bowlt, *The Silver Age: Russian Art of the Early Twentieth Century and the "World of Art" Group* (Newtonville, Mass.: Oriental Research Partners, 1979); and Viacheslav Shestakov, *Iskusstvo i mir v "Mire iskusstva"* (Moscow: "Slavianskii dialog," 1998).

3. See Vladimir Nabokov, "Diaghilev and a Disciple," review of *Serge Diaghilev, His Life, His Work, His Legend: An Intimate Biography,* by Serge Lifar, *The New Republic,* November 18, 1940, 699.

4. Translated by Gavriel Shapiro with Dmitri Nabokov. «Затем обедал

у милейших стариков Брайкевич; у них замечательная коллекция картин,—особенно целая россыпь сомовских, которыми я не мог насосаться». Quoted by permission of the Estate of Vladimir Nabokov. All rights reserved. Mikhail Braikevich (1874–1940), a construction engineer and economist by profession, was an art patron and collector, primarily of works by the *World of Art* painters.

5. In Nabokov's own words, "Malevich and Kandinsky mean nothing to me and I have always found Chagall's stuff intolerably primitive and grotesque," especially his later works; "the frescoes and windows he now contributes to temples and the Parisian Opera House *plafond* are coarse and unbearable" (*SO* 170). It is curious that Chagall imagery is suggested in *The Gift,* in Professor Anuchin's comparing Fyodor's book on Chernyshevsky to "some kind of impressionistic picture with a walking figure upside down against a green sky" (*Gift* 306). For relating this description to Chagall, see Marina Grishakova, "Vizual′naia poetika V. Nabokova," *Novoe literaturnoe obozrenie* 54 (2002): 209.

On the other hand, Nabokov thought highly of Cubism of the early (pre-*Guernica*) Picasso, admiring "the graphic aspect, the masterly technique, and the quiet colors" of his art (*SO* 167). Nabokov's passing interest in Cubism in the earlier years may be detected in his poem "The Cubes" (1924; for the original, see *Ssoch,* 1:618–19; for Dmitri Nabokov's English translation of the poem, see Grayson, McMillin, and Meyer, *Nabokov's World,* 2:4).

6. «Наивность, с которой изложены в «Эстетических отношениях [искусства к действительности]» плохо переваренные мысли западных социалистических и позитивных мыслителей»; see Alexander Benois, *Istoriia russkoi zhivopisi v XIX veke* (1902; reprint, Moscow: "Respublika," 1995), 220.

7. Benois' *Istoriia russkoi zhivopisi v XIX veke* is conceivably the best source of the *World of Art* perception of various trends and movements in nineteenth-century Russian art.

8. «Нас инстинктивно тянуло уйти [. . .] от тенденциозности передвижников [. . .], подальше от нашего упадочного академизма»; Alexander Benois, *Vozniknovenie "Mira Iskusstva"* (1928; reprint, Moscow: "Iskusstvo," 1994), 21.

9. Here is an illustrative expression of *The World of Art*'s creed: "We must be as free as gods," "We must seek in beauty a great justification for our humanity and in individuality—its supreme manifestation" («Мы должны быть свободны как боги», «Мы должны искать в красоте великого

оправдания нашего человечества и в личности—его высочайшего проявления»); see Sergei Diagilev, "Slozhnye voprosy," *Mir iskusstva* 3–4 (1899): 61.

10. See Nabokov, "Diaghilev and a Disciple," 699.

11. See I. S. Zil´bershtein and A. N. Savinov, eds., *Aleksandr Benua razmy-shliaet . . . (*Moscow: "Sovetskii khudozhnik," 1968), 231.

12. Ibid., 229.

13. See M. V. Dobuzhinsky, "Oblik Peterburga," publ. Galina Glushanok, *Zvezda* 5 (2003): 106.

14. See Sergei Makovsky, *Stranitsy khudozhestvennoi kritiki*, 2 vols. (St. Petersburg, 1909), 2:115; see also Zil´bershtein and Savinov, *Aleksandr Benua razmyshliaet . . .*, 501–2.

15. For a discussion of the role of memory in Nabokov's fiction, see Henry-Thommes, *Recollection, Memory and Imagination.*

16. For a detailed discussion on the subject, see Richard Borden, "Nabokov's Travesties of Childhood Nostalgia," *Nabokov Studies* 2 (1995): 104–34. For more on nostalgia in general and in Nabokov's oeuvre in particular, see Svetlana Boym, *The Future of Nostalgia* (New York: Basic Books, 2001).

17. See Dobuzhinsky, *Vospominaniia*, 185–87 and 407–9; and A. A. Sidorov, *Russkaia grafika nachala XX veka* (Moscow: "Iskusstvo," 1969), 42–47. For more on Maté and his impact on various Russian artists, see V. I. Fedorova, *V. V. Maté i ego ucheniki* (Leningrad: "Khudozhnik RSFSR," 1982).

18. See, respectively, Benois, *Moi vospominaniia*, 2:447, 1:517 and 683; Dobuzhinsky, *Vospominaniia*, 30, 139–40, 400; and Mstislav Dobuzhinsky, "Zapozdalyi venok na mogilu druga: K. A. Somov," n.p., n.d., 18 pages, Dobuzhinsky Papers, box 5, pp. 6–7, Bakhmeteff Archive, Columbia University Library, New York City.

19. For allusions to Aubrey Beardsley in *Lolita*, see Gavriel Shapiro, "*Lolita* Class List," *Cahiers du Monde Russe* 37 (1996): 326–27; and Gerard de Vries, "*Lolita* and Aubrey Beardsley," in de Vries and Johnson, *Vladimir Nabokov and the Art of Painting*, 59–66.

20. See Omry Ronen, "The Triple Anniversary of World Literature: Goethe, Pushkin, Nabokov," in Shapiro, *Nabokov at Cornell*, 178.

21. See *Sistematicheskii katalog biblioteki Vladimira Dmitrievicha Nabokova: Pervoe prodolzhenie*, 23 (# 2811).

22. See, for example, A. N. Benois, *Moi dnevnik, 1916–1917–1918* (Moscow: Russkii put´, 2003), 34, 45, 85, and 174–75.

23. It is worth noting that many years later Nabokov mentions Shahriar (spelled Scheher) and Scheherazade in *Ada* (217 and 218).

24. See, respectively, Yevgenia Petrova, ed., *The World of Art: On the Centenary of the Exhibition of Russian and Finnish Artists, 1898* (St. Petersburg and Helsinki: Palace Editions, 1998), illus. 99 and 58; Alexander Schouvaloff, *Léon Bakst: The Theatre Art* (London: Sotheby's Publications, 1991), 90–91; and Irina Pruzhan, *Konstantin Somov* (Moscow: "Izobrazitel´noe iskusstvo," 1972), illus. 46. See also Susan Elizabeth Sweeney, "'Ballet Attitudes': Nabokov's *Lolita* and Petipa's *The Sleeping Beauty*," in Zunshine, *Nabokov at the Limits*, 114.

It is quite possible that in referring to *Turks,* Nabokov had in mind a composite image of Bakst's sketches and of those by Boris Anisfeld (1878–1973), whose style was very much influenced by Bakst. Anisfeld's several costume sketches, such as *Moor* and *Eunuch,* for the *Islamey* ballet, which was set to Mily Balakirev's music by Mikhail Fokine and premiered in the spring of 1912 at the Mariinsky Theater, were originally in the possession of V. D. Nabokov. See Petrova, *The World of Art,* 253–54.

25. «вертикально падающий крупный снег «Мира Искусства»» (*Ssoch,* 5:289). It is worth noting that many émigré memoirists retrospectively looked at St. Petersburg through the prism of *The World of Art's* pictorial imagery. See Al´bin Konechnyi, "Peterburg 's togo berega' (v memuarakh emigrantov 'pervoi volny')," *Blokovskii sbornik* 13 (1996): 130.

26. Translated by Dmitri Nabokov. Quoted by permission of the Estate of Vladimir Nabokov. All rights reserved. For the original lines, see chapter 2, note 53.

27. See also Shapiro, "Setting His Myriad Faces in His Text," 23.

28. See also Nabokov's longer poem "Petersburg" (1923), in which he describes the city's skating rinks (*Ssoch,* 1:597–98).

29. The motif of skating in the poem evokes Somov's painting *Winter. Skating Rink* (1915; State Russian Museum, St. Petersburg).

30. See Boyd, *Vladimir Nabokov: The Russian Years,* 241.

31. «валил отвесно крупный мягкий снег в сером, как матовое стекло, воздухе» (*Ssoch,* 2:96).

32. «И только в ноябре Машенька переселилась в Петербург. Они встретились под той аркой, где—в опере Чайковского—гибнет Лиза» (ibid.).

33. Ironically, both Benois and Dobuzhinsky created stage and costume

designs for the production of Tchaikovsky's *The Queen of Spades,* respectively, at the Petrograd Theater of Opera and Ballet (formerly Mariinsky; 1921) and at the Kaunas State Theater (1925 and 1934).

34. See Alexander Pushkin, *The Complete Works of Alexander Pushkin,* ed. Iain Sproat et al., 15 vols. (Norfolk, Eng.: Milner, 1999–2003), 9:217; «мокрый снег падал хлопьями», see A. S. Pushkin, *Polnoe sobranie sochinenii,* 17 vols. (Moscow and Leningrad: Izdatel´stvo Akademii Nauk SSSR, 1937–59), 8:239.

35. «с Вашего «Петра и Исаакия» я перед самой выставкой сделал копию, но она очень разнится от самого оригинала, где много *угля* и мало *краски.* Тут я сделал гуашью и прибавил падающий снег, так что это совсем не дубликат, и я только Вам благодарен за то, что мог, делая эту вещь, вспомнить и погрузиться в наши петербургские настроения . . . А как их забыть? Когда все встает, точно было вчера»; M. V. Dobuzhinsky, *Pis´ma* (St. Petersburg: Izdatel´stvo "Dmitri Bulanin," 2001), 322.

36. The phrase "frost-dust" (*CE* 61 and *SM* 100), which is rendered as «морозной пылью» in *Other Shores* (*Ssoch,* 5:204), alludes to Pushkin's *Eugene Onegin,* where it appears in chapter 1, canto XVI, in the episode, set in wintry St. Petersburg, of Onegin's riding in a sleigh to dinner at the famous Talon restaurant. In his English translation of the novel in verse, Nabokov renders the phrase as "frostdust" (*EO,* 1:101), which, as he explains, he preferred over "the more elegant but less accurate: 'the powder of the frost'" (*EO,* 2:70).

37. For Nabokov's entering the Tenishev School in 1910 rather than in 1911 (*SM* 180), see Ol´ga Skonechnaia, "Nabokov v Tenishevskom uchilishche," *Nashe nasledie* 1 (1991): 109–10. It is worth noting that Nabokov the schoolboy had demonstrated the most steady and obvious accomplishments in drawing (ibid., 111).

On the other famous Tenishev School graduates, see Mets, *Osip Mandel´shtam i ego vremia,* 268, 269, 272, and 274. Incidentally, Levinson-Lessing was Iaremich's colleague at the Hermitage Museum (see chapter 1, note 48).

38. It is noteworthy that Pavel Chistiakov (1832–1919), the renowned pedagogue at the St. Petersburg Academy of Fine Arts and a teacher of Vasily Maté, spoke highly of the Ažbe School. See Benois, *Moi vospominaniia,* 1:556 and 2:97 and 651.

39. Once again, for an account of Dobuzhinsky's life, aside from the

artist's own memoirs (*Vospominaniia*), see Chugunov, *Mstislav Valerianovich Dobuzhinsky.*

40. For some comparison between Nabokov and Dobuzhinsky, see Igor´ Kozitsky, "Nabokov i Dobuzhinsky: sviazi formal´nye i ne tol´ko," *Neva* 11 (1997): 214–20.

41. On Dobuzhinsky's collecting butterflies in his boyhood, see his *Vospominaniia,* 34. Nabokov's lifelong lepidopteral passion is manifest in a great many of his literary works. For extensive information on the subject, see Zimmer, *A Guide to Nabokov's Butterflies and Moths.*

42. About Dobuzhinsky the pedagogue, see the reminiscences of some of his students, such as Georgy Vereisky, Vladimir Milashevsky, and Alexander Shenderov, in *Vospominaniia o Dobuzhinskom,* comp. G. I. Chugunov (St. Petersburg: "Akademicheskii proekt," 1997), 46–82.

43. Respectively, Cornell University alumni Joseph F. Martino Jr., class of 1953, who later became a high school teacher of English literature, in a telephone communication in the spring of 1998; and Moses Zevi Blum, class of 1957, later Cornell University art professor, in a personal communication in the summer of 2002.

44. «Удивляет при этом необъяснимое обилие фальши и исторических неточностей, которыми полон фильм. Ведь там, в Москве, под рукой в Оружейной Палате и в Историческом Музее непочатое богатство всяческих реликвий этой эпохи. И следует признать отсутствие у постановщиков такта и простой добросовестности, не говоря о вкусе, если они могли наряду с вещами убедительными уснастить фильм тем, что называется «клюквой». Ни в театре, ни в фильме мелочей не существует, и скверно, если говорят: «публика этого не заметит». Имеющие очи видеть всегда увидят погрешности и недочеты»; Mstislav Dobuzhinsky, "Susal´nyi fil´m," n.p., 1947, Dobuzhinsky Papers, box 5, p. 1, Bakhmeteff Archive, Columbia University Library, New York City.

45. «Я заметил у тебя только одну ошибку: ампирный дом на Невском между Литейной и Надеждинской, где устраивали выставки,—дом не Радоконаки, как ты пишешь, а *Бернардакки* (или Бернардацци)—я уверен. Да, и еще—у военных врачей эполеты были не золотые, а серебряные (у меня был дядя военный доктор, так что хорошо помню)»; Dobuzhinsky, *Pis´ma,* 321.

46. See Dobuzhinsky, *Vospominaniia,* between 224 and 225; and Chugunov, *Mstislav Valerianovich Dobuzhinsky,* 45.

47. «Пересматривая свои детские рисунки, я удивляюсь, действительно, как рано у меня явилось чувство комизма: есть явные гротески уже в моих трехлетних рисунках»; Dobuzhinsky, *Pis'ma*, 78.

48. On Nabokov's predilection for and attitude toward comic art and for the important role of comic art in his oeuvre, see Gavriel Shapiro, "Nabokov and Comic Art," in Zunshine, *Nabokov at the Limits*, 213–34; Clarence Brown, "Krazy, Ignatz, and Vladimir: Nabokov and the Comic Strip," in Shapiro, *Nabokov at Cornell*, 251–63; and Gavriel Shapiro, "Nabokov and Comic Art: Additional Observations and Remarks," *The Nabokovian* 59 (Fall 2007): 21–31.

49. See Dobuzhinsky, *Pis'ma*, the front and back flyleafs and 385–86.

50. For a much broader context in which childhood and youth play the essential role in Russian memoir literature, see Andrew Baruch Wachtel, *The Battle for Childhood: Creation of a Russian Myth* (Stanford, Calif.: Stanford University Press, 1990).

51. Translated by Gavriel Shapiro with Dmitri Nabokov. «ваши воспоминания о Мире Иск<усства> очаровательны: это настоящий Добужинский. Эти овалы, врисованные как бы в текст, с портретами Сомова, Бакста, Бенуа, Грабаря [. . .] необыкновенно хороши»; «Единственная маленькая придирка: избегайте кавычек! Слову не нужны типографские подпорки»; Vadim Stark, "Perepiska Vladimira Nabokova s M. V. Dobuzhinskim," *Zvezda* 11 (1996): 99.

52. «жил среди преданий»; «Было интересно ходить и вокруг памятника тысячелетия России напротив собора и узнавать в нем разных царей и героев в кольчугах и латах»; Dobuzhinsky, *Vospominaniia*, 46 and 47.

53. Dobuzhinsky, *Pis'ma*, 79 and 337.

54. «родной город», «*коренной* Петербуржец»; Dobuzhinsky, *Pis'ma*, 270. See also Dobuzhinsky, "Oblik Peterburga," 101–7.

55. «С самого начала (1901) меня интересовала более всего «изнанка города» [. . .], и я рисовал «Питер», его уголки, а красотами Петербурга любовался, но рисовать их не подмывало. Этим занимались Остроумова, отчасти Бенуа и Лансере, и за «парадный» С.-Петербург я взялся попутно лишь по настоянию друзей и «заказчиков»»; «мне стало противно, что меня провозгласили каким-то «певцом Петербурга»»; Dobuzhinsky, *Pis'ma*, 311. For examples of the latter proclamation, both in Dobuzhinsky's lifetime and posthumously, see S. K. Makovsky, *Grafika M. V. Dobuzhinskogo* (Berlin: "Petropolis," 1924),

18; Vera Kovarsky, "M. V. Dobujinsky—Pictorial Poet of St. Petersburg," *Russian Review* 19, no. 1 (January 1960): 24–37; and Susan Cook Summer, "The Poet of St. Petersburg," *Columbia Library Columns* 33, no. 2 (February 1984): 3–11.

56. For a detailed discussion of the image of St. Petersburg in Nabokov's oeuvre, see Pekka Tammi, "The St. Petersburg Text and Its Nabokovian Texture," in his *Russian Subtexts in Nabokov's Fiction: Four Essays* (Tampere, Finland: Tampere University Press, 1999), 67–90; Anna Lisa Crone and Jennifer Jean Day, *My Petersburg / Myself: Mental Architecture and Imaginative Space in Modern Russian Letters* (Bloomington, Ind.: Slavica, 2004); and Aleksandr Dolinin, "Proza Nabokova i 'Peterburgskii Tekst' russkoi literatury," in his *Istinnaia zhizn' pisatelia Sirina*, 346–66. In their perceptions of St. Petersburg, these authors are indebted to the works on the city as a myth- and text-generating entity by Yuri Lotman and Vladimir Toporov, first and foremost. See the collection *Semiotika goroda i gorodskoi kul'tury: Peterburg*, in *Trudy po znakovym sistemam* 18 (1984). See also Grigory Kaganov, *Images of Space: St. Petersburg in the Visual and Verbal Arts*, trans. Sidney Monas (Stanford, Calif.: Stanford University Press, 1997).

57. Dobuzhinsky, *Vospominaniia*, 207.

58. Dobuzhinsky, *Pis'ma*, 318.

59. «Какая ласка для глаза, какое очарование для памяти!»; Stark, "Perepiska Vladimira Nabokova s M. V. Dobuzhinskim," 97.

60. See Boyd, *Vladimir Nabokov: The Russian Years*, 258–59.

61. Dobuzhinsky, *Pis'ma*, 200.

62. Translated by Gavriel Shapiro with Dmitri Nabokov. «Вчера с Бенуа и Сомовым сидел у милейшего Добужинского»; «Провожу день рождения так: завтракаю у Татариновых, затем солнце, затем еду к Sylvia Beach, затем в *Candide* с Дусей, затем к Leon, а если успею, к Добужинскому, который пишет мой портрет»; «Добужинский сделал мой портрет; по-моему, похоже». Quoted by permission of the Estate of Vladimir Nabokov. All rights reserved.

Vladimir (1892–1961) and Raisa (née Fleishits, pseud. Raissa Tarr, 1890–1974) Tatarinov were poets and Nabokov's friends. Incidentally, Vladimir Tatarinov wrote a review of S. K. Makovsky's monograph, *Grafika Dobuzhinskogo*, in which he speaks very highly of both the book and the artist; see his "Grafika Dobuzhinskogo," *Zhar-ptitsa* 13 (1925): 33–34. Sylvia Woodbridge Beach (1887–1962) was a writer, bookseller, and publisher and a friend of James Joyce. *Candide* was a weekly literary magazine (1924–44); Doussia Ergaz (1904–67) was Nabokov's French literary agent between the early 1930s and 1965; Paul (1893–1942) and Lucie (née Ponizovsky, pseud. Noel, 1899–1972) Léon were mutual friends of Nabokov and Joyce and introduced the two writers to each other in the late 1930s in Paris. Nabokov met Lucie, who later "checked his manuscript" of *The Real Life of Sebastian Knight* "for solecisms," as early as 1920, the year her brother, Alex, whom Nabokov befriended, entered Cambridge University. See Boyd, *Vladimir Nabokov: The Russian Years,* 503 and 178. See also Lucie Léon Noel, "Playback," *TriQuarterly* 17 (Winter 1970): 209–19.

63. «с очень большой просьбой»; Stark, "Perepiska Vladimira Nabokova s M. V. Dobuzhinskim," 95.

64. Translated by Gavriel Shapiro with Dmitri Nabokov. «наша гостиная отделана . . . Добужинским: мы развесили по стенам «фотографии» и «тарелку» от «События», и получился какой-то будуар начала века»; see Stark, "Perepiska Vladimira Nabokova s M. V. Dobuzhinskim," 99 and 106.

65. «Очень мне не терпится пожать вашу большую умную руку»; «Я часто думаю, какой пробел у меня, что Вы не здесь»; see Stark, "Perepiska Vladimira Nabokova s M. V. Dobuzhinskim," 96 and 100.

66. «Как на зло, те, с кем особенно дружен, живут не в N<ew> Y<ork'e>», «Влад. Набоков-Сирин—в Бостоне»; «Влад: Набоков-Сирин тоже давно уехал (сидит в «Итаке», в университете, читает о русск<ой> литературе лекции и пишет *только* по-английски)»; Dobuzhinsky, *Pis'ma,* 277–78 and 297. In those years, Nabokov resided first in Cambridge, Mass. (1941–48), and then in Ithaca, N.Y. (1948–59), teaching, respectively, at Wellesley College and Cornell University.

67. Translated by Dmitri Nabokov; see *The Nabokovian* 51 (Fall 2003): 4.

68. For a very different treatment of the subject, devoid of any obvious parallels with Dobuzhinsky's sketch, see Georgy Ivanov's eponymous poem (1914) in his *Sobranie sochinenii v trekh tomakh* (Moscow: "Soglasie," 1994), 1:174.

69. See Chugunov, *Mstislav Valerianovich Dobuzhinsky,* 124–25.

70. For the image of this oval plaque, see C. H. de Jonge, *Delft Ceramics,* trans. Marie-Christine Hellin (London: Pall Mall, 1970), plate XIV (between pp. 72 and 73). For information on Delft ceramics, see Henry Pierre Fourest, *Delftware: Faience Production at Delft,* trans. Katherine Wat-

son (New York: Rizzoli, 1980); and Jan Daniel van Dam, *Delffse Porceleyne: Dutch Delftware 1620–1850* (Amsterdam and Zwolle: Rijksmuseum and Uit-geverij Waanders, 2004).

71. S. L. Sobol′, *Istoriia mikroskopa i mikroskopicheskikh issledovanii v Rossii v XVIII veke* (Moscow and Leningrad: Izdatel′stvo Akademii Nauk SSSR, 1949), 30–45; V. F. Levinson-Lessing, "Pervoe puteshestvie Petra I za gra-nitsu," in *Kul′tura i iskusstvo petrovskogo vremeni*, ed. G. N. Komelova (Len-ingrad: "Avrora," 1977), 11–12 and 32. Nabokov could have come across an account of this meeting between the Russian tsar and the Dutch scientist in Scheltema, "Petr Velikii, imperator Rossii, v Gollandii i v Zaandame v 1697 i 1717 gg.," trans. A. S. Latsinsky, *Russkaia Starina* 3 (1916): 387; as cited in Sobol′, *Istoriia mikroskopa,* 31.

72. For the poem's date of composition, see Vladimir Nabokov, *Kak ia liubliu tebia* (Moscow: "Tsentr-100," 1994), 25.

73. See Pushkin, *Complete Works of Alexander Pushkin*, 5:298 and 299; «Петра творенье» and «град Петров», Pushkin, *Polnoe sobranie sochi-nenii*, 5:136 and 137.

74. George Heard Hamilton, *The Art and Architecture of Russia* (New York: Penguin Books, 1983), 265.

75. It is worth noting that almost ten years earlier, in 1917, Nabokov composed a poem, "A Stroll with Jean-Jacques Rousseau" («Прогулка с J.-J. Rousseau»), which he inscribed to Alexander Benois. See A. Terekhov, "Neizdannoe stikhotvorenie V. Nabokova," *Rossiiskii literaturovedcheskii zhurnal* 11 (1997): 316–26.

76. Compare *The Defense*, where Luzhin prefers pencil drawing over oil painting and especially enjoys "to shade, tenderly and evenly, not pressing too hard, in regularly applied strokes" (*Def* 207).

77. Translated by Dmitri Nabokov; see *The Nabokovian* 51 (Fall 2003): 28–31.

78. The barbershop images, evoked by Dobuzhinsky's paintings, appear in *The Defense*. Dobuzhinsky's stage design image is apparently alluded to in a sentence from *Mary*: "They met under the same arch where Liza dies in Tchaikovsky's *The Queen of Spades*" (*Mary* 69). In Tchaikovsky's opera, in contradiction to Pushkin's tale, Liza commits suicide by throwing herself from the bridge over the Zimniaia Kanavka (lit. a "wintry small ditch"); see *Ssoch*, 2:695. Compare the earlier "snow" allusion to Benois' illustra-tion of Pushkin's eponymous tale, *Hermann at the Countess's Driveway*.

79. Compare Vadim Vadimovich's admission: "As to summers, to my

young summers, all of them had bloomed for me on the great country estates of my family. Thus I realized with silly astonishment that, except for picture postcards [. . .], I had never seen my native city in June or July" (*LATH* 210).

80. In a letter to Dobuzhinsky in summer 1940, Nabokov admits that he "was once 'copying'" one of the artist's works, namely his *Okhta Woman* («Охтенка»), which he calls "A Peasant Woman" («Баба»). See Stark, "Perepiska Vladimira Nabokova s M. V. Dobuzhinskim," 97 and 105.

81. On the competitive spirit of ekphrasis, see Marianne Shapiro, "Ecphrasis in Virgil and Dante," *Comparative Literature* 42 (Spring 1990): 97. Similarly, on the "paragonal energy" of ekphrasis and its staging "a contest between rival modes of representations," see Heffernan, *Museum of Words*, 6.

82. «Вы когда-то написали маленькие стихи, посвященные мне. Их у меня нет, а я очень ими дорожу как знаком отличия. Это для меня *Владимир 1-ой* степени и с короной. Если Вы найдете у себя или вспомните, пришлите мне эту регалию»); Stark, "Perepiska Vladimira Nabokova s M. V. Dobuzhinskim," 100.

83. Stark, "Perepiska Vladimira Nabokova s M. V. Dobuzhinskim," 93.

84. I am indebted to Ilya Astrov for his assistance with Russian military awards (electronic communication of June 23, 2000).

85. In *Conclusive Evidence*, this inability is stated but not exemplified, whereas in *Speak, Memory*, another example—"mama"—is added. See, respectively, *CE* 10 and *SM* 28.

86. It is noteworthy that this image can be found already in *The Gift*, set in Berlin: "Among the signs over chemists' shops, stationers' and grocers', which swam before the eyes and, at first, were even incomprehensible, only one could still appear to be written in Russian: Kakao" (*Gift* 80).

87. See Alla Gusarova, comp., *Mstislav Dobuzhinsky: Zhivopis´, grafika, teatr* (Moscow: "Izobrazitel´noe iskusstvo," 1982), 18.

88. «Чижик, чижик, где ты был? На Фонтанке водку пил». It is worth noting that Nabokov employed an amusing version of this ditty in his translation of Lewis Carroll's *Alice's Adventures in Wonderland*—*Ania v strane chudes* (1923); see *Ssoch*, 1:399.

89. See S. S. Nabokov, "Profili," *Nabokovskii vestnik* 2 (1998): 152.

90. See Zil´bershtein and Samkov, *Sergei Diagilev i russkoe iskusstvo*, 2:287.

91. Translated by Gavriel Shapiro with Dmitri Nabokov. «Катки, катки

—на Мойке, на Фонтанке, / в Юсуповском серебряном раю» (*Ssoch,* 1:597). With the line "in the Iusupov silver paradise" Nabokov refers to the Iusupov Garden. At the turn of the twentieth century, in wintertime, its pond would become a skating rink, where skating contests and dancing balls on ice, with fireworks and illuminations, were held. See S. F. Svetlov, *Peterburgskaia zhizn´ v kontse XIX stoletiia (v 1892 godu)* (St. Petersburg: "Giperion," 1998), 45.

92. See Dobuzhinsky, *Vospominaniia,* 15. About the Obvodny Canal, see Naum Sindalovsky, *Peterburg v fol´klore* (St. Petersburg: "Letnii sad," 1999), 191–92.

93. «приторными и фальшивыми»; see Dobuzhinsky, *Vospominaniia,* 127.

94. For a discussion of Semiradsky and some other Russian painters in the novel, see Gavriel Shapiro, "References to Russian Art in *The Defense,*" *The Nabokovian* 50 (Spring 2003): 58.

95. «очень посредственный, но очень знаменитый маринист того времени» (*Ssoch,* 5:172).

96. «мертвечина», «Проталина», «Начало теплых дней» (*Ssoch,* 5: 172 and 686). «Ранняя весна»; for the latter painting, see Vitaly Manin, *Russkii peizazh* (Moscow: "Belyi gorod," 2001), 267.

97. On Nabokov's attitude toward Moscow, see Tammi, "St. Petersburg Text and Its Nabokovian Texture," 78–79.

98. «Идейность и тенденциозность передвижников неизменно отставляли на второй план живописные задачи. Всякая «эстетика» благодаря проповедям Чернышевского и Писарева была изгнана, и «реализм» передвижников был лишен всякого художественного чувства»; Mstislav Dobuzhinsky, "Mir Iskusstva," n.p., 1942, Dobuzhinsky Papers, box 4, p. 27, Bakhmeteff Archive, Columbia University Library, New York City.

99. «многие находят в них известные достоинства, главным образом потому, что они весьма внимательно запечатлевали подробности быта, чисто реалистические»; "Beseda s M. V. Dobuzhinskim," Massapequa, N.Y., November 19, 1957, p. 8, Dobuzhinsky Papers, box 4, Bakhmeteff Archive, Columbia University Library, New York City.

100. See Nabokov, "Diaghilev and a Disciple," 699.

101. Translated by Gavriel Shapiro with Dmitri Nabokov. «громадного прилизанного перовского «Прибоя»» (*Ssoch,* 5:172).

102. «истинно талантливый художник, хотя и ужасал тем, что порой бывал безвкусен»; Dobuzhinsky, *Vospominaniia*, 184.

103. Translated by Gavriel Shapiro with Dmitri Nabokov. «ту бездарнейшую картину бездарного Репина, на которой сорокалетний Онегин целится в кучерявого Собинова» (*Ssoch*, 5:270). Leonid Sobinov (1872–1934) was a famous opera singer (lyrical tenor); one of his best and most memorable parts was that of Vladimir Lensky.

104. For a detailed discussion of Symbolism in Russian art, see A. A. Rusakova, *Simvolizm v russkoi zhivopisi* (Moscow: "Iskusstvo," 1995).

105. Dobuzhinsky, *Vospominaniia*, 141 and 217.

106. «то же видение иных миров и почти одинаковый конец, и тот и другой одиноки в искусстве»; Dobuzhinsky, *Pis′ma*, 112.

107. See Shapiro, "Setting His *Myriad* Faces in His Text," 18.

108. For the *Despair* and *Ada* references to Vrubel, see, respectively, Ol′ga Burenina, "'Otchaianie' kak olakrez russkogo simvolizma," in *Hypertext "Otchaianie" / Sverkhtekst "Despair": Studien zu Vladimir Nabokovs Roman-Rätsel*, ed. Igor Smirnov (Munich: Verlag Otto Sagner, 2000), 184n23; Simon Karlinsky, "Nabokov's Russian Games," in *Critical Essays on Vladimir Nabokov*, ed. Phyllis A. Roth (Boston: G. K. Hall, 1984), 89; and D. Barton Johnson, "A Shimmer of Exact Details: *Ada*'s Art Gallery," in de Vries and Johnson, *Vladimir Nabokov and the Art of Painting*, 106–8.

109. «первых новых настоящих проникновенных русских пейзажистов»; Dobuzhinsky, "Mir Iskusstva," n.p., 1942, Dobuzhinsky Papers, box 4, p. 45, Bakhmeteff Archive, Columbia University Library, New York City.

110. See Vladimir Nabokov, "Natasha," Manuscript Division, Vladimir Nabokov Archives, container 19, p. 11, Library of Congress, Washington D.C. (the sentence, although easily discernible, is crossed out in the manuscript). For the English translation of the story, see Vladimir Nabokov, "Natasha," trans. Dmitri Nabokov, *The New Yorker*, June 9 and 16, 2008, 54–60 (for the mention of "Levitan's landscapes," see p. 59).

111. Nabokov is perfectly on target here: Levitan's "Volga" period lasted from 1887 to 1890. See A. A. Fedorov-Davydov, *Isaak Il′ich Levitan*, 2 vols. (Moscow: "Iskusstvo," 1966), 1:67–141.

112. For a comprehensive discussion of Serov's life and artistic career, see Elizabeth Kridl Valkenier, *Valentin Serov: Portraits of Russia's Silver Age* (Evanston, Ill.: Northwestern University Press, 2001).

113. «замечательного человека», «Он был необыкновенный труженик в искусстве, и, несмотря на длительность, с которой создавались его вещи, они были прекрасны именно своей необычайной свежестью»; Dobuzhinsky, *Vospominaniia,* 203.

114. «Чтобы еще раз увидеть «Девушку [sic] с персиками», мы отправлялись (гостя на Рождественские каникулы в Москве) в лютый холод, в плохо отопленных вагонах, а затем в розвальнях в Мамонтовское «Абрамцево»—и каково было наше разочарование, когда нас даже не впустили (по распоряжению отсутствовавших хозяев) в пустой дом»; Dobuzhinsky, "Zapozdalyi venok na mogilu druga: K. A. Somov," 1.

115. Ada Bredow is looking, of course, for a five-petaled lilac flower, which, according to Russian popular belief, is supposed to bring luck to its finder.

116. Christine Raguet-Bouvart errs when suggesting that the portrait described in *LATH* "could as well be" that of Praskovia Mamontova (1873–1945), Savva Mamontov's niece and Véra's cousin: at the time of Serov's painting her portrait (1889) Praskovia was sixteen, not a "girl of twelve or so"; and although her arms are resting on a garden table, there is no indication that she is holding anything in her hands. See Raguet-Bouvart, "European Art: A Framing Device?" 184–85.

117. Dobuzhinsky, *Vospominaniia,* 141.

118. See O. L. Leikind, K. V. Makhrov, and D. Ia. Severiukhin, comps., *Khudozhniki Russkogo Zarubezh´ia, 1917–1939* (St. Petersburg: "Notabene," 1999), 536–37.

119. «Вернулся Сорин, но его еще не видел. Он продолжает быть хорошим товарищем, но ты сам понимаешь—его искусство ничего мне не говорит»; Dobuzhinsky, *Pis´ma,* 297.

120. On Sorin's ties with the artists, see I. I. Vydrin, comp., *A. N. Benua i M. V. Dobuzhinsky—Perepiska* (St. Petersburg: "Sad iskusstv," 2003).

121. For information on Melita Cholokashvili and Meri Shervashidze, who was also known under her married name, Eristavi, or Eristova in the Russified form, see Alexandre Vassiliev, *Beauty in Exile* (New York: Harry N. Abrams, 2000).

122. See Sergei Makovsky, "Portrety S. A. Sorina," *Zhar-ptitsa* 8 (1922): 2–6.

123. See, for example, the obituary for Marina de Kovalevskaya, *Rus-*

skaia Mysl´, December 23, 1993–January 5, 1994, 23. Compare Nabokov's own invention—Dmitri de Midoff (*LATH* 90).

124. See L. Ia. Abramov et al., eds., *Shakhmatnyi slovar´* (Moscow: "Fizkul´tura i sport," 1964), 199.

125. «Тут выставка Малявина, мы были в субботу с Додей—какой это ужас, какая безвкусица, просто позор / . . . / Какой дурак—позор русского искусства!»; Dobuzhinsky, *Pis´ma,* 260. Dodia was the nickname of Dobuzhinsky's younger son, Vsevolod.

126. «била в глаза» (*Ssoch,* 2:375).

127. «сарафан—кумачевый огонь», «резкая, исчерна-синяя тень на лбу, почти неправдоподобная тень—к ней надо привыкнуть»; Sergei Makovsky, "Maliavin," *Zhar-ptitsa* 10 (1923): 2.

128. «Баба в кумачовом платке до бровей ела яблоко», «ее черная тень на заборе ела яблоко побольше» (*Ssoch,* 2:375).

129. «ухмыляясь и жмурясь от знойного света»; «электрический свет жирно ее обливал, и краски поразили его, как солнечный удар». See, respectively, Makovsky, "Maliavin," 2; and *Ssoch,* 2:375.

130. «С ней [Гончаровой] и Ларионов<ым> вижусь. Она здорово талантливый человек, талантливее его»; «Дягилевская выставка закрывается 16 янв., и жаль, если Вы ее не увидите, собрано много превосходных произведений, доминируют Бакст, Бенуа, Гончарова, больше всего последняя—самый театральный талант, по-моему»; Dobuzhinsky, *Pis´ma,* 173 and 307.

131. For a discussion of Nabokov's pen name Sirin and its various meanings, see Shapiro, *Delicate Markers,* 9–29.

CHAPTER 5

The first epigraph for this chapter is from Benois, *Moi vospominaniia,* 1:684: ««История живописи в XIX веке» была очень скоро переведена на многие языки, и всюду она порождала страстные толки; всюду старики были возмущены ею, ее жестокими переоценками, всюду молодежь приходила от нее в восторг».

The second epigraph is from Dobuzhinsky, *Vospominaniia,* 156: «я запоем читал и Мутера (мне прислал отец многотомное русское издание его «Истории живописи»)».

1. One notable recent exception is the monograph by Rotraud Schlei-nitz, *Richard Muther—Ein provokativer Kunstschriftsteller zur Zeit der Münchener Secession* (Hildesheim, Ger.: Georg Olms Verlag, 1993).

2. Many years later (in 1914), Zinaida Vengerova, who translated Muther's three-volume set into Russian, did not make a good impression on Nabokov. The writer recalls how Vengerova, who was translating the works of H. G. Wells at the time and who attended a dinner in his honor at the Nabokov residence, made an embarrassing mistake when she told the English guest that her favorite novel of his was *The Lost World,* the novel by Sir Arthur Conan Doyle, when evidently thinking about *The War of the Worlds* (*SO* 104).

3. «Редакция «Мир Искусства» начала свое существование шесть лет до того, что был затеян и появился в свет наш журнал»; Benois, *Moi vospominaniia,* 1:683.

4. «Более отчетливую форму получило наше художественное вожделение благодаря толчку, полученному извне. Таким толчком явилась книга [. . .] «Geschichte der Malerei im XIX. Jahrhundert» Рихарда Мутера»; «Первый же выпуск [. . .] произвел на меня впечатление какого-то откровения»; «успех ее был прямо-таки *мировым*»; «Постепенно с нее началось изменение самого «тона» художественной критики. Она же дала общественному мнению по вопросам современного искусства род нити Ариадны, новые мерила и новые формулировки»); Benois, *Moi vospominaniia,* 1:683–84.

5. «Мутер виноват тем, что написал лучшую в европейской ли-тературе книгу о современной живописи»; Igor´ Grabar´, "Otvet g. Zhanu Broshe," *Mir iskusstva* 10 (1899), "Khudozhestvennaia khronika" section, 116. Nabokov was apparently familiar with this article and other references to Muther in the journal, as it was available to him in his fa-ther's library. See *Sistematicheskii katalog biblioteki Vladimira Dmitrievicha Nabokova,* 38 (# 882).

6. «историко-критическую деятельность»; Benois, *Moi vospomina-niia,* 1:685.

7. See Zil´bershtein and Savinov, *Aleksandr Benua razmyshliaet . . .,* 41, 6, and 45.

8. «просветившей» его ««Истории живописи» Мутера», которую он читал «запоем» и «продолжал с увлечением штудировать»; see Dobuzhinsky, *Vospominaniia,* 127, 156, 163, and 383–84.

9. *Sistematicheskii katalog biblioteki Vladimira Dmitrievicha Nabokova*, 45 (# 1015).

10. «сделались общим достоянием и так пропитали общество, что даже самые консервативные люди и те стали говорить «словами Мутера»»; Alexander Benois, "Khudozhestvennye pis´ma: Muter," *Rech´*, July 23 (August 5), 1909, 2.

11. «носились в воздухе и до книги Мутера, но лишь она дала им плотность и стройность, полную убедительность и смелую исключительность»; Benois, "Khudozhestvennye pis´ma: Muter."

12. «по Мутеру историческое значение художника зависит от его роли в «общеевропейском духовном концерте», важнейшим критерием оценки является индивидуальное своеобразие мастера, а качество картины, минуя социологию и требования «злобы дня», определяется прежде всего живописными достоинствами»; Mark Etkind, *A. N. Benua i russkaia khudozhestvennaia kul´tura* (Leningrad: "Khudozhnik RSFSR," 1988), 40.

13. «культом красоты и высокой художественной культуры»; Sergei Lifar´, *Diagilev* (St. Petersburg: "Kompozitor," 1993), 67.

14. «Великая сила искусства заключается именно в том, что оно самоцельно, самополезно и главное—свободно»; «Творец должен любить лишь красоту и лишь с нею вести беседу во время нежного, таинственного проявления своей божественной природы»; Sergei Diagilev, "Slozhnye voprosy," *Mir iskusstva* 1–2 (1899): 15 and 16.

15. I employ the phrase "by a nail" to indicate the predestination that Millais had in mind rather than the more customary expression "on a nail," which suggests an accident.

16. Muther, *History of Modern Painting*, 3:22 and 25; for this passage in the Russian translation, see Muther, *Istoriia zhivopisi v XIX veke*, 2:358.

17. «стружки на полу» (*Ssoch*, 1:546).

18. Translated by Gavriel Shapiro with Dmitri Nabokov. «он вспомнил домик в переулке пестром, / и голубей, и стружки на полу» (ibid.).

19. For a discussion of the painting, see Malcolm Warner, "John Everett Millais, *Christ in the Carpenter's Shop* (*Christ in the House of His Parents*), 1849–50," in *The Pre-Raphaelites*, ed. Leslie Parris (London: Tate Gallery, 1994), 77–79.

20. For the painting's provenance at the Tate Gallery I am indebted to Jessica Collins, assistant archivist of the National Gallery (London).

21. Vladimir Nabokov, "The Glasses of St. Joseph," trans. Dmitri Nabokov, *The Nabokovian* 54 (Spring 2005): 4.

22. Warner, "John Everett Millais, *Christ in the Carpenter's Shop*," 78.

23. See Muther, *Istoriia zhivopisi v XIX veke*, 3:415. Strictly speaking, in the 1880s Böcklin had created at least five variants on the subject. In his book, however, Muther reproduces the last version.

24. On the recurrent manifestation of death in the novel, see M. A. Dmitrovskaia, "Ot pervoi metafory k poslednei: Smysl finala romana V. Nabokova 'Mashen´ka'," in *Tekst, intertekst, kul´tura: Sbornik dokladov mezhdunarodnoi nauchnoi konferentsii, Moskva, 4–7 aprelia 2001 goda*, ed. V. P. Grigor´ev and N. A. Fateeva (Moscow: "Azbukovnik," 2001), 306–7.

25. On the popularity of *The Isle of the Dead* in Russia at the turn of the twentieth century, see Iu. K. Shcheglov, *Romany I. Il´fa i E. Petrova: Sputnik chitatelia*, 2 vols. (Vienna: Wiener Slawistischer Almanach, 1990–91), 1:179–80.

26. For a detailed discussion of both versions of Delacroix's painting in their relation to *Invitation to a Beheading*, see Shapiro, *Delicate Markers*, 194–96.

27. The painting's title that Muther employs in his book invokes that of Charles Baudelaire's sonnet inspired by Delacroix's painting. For the first mention of this connection, see Aleksandr Dolinin, "Tsvetnaia spiral´ Nabokova," in *Rasskazy. Priglashenie na kazn´. Roman. Esse, interv´iu, retsenzii*, by Vladimir Nabokov (Moscow: "Kniga," 1989), 466–67. For the connection between Nabokov's novel and Baudelaire's sonnet inspired by Delacroix, see also Shapiro, *Delicate Markers*, 192–93.

28. See also Shapiro, *Delicate Markers*, 96.

29. «вся фигура девушки написана в белых тонах»; Muther, *Istoriia zhivopisi v XIX veke*, 1:297. The painting exists in three known versions: the original, privately owned until 1995, since then has been at the National Gallery (Prague, Czech Republic), and two copies, one at the Hermitage Museum (St. Petersburg, Russia) and the other at the Frye Art Museum (Seattle, Wash.). For the provenance of the first and third versions of the painting, I am indebted to Veronika Hulikova and Donna Kovalenko, respectively. The provenance information about the Hermitage variant may be found on the museum's website—http://www.hermitagemuseum.org. The site lists as its source of entry the Leningrad State Purchasing Commission (1936) and indicates that the painting was formerly in the collec-

tion of the industrialist Franz San-Galli (Sangalli), St. Petersburg. (Curiously, Nabokov describes "weighty belly sleds from Sangalli's" in *The Gift* [*Gift* 20].) On all three variants, the roses are depicted as pink. Since the European variants were in private hands and the American variant was inaccessible to Nabokov at the time of his composing the novel, it is safe to conclude that the writer's sole familiarity with the painting was through Muther's book, where the flowers appear very light in tone, presumably white. Nabokov apparently had no doubts about the color of the roses, as it is usually white that is associated with death and martyrdom. See, for example, Nabokov's early poem "Childhood" ("Detstvo," 1922), in which its lyrical "I" recalls a picture that portrays a dead maiden amidst white roses; see *Ssoch,* 1:514.

30. «изображала сцену мученичества и всегда героем их [были] или беспомощная женщина, или жалкое дитя»; Muther, *Istoriia zhivopisi v XIX veke,* 1:297.

31. Luba Freedman, *Titian's Portraits Through Aretino's Lens* (University Park: Pennsylvania State University Press, 1995), 71 and 137.

32. «Что это у тебя, сказочный огородник? Мак-с. А то? Лук-с, ваша светлость» (*Ssoch,* 4:215).

33. Presently, this painting is located at the Museum Ostdeutsche Galerie in Regensburg. The museum had acquired the painting in 1970; prior to its acquisition by the museum, the painting was privately owned. I am indebted to Dr. Gerhardt Leistner, head of the museum's art and sculpture collection, for this information (electronic communication of April 3, 2000).

34. On various manifestations of blindness (physical, moral, etc.) in Nabokov's characters, and specifically in Albert Albinus (Bruno Krechmar [Kretschmar] in the Russian original), see Khasin, "The Theatre of Privacy," 111–12.

35. «Угрюмых тройка есть певцов—/Шихматов, Шаховской, Шишков». For more details, see Gavriel Shapiro, "Nabokov's Allusions: Dividedness and Polysemy," *Russian Literature* 43 (1998): 330–32.

36. See Stephen Duffy, *Paul Delaroche, 1797–1856: Paintings in the Wallace Collection* (London: Trustees of the Wallace Collection, 1997), 21–22.

37. See Muther, *Istoriia zhivopisi v XIX veke,* 1:229.

38. Ibid., 1:22–23.

39. Ibid., 1:243 and 246.

40. On the numerous pictorial representations of the assassination, see Claude Mazauric et al., *Charlotte Corday: Une Normande dans la Révolution* (Versailles: Musée Lambinet, 1989).

41. In Nabokov's own translation of the novel into Russian, a "maiden" is rendered as «девочка», that is, a "little girl" (*LoR* 17).

42. See Muther, *Istoriia zhivopisi v XIX veke*, 3:352.

43. See Gennady Barabtarlo, "Those Who Favor Fire (On *The Enchanter*)," *Russian Literature Triquarterly* 24 (1991): 105–7.

44. See, respectively, Claude Keisch and Marie Ursula Riemann-Reyher, eds., *Adolph Menzel, 1815–1905: Between Romanticism and Impressionism* (New Haven, Conn.: Yale University Press, 1996), 234; and Jens Christian Jensen, *Adolph Menzel* (Cologne: DuMont Buchverlag, 1982), 82.

45. *The Flute Concert of Frederick the Great at Sans Souci* was considered by far Menzel's most popular painting and frequently served as the model for *tableaux vivants*. See Keisch and Riemann-Reyher, *Adolph Menzel*, 245.

CHAPTER 6

The original Russian for this chapter's second epigraph reads: «но наши скитания не всегда бывают унылы, и мужественная тоска по родине не всегда мешает нам насладиться чужой страной, изощренным одиночеством в чужую электрическую ночь, на мосту, на площади, на вокзале»; see *Ssoch*, 2:646–47.

1. Ralph M. Leck, *Georg Simmel and Avant-Garde Sociology: The Birth of Modernity, 1880–1920* (Amherst, N.Y.: Humanity Books, 2000), 33.

2. For the emergence of Berlin as the capital of Germany and its chief metropolis, as well as for a historical survey of German Expressionism, I consulted Otto Friedrich, *Before the Deluge: A Portrait of Berlin in the 1920's* (New York: Harper and Row, 1972); Giles MacDonogh, *Berlin* (New York: St. Martin's, 1998); Dorothy Rowe, *Representing Berlin: Sexuality and the City in Imperial and Weimar Germany* (Aldershot, Eng., and Burlington, Vt.: Ashgate, 2003); John Willett, *Expressionism* (London: Weidenfeld and Nicolson, 1970); Paul Vogt, *Expressionism: German Painting 1905–1920,* trans. Antony Vivis and Robert Erich Wolf (New York: Harry N. Abrams, 1980); Stephanie Barron and Wolf-Dieter Dube, *German Expressionism: Art and Society* (London: Thames and Hudson, 1997); Shulamith Behr, *Expressionism* (London: Tate Gallery, 1999); and Sabine Rewald, with essays by Ian Bu-

ruma and Matthias Eberle, *Glitter and Doom: German Portraits from the 1920s* (New York: Metropolitan Museum of Art, 2006).

3. See Henrik Reeh, *Ornaments of the Metropolis: Siegfried Kracauer and Modern Urban Culture* (Cambridge, Mass.: MIT Press, 2004), 19.

4. Dieter E. Zimmer, "*Mary,*" in Alexandrov, ed., *Garland Companion to Vladimir Nabokov,* 350.

5. It is noteworthy that Evgeny Zamiatin (1884–1937), Nabokov's compatriot and fellow writer, perceived Berlin "as a condensed, 80-percent version of Petersburg." See his "Autobiography, 1929," in *A Soviet Heretic: Essays by Yevgeny Zamyatin,* ed. and trans. Mirra Ginsburg (Chicago: University of Chicago Press, 1970), 13.

6. For an illuminating account of Grosz's life and artistic career, see Herbert Knust, "George Grosz: Literature and Caricature," in *Montage, Satire and Cultism: Germany Between the Wars,* ed. Herbert Knust (Champaign: University of Illinois Press, 1975), 20–49.

7. M. Kay Flavell, *George Grosz: A Biography* (New Haven, Conn., and London: Yale University Press, 1988), 314.

8. For a detailed discussion of the painting, see Peter Springer, *Hand and Head: Ernst Ludwig Kirchner's "Self-Portrait as Soldier,"* trans. Susan Ray (Berkeley: University of California Press, 2002).

9. Anton Denikin (1872–1947) was the commander (April 1918–April 1920) of the White (Volunteer) Army.

10. Boyd, *Vladimir Nabokov: The Russian Years,* 133.

11. Vladimir Nabokov, "Revolution," trans. Dmitri Nabokov, *Paris Review* 175 (Fall/Winter 2005): 171–73.

12. It is noteworthy that Kirchner's *Self-Portrait as Soldier* served as the cover for a recent edition of this novel by Remarque. See Springer, *Hand and Head,* 11.

13. By the late 1920s, however, Grosz found himself more and more at odds with the German Communist Party (KPD). For a detailed discussion on the subject, see Barbara McCloskey, *George Grosz and the Communist Party: Art and Radicalism in Crisis, 1918 to 1936* (Princeton, N.J.: Princeton University Press, 1997).

14. See, respectively, Rose-Carol Washton Long, ed. and annot., *German Expressionism: Documents from the End of the Wilhelmine Empire to the Rise of National Socialism* (New York: G. K. Hall, 1993), illus. 34 and 26; and Frank Whitford, *The Berlin of George Grosz* (New Haven, Conn., and London: Yale University Press, 1997), illus. 72.

Being affiliated with the German Socialist Party, Pechstein initially objected to the KPD uprising and produced a number of anti-Spartacist posters. Later, however, in the spirit of reconciliation, he altogether stopped his anti-KPD propaganda and accepted the success of the Spartacist takeover. See Joan Weinstein, *The End of Expressionism: Art and the November Revolution in Germany, 1918–19* (Chicago and London: University of Chicago Press, 1990), 51–55.

15. On Nabokov's being a stranger in Berlin, see Karl Schlögel, "Stadtwahrnehmung: Nabokov und die Taxifahrer," in his *Berlin Ostbahnhof Europas: Russen und Deutsche in ihrem Jahrhundert* (Berlin: Siedler Verlag, 1998), 159–76.

16. See G. I. Chugunov, "M. V. Dobuzhinsky i ego 'Vospominaniia,'" in Dobuzhinsky, *Vospominaniia*, 359.

17. «вывороченные кишки сифилитических баб и прочие паскудства»; «это человек, ушибленный войной и, вероятно, безнадежно»; Dobuzhinsky, *Pis'ma*, 191.

18. About the Malik Press's "hit-and-run" distribution of Grosz's artwork in Berlin, see Rainer Rumold, *The Janus Face of the German Avant-Garde: From Expressionism Toward Postmodernism* (Evanston, Ill.: Northwestern University Press, 2002), 54.

19. On Berlin's Museum of the Contemporary Art and its founder, Ludwig Justi (1876–1957), the then director of the Nationalgalerie, see Kurt Winkler, "Ludwig Justi—Der Konservative Revolutionär," in *Avantgarde und Publikum: Zur Rezeption avantgardistischer Kunst in Deutschland 1905–1933*, ed. Henrike Junge (Cologne: Böhlau Verlag, 1992), 181–83; and Thomas W. Gaehtgens and Kurt Winkler, eds., *Ludwig Justi: Werden—Wirken—Wissen: Lebenserinnerungen aus fünf Jahrzehnten*, 2 vols. (Berlin: Nicolai, 2000), 1:433–68.

20. See Kjeld Bülow, *George Grosz: A Bibliography and Other Check Lists* (Copenhagen: Booktrader, 1993), 86–87.

21. Flavell, *George Grosz*, 312. By the late 1930s, however, Grosz abandoned this sociopolitically charged attitude altogether; see McCloskey, *George Grosz and the Communist Party*, 193.

22. See Boyd, *Vladimir Nabokov: The Russian Years*, 88–89, 173, and 376–77. «Сегодня иду на футбольный матч с Кянджунцевыми»; Vladimir Nabokov Archives, Montreux. Quoted by permission of the Estate of Vladimir Nabokov. All rights reserved. Savely Kiandzhuntsev was Nabokov's Tenishev School classmate.

23. Dmitri Nabokov in a telephone communication on March 28, 2004. Dmitri Nabokov also writes about his father: "He did enjoy watching Lev Yashin [1929–90, the renowned Russian soccer goalkeeper of the 1950s and 1960s]. Among other reasons, besides the moon landing, that my parents temporarily ordered a TV, were the Olympics, major tennis finals, and sometimes hockey championships." See Nabokv-L, Dmitri Nabokov's posting of August 6, 2003.

24. Boyd, *Vladimir Nabokov: The Russian Years,* 100, 173, and 267. It looks like Nabokov inherited his fondness for boxing from his father. Benois reported that V. D. "Nabokov is himself a great admirer as well as virtuoso of boxing; it is not for nothing that he is daily engaged in exercising this art together with his sons" («Набоков сам большой поклонник и тоже виртуоз бокса; недаром он ежедневно предается упражнениям в этом искусстве вместе с сыновьями»). See Benois, *Moi dnevnik,* 175. And the senior Nabokov passed this fondness on to his eldest son. Nabokov brought to the United States "the two pairs of boxing gloves" that he "used for coaching sessions with Dmitri." See Boyd, *Vladimir Nabokov: The American Years,* 12.

25. See *Ssoch,* 1:749–54 and 814. For a detailed description of the match, see Dieter E. Zimmer, *Nabokovs Berlin* (Berlin: Nicolai, 2001), 78–79.

26. Translated by Gavriel Shapiro with Dmitri Nabokov. «Греки играли в хоккей и били по punching ball. Спорт, будь это охота, или рыцарский турнир, или петушиный бой, или добрая русская лапта, всегда веселил и увлекал человечество. Искать в нем признаки варварства уже потому бессмысленно, что настоящий варвар–всегда прескверный спортсмен»; Vladimir Nabokov, "On Generalities," publ. Aleksandr Dolinin, *Zvezda* 4 (1999): 13–14. *Lapta* is mentioned in *Podvig* and is translated in *Glory* as "tag-bat"; see, respectively, *Ssoch,* 3:226 and *Glory* 175.

27. On Nabokov's outlook toward athletics, reminiscent of those of the ancient Greeks and Romans, specifically in *Glory,* see Buhks, *Eshafot v khrustal'nom dvortse,* 80. See also Giovanni de' Bardi's *Discourse on the Game of Florentine Calcio* (1580), in which the Renaissance author speaks of *calcio,* a precursor of soccer, as "a public game, of two teams of young men, on foot and without arms, who, in an affable manner and for the sake of honor, contend to pass an inflated ball from the *posta* (on one end of the middle line) forward to the opposite goal." Bardi argues that "from *calcio* there result all the fruits of the gymnastic art which are so much praised

by so many philosophers, physicians, *grammatici,* and other serious and learned writers. These fruits are in substance: to make the body sound, dexterous, and robust, and to make the mind awake, sharp and desirous of virtuous victory." As cited in Theodor E. Mommsen, "Football in Renaissance Florence," *Yale University Library Gazette* 16, no. 1 (July 1941): 14 and 16–17.

28. See Whitford, *The Berlin of George Grosz,* illus. 8 and 9.

29. See, respectively, Peter Selz, *Max Beckmann* (New York: Abbeville, 1996), illus. 104; Donald E. Gordon, *Ernst Ludwig Kirchner* (Cambridge, Mass.: Harvard University Press, 1968), illus. 974–76 and esp. pl. 108; Jill Lloyd, *German Expressionism: Primitivism and Modernity* (New Haven, Conn., and London: Yale University Press, 1991), illus. 107; and Peter-Klaus Schuster, ed., *George Grosz: Berlin–New York* (Berlin: Ars Nicolai, 1994), pl. IX.29. On the history of Grosz's portrait of Schmeling, see Max Schmeling, *Max Schmeling: An Autobiography,* trans. George B. von der Lippe (Chicago: Bonus Books, 1998), 28–30. For Grosz's fascination with boxing, see Schuster, *George Grosz,* 268–69. For Grosz's seeing in boxing "a parallel activity for his own strategy as a critic of the status quo" (129), and more broadly, for the attitude to boxing and sports in general in Weimar Germany, see David Bathrick, "Max Schmeling on the Canvas: Boxing as an Icon of Weimar Culture," *New German Critique* 51 (Autumn 1990): 113–36.

30. For a detailed analysis of the story, see Julian W. Connolly, "The Play of Light and Shadow in 'The Fight,'" in *A Small Alpine Form: Studies in Nabokov's Short Fiction,* ed. Charles Nicol and Gennady Barabtarlo (New York and London: Garland, 1993), 25–37.

31. See Whitford, *The Berlin of George Grosz,* 49.

32. Serge Sabarsky, *George Grosz: The Berlin Years* (New York: Rizzoli, 1985), 30. For a detailed discussion on the subject of sex murder, see Maria Tatar, *Lustmord: Sexual Murder in Weimar Germany* (Princeton, N.J.: Princeton University Press, 1995).

33. For the most recent discussion on the subject, see Michael White, "The Grosz Case: Paranoia, Self-Hatred and Anti-Semitism," *Oxford Art Journal* 30, no. 3 (2007): 431–53.

34. Hermann Karlovich apparently "borrowed" this idea from Thomas de Quincey's "On Murder Considered as One of the Fine Arts" (1827). See Davydov, *"Teksty-matreški" Vladimira Nabokova,* 93–97.

35. Once again, on Nabokov's penchant for comic art, see Shapiro, "Nabokov and Comic Art"; Brown, "Krazy, Ignatz, and Vladimir: Nabokov

and the Comic Strip"; and Shapiro, "Nabokov and Comic Art: Additional Observations and Remarks."

36. For a more elaborate analysis of this painting by Dix, see Rowe, *Representing Berlin*, 161–62.

37. The Schuster catalogue, for example, lists the painting as *Ehepaar. Mann und Frau.* See Schuster, *George Grosz*, 349.

38. On the cult of the machine and a fascination with robots in literature and the performing arts with regard to *King, Queen, Knave,* see Jeff Edmunds, "Look at Valdemar! (A Beautified Corpse Revived)," *Nabokov Studies* 2 (1995): 163–64.

39. Boyd confirmed establishing this connection, but was unable to retrieve his old files, and suggested I rely on Zimmer's reference as the source (electronic communication of September 2, 2005). See Zimmer, *Nabokovs Berlin*, 66. Incidentally, Nabokov implicitly expressed his opinion on KaDeWe in *The Gift*, in which Fyodor dubs it "a huge department store that sold all forms of local bad taste"; that Nabokov has KaDeWe in mind is clear from his mentioning his protagonist "crossing Wittenberg Square" (*Gift* 166), on one side of which the department store stands.

40. For a more detailed discussion, see Nora Buhks, "*Locus-poeticus: Salon de coiffure* v russkoi kul´ture nachala XX veka," *Slavic Almanac* 10, no. 1 (2004): 9–10.

41. Zimmer, *Nabokovs Berlin*, 141.

42. For a discussion of the mannequin motif in *King, Queen, Knave* and for linking this motif to the German literary tradition, specifically to Johann Ludwig Tieck and E. T. A. Hoffmann, see Maria Virolainen, "Angloiazychnoe tvorchestvo Nabokova kak inobytie russkoi slovesnosti," in her *Istoricheskie metamorfozy russkoi slovesnosti* (St. Petersburg: "Amfora," 2007), 446.

43. Boyd, *Vladimir Nabokov: The Russian Years*, 282.

44. Nicole Parrot, *Mannequins* (Paris: Editions Colona, 1981), 101.

45. «Выброшенный из России через Крым, где пришлось пережить один из самых тяжких эпизодов братоубийственной смуты, Сирин побывал в Греции, Лондоне, Париже, в Швейцарии, Германии. Что же мог видеть в эти годы его зоркий глаз, кроме настойчивого извращения человеческой природы, угашения смысла жизни, усилий создать робота и таких симптоматических успехов в этом направлении»; I. V. Gessen, *Gody izgnaniia: Zhiznennyi otchet* (Paris: YMCA, 1979), 99.

46. Whitford, *The Berlin of George Grosz*, 122. For a detailed, nuanced reading of this piece, see Brigid Doherty, "Berlin Dada: Montage and Embodiment of Modernity, 1916–1920" (Ph.D. diss., University of California, Berkeley, 1996), 159–69.

47. For a discussion of Nabokov's perception of automatism being at the core of totalitarianism, see Michael Glynn, *Vladimir Nabokov: Bergsonian and Russian Formalist Influences in His Novels* (New York: Palgrave Macmillan, 2007), 150–51.

48. See Dobuzhinsky, *Vospominaniia,* between 224 and 225.

49. For Dix's *War Cripples,* see Fritz Löffler, *Otto Dix: Life and Work,* trans. R. J. Hollingdale (New York: Holmes and Meier, 1982), illus. 28.

50. George Grosz, *The Autobiography of George Grosz: A Small Yes and a Big No,* trans. Arnold J. Pomerans (London and New York: Allison and Busby, 1982), 95.

51. For the painting, see Whitford, *The Berlin of George Grosz,* illus. 75.

52. For a detailed analysis of this painting, see Rowe, *Representing Berlin,* 167–79.

53. It is worth noting that, unlike Nabokov, most Russian émigrés in and visitors to Berlin in the 1920s and 1930s had a rather one-sided, negative perception of the city. See Thomas Urban, "Berlin—'Stiefmutter der russischen Städte'" in his *Vladimir Nabokov: Blaue Abende in Berlin* (Berlin: Propyläen Verlag, 1999), 15–42; Alexander Dolinin, "'The Stepmother of Russian Cities': Berlin of the 1920s Through the Eyes of Russian Writers," in *Cold Fusion: Aspects of the German Cultural Presence in Russia,* ed. Gennady Barabtarlo (New York: Berghahn Books, 2000), 225–40. For a somewhat different treatment of the subject, in which "Nabokov's position with respect to Berlin" is compared to that of "a Baudelairean *flâneur,*" see Alexander Dolinin, "Clio Laughs Last: Nabokov's Answer to Historicism," in Connolly, *Nabokov and His Fiction,* 202–3.

54. Georg Simmel, "The Metropolis and Mental Life," in *The Sociology of Georg Simmel,* ed. and trans. Kurt H. Wolff (New York: Free Press of Glencoe, 1964), 424.

55. Thus in his 1920 essay, Friedrich Markus Huebner names Simmel among the philosophical precursors of Expressionism. See Huebner's "Der Expressionismus in Deutschland, 1920," in *Expressionismus: Der Kampf um eine literarische Bewegung,* ed. Paul Raabe (Zurich: Arche Verlag, 1987), 139.

56. Nabokov's substantial measure of dispassionate objectivity in his

portrayal of life in Berlin calls to mind another essay by Simmel—"The Stranger," in *Sociology of Georg Simmel*, 402–8.

57. In this poem of 1922, the young Nabokov vows: "neither by thought nor by word shall I sin against your Muse" («ни помыслом, ни словом не согрешу пред музою твоей») (*Stikhi* 38). For a brief discussion of the poem, see Shrayer, *World of Nabokov's Stories*, 244.

CONCLUSION

1. For a detailed discussion of epiphanies in literature, those "sudden gifts of vision" (p. 1), see Martin Bidney, *Patterns of Epiphany: From Wordsworth to Tolstoy, Pater, and Barrett Browning* (Carbondale and Edwardsville: Southern Illinois University Press, 1997).

2. Gerard de Vries erroneously takes this good-humored remark by Dobuzhinsky at its face value when he asserts that Nabokov as a painter "lacked the talent with which so many Russian authors, such as Zhukovsky and Lermontov, were endowed"; see de Vries and Johnson, *Vladimir Nabokov and the Art of Painting*, 16.

3. I foresee some critics pointing to the novels *Invitation to a Beheading* and *Bend Sinister,* and the story "Conversation Piece, 1945." I obviously speak here about the prevailing tendency in Nabokov's aesthetics. "Conversation Piece, 1945" is somewhat of an aberration in Nabokov's literary canon and is probably the weakest of his stories. As for the two novels, they may indeed be read, in Nabokov's own words, as "absolutely final indictments of Russian and German totalitarianism" (*SO* 156). But it would be a gross oversimplification to reduce them to this single reading, which constitutes merely one of multitudinous semantic strands, whereas the German Expressionist painters intended the sociopolitical to be the main, if not the sole, interpretation of their art.

4. For Stalin's pronouncement, see, for example, Mikhail Vaiskopf, *Pisatel' Stalin* (Moscow: Novoe literaturnoe obozrenie, 2001), 343.

5. Boyd has remarked with regard to Nabokov's early story "A Letter That Never Reached Russia": "Here again Nabokov serves up the world according to his secret recipe for happiness: detach the mind from accepting a humdrum succession of moments, and everything becomes magical, a masterpiece of precision and harmony, a gift of absurd generosity," and

Boyd has noted more generally that "Nabokov had two great gifts as a writer and a man: literary genius and a genius for personal happiness." See, respectively, Boyd, *Vladimir Nabokov: The Russian Years*, 238 and 10.

6. For a fairly extensive list of the painters and paintings mentioned in Nabokov's oeuvre, see de Vries and Johnson, *Vladimir Nabokov and the Art of Painting*, 178–80 and 219–23.

7. This Cornell lecture passage invokes a pronouncement of Saint Augustine with which Nabokov was undoubtedly familiar: "When we see a beautiful script, it is not enough to praise the skill of the scribe for making the letters even and alike and beautiful; we must also read what he has signified to us through those letters. With pictures it is different. For when you have looked at a picture, you have seen it all and have praised it"; as cited in Meyer Schapiro, *Romanesque Art* (New York: George Braziller, 1977), 25. For a discussion of Nabokov's works in relation to those of Saint Augustine, see Henry-Thommes, *Recollection, Memory and Imagination*.

Bibliography

WORKS BY AND ABOUT NABOKOV

For the main corpus of Nabokov's works, see the list of abbreviations.

Aleksandrov, Daniil. "Nabokov—naturalist i entomolog." In *V. V. Nabokov: Pro et contra,* comp. B. V. Averin, M. E. Malikova, and A. A. Dolinin, 2 vols., 1:429–38. St. Petersburg: Izdatel´stvo Russkogo Khristianskogo gumanitarnogo instituta, 1997–2001.

Alexandrov, Vladimir E., ed. *The Garland Companion to Vladimir Nabokov.* New York and London: Garland, 1995.

Appel, Alfred, Jr. *Nabokov's Dark Cinema.* New York: Oxford University Press, 1974.

Averin, B. V., M. E. Malikova, and A. A. Dolinin, comps. *V. V. Nabokov: Pro et contra.* 2 vols. St. Petersburg: Izdatel´stvo Russkogo Khristianskogo gumanitarnogo instituta, 1997–2001.

Babikov, Andrei. "Izobretenie teatra." In Vladimir Nabokov, *Tragediia gospodina Morna. P´esy. Lektsii o drame,* 5–42. St. Petersburg: "Azbuka-klassika," 2008.

Barabtarlo, Gennady. *Phantom of Fact: A Guide to Vladimir Nabokov's "Pnin."* Ann Arbor, Mich.: Ardis, 1989.

———. "Those Who Favor Fire (On *The Enchanter*)." *Russian Literature Tri-quarterly* 24 (1991): 89–112.

Beloshevskaia, L. N., and V. P. Nechaev. "Kirill Nabokov." In *"Skit": Praga, 1922–1940: Antologiia, biografii, dokumenty,* comp. L. N. Beloshevskaia and V. P. Nechaev, 553–64. Moscow: Russkii put´, 2006.

Berdjis, Nassim Winnie. *Imagery in Vladimir Nabokov's Last Russian Novel ("Дар"), Its English Translation ("The Gift"), and Other Prose Works of the 1930s.* Frankfurt am Main: Peter Lang, 1995.

Bodenstein, Jürgen. "'The Excitement of Verbal Adventure': A Study of

Vladimir Nabokov's English Prose." Ph.D. diss., Ruprecht-Karl University at Heidelberg, 1977.

Borden, Richard. "Nabokov's Travesties of Childhood Nostalgia." *Nabokov Studies* 2 (1995): 104–34.

Bouchet, Marie C. "Crossbreeding Word and Image: Nabokov's Subversive Use of Ekphrasis." www.ucl.ac.uk/english/graduate/issue/2/marie.htm.

Boyd, Brian. *Ada*online. www.libraries.psu.edu/nabokov/ada.

———. "The Nabokov Biography and the Nabokov Archive." *Biblion* 1, no. 1 (Fall 1992): 15–36.

———. *Vladimir Nabokov: The American Years*. Princeton, N.J.: Princeton University Press, 1991.

———. *Vladimir Nabokov: The Russian Years*. Princeton, N.J.: Princeton University Press, 1990.

———. "'Welcome to the Block': *Priglashenie na kazn´/ Invitation to a Beheading*, A Documentary Record." In *Nabokov's "Invitation to a Beheading": A Critical Companion*, ed. Julian W. Connolly, 141–79. Evanston, Ill.: Northwestern University Press, 1997.

Boyd, Brian, and Robert Michael Pyle, eds. *Nabokov's Butterflies: Unpublished and Uncollected Writings*. Boston: Beacon, 2000.

Brown, Clarence. "Krazy, Ignatz, and Vladimir: Nabokov and the Comic Strip." In *Nabokov at Cornell*, ed. Gavriel Shapiro, 251–63. Ithaca, N.Y., and London: Cornell University Press, 2003.

Buhks, Nora. *Eshafot v khrustal´nom dvortse: O russkikh romanakh Vladimira Nabokova*. Moscow: Novoe literaturnoe obozrenie, 1998.

———. "Les fantômes de l'opéra dans les romans de Nabokov." *Revue des Études Slaves* 72, nos. 3–4 (2000): 453–66.

———. *"Locus-poeticus: Salon de coiffure* v russkoi kul´ture nachala XX veka." *Slavic Almanac* 10, no. 1 (2004): 2–23.

———. "Sur la structure du roman de Vl. Nabokov 'Roi, dame, valet.'" *Revue des Études Slaves* 59 (1988): 799–810.

Burenina, Ol´ga. "'Otchaianie' kak olakrez russkogo simvolizma." *Hypertext "Otchaianie"/Sverkhtekst "Despair": Studien zu Vladimir Nabokovs Roman-Rätsel*, ed. Igor Smirnov, 163–86. Munich: Otto Sagner, 2000.

Ciancio, Ralph A. "Nabokov's Painted Parchments." In *Nabokov at the Limits: Redrawing Critical Boundaries*, ed. Lisa Zunshine, 235–69. New York and London: Garland, 1999.

Connolly, Julian W., ed. *The Cambridge Companion to Vladimir Nabokov.* Cambridge: Cambridge University Press, 2005.

———. *"Invitation to a Beheading:* Nabokov's 'Violin in a Void.'" In *Nabokov's "Invitation to a Beheading": A Critical Companion,* ed. Julian W. Connolly, 3–44. Evanston, Ill.: Northwestern University Press, 1997.

———, ed. *Nabokov and His Fiction: New Perspectives.* Cambridge: Cambridge University Press, 1999.

———, ed. *Nabokov's "Invitation to a Beheading": A Critical Companion.* Evanston, Ill.: Northwestern University Press, 1997.

———. "The Play of Light and Shadow in 'The Fight.'" In *A Small Alpine Form: Studies in Nabokov's Short Fiction,* ed. Charles Nicol and Gennady Barabtarlo, 25–37. New York and London: Garland, 1993.

———. "The Quest for a Natural Melody in the Fiction of Vladimir Nabokov." In *Nabokov at the Limits: Redrawing Critical Boundaries,* ed. Lisa Zunshine, 69–85. New York and London: Garland, 1999.

Cornwell, Neil. "Paintings, Governesses and 'Publishing Scoundrels': Nabokov and Henry James." In *Nabokov's World,* ed. Jane Grayson, Arnold McMillin, and Priscilla Meyer, 2 vols., 2:96–116. New York: Palgrave, 2002.

Dann, Kevin T. "*The Gift:* Vladimir Nabokov's Eidetic Technique." In his *Bright Colors Falsely Seen: Synaesthesia and the Search for Transcendental Knowledge,* 120–64. New Haven, Conn.: Yale University Press, 1998.

Davydov, Sergei. *"Teksty-matreški" Vladimira Nabokova.* Munich: Otto Sagner, 1982.

Delage-Toriel, Lara. "Brushing Through 'Veiled Values and Translucent Undertones': Nabokov's Pictorial Approach to Women." *Transatlantica* 1 (2006). http://www.transatlantica.revues.org/document760.html.

de Vries, Gerard. "Sandro Botticelli and Hazel Shade." *The Nabokovian* 49 (Fall 2002): 12–23.

de Vries, Gerard, and D. Barton Johnson, with an essay by Liana Ashenden. *Vladimir Nabokov and the Art of Painting.* Amsterdam: Amsterdam University Press, 2006.

Diment, Galya. *Pniniad: Vladimir Nabokov and Marc Szeftel.* Seattle and London: University of Washington Press, 1997.

Dirig, Robert. "Theme in Blue: Vladimir Nabokov's Endangered Butterfly." In *Nabokov at Cornell,* ed. Gavriel Shapiro, 205–18. Ithaca, N.Y., and London: Cornell University Press, 2003.

Dmitrovskaia, M. A. "Ot pervoi metafory k poslednei: Smysl finala romana V. Nabokova 'Mashen´ka.'" In *Tekst, intertekst, kul´tura: Sbornik dokladov mezhdunarodnoi nauchnoi konferentsii, Moskva, 4–7 aprelia 2001 goda,* ed. V. P. Grigor´ev and N. A. Fateeva, 305–18. Moscow: "Azbukovnik," 2001.

Dolinin, Alexander. "Clio Laughs Last: Nabokov's Answer to Historicism." In *Nabokov and His Fiction: New Perspectives,* ed. Julian W. Connolly, 197–215. Cambridge: Cambridge University Press, 1999.

———. *Istinnaia zhizn´ pisatelia Sirina.* St. Petersburg: "Akademicheskii proekt," 2004.

———. "'The Stepmother of Russian Cities': Berlin of the 1920s Through the Eyes of Russian Writers." In *Cold Fusion: Aspects of the German Cultural Presence in Russia,* ed. Gennady Barabtarlo, 225–40. New York: Berghahn Books, 2000.

———. "Tsvetnaia spiral´ Nabokova." In Vladimir Nabokov, *Rasskazy. Priglashenie na kazn´. Roman. Esse, interv´iu, retsenzii,* 438–69. Moscow: "Kniga," 1989.

Edmunds, Jeff. "Look at Valdemar! (A Beautified Corpse Revived)." *Nabokov Studies* 2 (1995): 153–71.

Ferrand, Jacques. *Les Nabokov: Essai généalogique.* Montreuil, France: J. Ferrand, 1982.

Field, Andrew. *Nabokov: His Life in Art.* Boston and Toronto: Little, Brown, 1967.

———. *Nabokov: His Life in Part.* New York: Viking, 1977.

Flannagan, Roy C., III. "'Beauty of Distance': The Centrality of Landscape Description in Vladimir Nabokov's *Lolita.*" Ph.D. diss., Southern Illinois University at Carbondale, 1996.

Foster, John Burt, Jr. "Nabokov and Proust." In *The Garland Companion to Vladimir Nabokov,* ed. Vladimir E. Alexandrov, 472–81. New York and London: Garland, 1995.

Frank, Siggy. "Exile in Theatre / Theatre in Exile—Nabokov's Early Plays, *Tragediia gospodina Morna* and *Chelovek iz SSSR.*" *Slavonic and East European Review* 85, no. 4 (October 2007): 629–57.

Funke, Sarah. *Véra's Butterflies: First Editions by Vladimir Nabokov Inscribed to His Wife.* New York: Glenn Horowitz, 1999.

Glebov, Iu. I. "'Vliublennost´' Vladimira Nabokova: Potainoi istochnik." *Russian Studies* 1, no. 3 (1995): 273–77.

Glynn, Michael. *Vladimir Nabokov: Bergsonian and Russian Formalist Influences in His Novels.* New York: Palgrave Macmillan, 2007.

Golubovsky, Mikhail. "Anagrammnye variatsii: Sostukivanie slov." *Vestnik Online* 24 (335), November 26, 2003. http://www.vestnik.com/issues/2003/1126/koi/golubovsky.htm.

Grams, Paul. "*Pnin:* The Biographer as Meddler." In *A Book of Things About Vladimir Nabokov,* ed. Carl R. Proffer, 193–202. Ann Arbor, Mich.: Ardis, 1974.

Grayson, Jane, Arnold McMillin, and Priscilla Meyer, eds. *Nabokov's World,* 2 vols. New York: Palgrave, 2002.

Grishakova, Marina. "Vizual'naia poetika V. Nabokova." *Novoe literaturnoe obozrenie* 54 (March 2002): 205–28.

Haber, Edythe C. "Nabokov's *Glory* and the Fairy Tale." *Slavic and East European Journal* 21, no. 2 (Summer 1977): 214–24.

Henry-Thommes, Christoph. *Recollection, Memory and Imagination: Selected Autobiographical Novels of Vladimir Nabokov.* Heidelberg: Universitätsverlag Winter, 2006.

Hyde, G. M. *Vladimir Nabokov: America's Russian Novelist.* London: Marion Boyars, 1977.

Johnson, D. Barton. *Worlds in Regression: Some Novels of Vladimir Nabokov.* Ann Arbor, Mich.: Ardis, 1985.

Johnson, Kurt, and Steve Coates. *Nabokov's Blues: The Scientific Odyssey of a Literary Genius.* Cambridge, Mass.: Zoland Books, 1999.

Juliar, Michael. *Vladimir Nabokov: A Descriptive Bibliography.* New York and London: Garland, 1986.

Karlinsky, Simon. "Nabokov's Russian Games." In *Critical Essays on Vladimir Nabokov,* ed. Phyllis A. Roth, 86–92. Boston: G. K. Hall, 1984.

Khasin, Gregory. "The Theatre of Privacy: Vision, Self, and Narrative in Nabokov's Russian Language Novels." Ph.D. diss., University of Chicago, 1999.

Klimenko, L. F. "Biblioteka doma Nabokovykh." *Nabokovskii vestnik* 1 (1998): 193–200.

Kozitsky, Igor'. "Nabokov i Dobuzhinsky: Sviazi formal'nye i ne tol'ko." *Neva* 11 (1997): 214–20.

Ledkovskaia, M. V. "Zabytyi poet: Kirill Vladimirovich Nabokov." *Nabokovskii vestnik* 2 (1998): 130–38.

Léon Noel, Lucie. "Playback." *TriQuarterly* 17 (Winter 1970): 209–19.

Levinton, G. A. "The Importance of Being Russian ili Les allusions perdues." In *V. V. Nabokov: Pro et contra*, comp. B. V. Averin, M. E. Malikova, and A. A. Dolinin, 2 vols., 1:308–39. St. Petersburg: Izdatel´stvo Russkogo Khristianskogo gumanitarnogo instituta, 1997–2001.

Liuksemburg, A. M., and G. F. Rakhimkulova. *Magistr igry Vivian van Bok: Igra slov v proze Vladimira Nabokova v svete teorii kalambura*. Rostov-on-Don: Izdatel´stvo instituta massovykh kommunikatsii, 1996.

Long, Michael. *Marvell, Nabokov: Childhood and Arcadia*. London: Oxford University Press, 1984.

McCarthy, Penny. "Nabokov's *Ada* and Sidney's *Arcadia:* The Regeneration of a Phoenix." *Modern Language Review* 99, no. 1 (January 2004): 17–31.

Merkel, Stephanie L. "Vladimir Nabokov's *King, Queen, Knave* and the *Commedia Dell'Arte*." *Nabokov Studies* 1 (1994): 83–102.

Miagkov, P. I. "Zapadnoevropeiskaia zhivopis´ v sobranii sem´i Nabokovykh." *Nabokovskii vestnik* 1 (1998): 209–16.

Nabokov, Dmitri. "Nabokov i teatr." In Vladimir Nabokov, *Tragediia gospodina Morna. P´esy. Lektsii o drame*, 519–38. St. Petersburg: "Azbuka-klassika," 2008.

———. "Zapis´ vystupleniia v Natsional´noi Rossiiskoi biblioteke. S.-Peterburg, 12 iiunia 1995 g." *Zvezda* 11 (1996): 3–9.

Nabokov, Nicolas. *Bagazh: Memoirs of a Russian Cosmopolitan*. New York: Atheneum, 1975.

Nabokov, S. S. "Profili." *Nabokovskii vestnik* 2 (1998): 143–66.

Nabokov, V. D. "Charl´z Dikkens." In *Istoriia zapadnoi literatury*, ed. F. D. Batiushkov, 4 vols., 4:52–70. Moscow: "Mir," 1912–17.

———. "Charl´z Dikkens (K 100-letiiu so dnia ego rozhdeniia)." *Rech´*, January 25 (February 7), 1912, 3.

———. "Charl´z Dikkens, kak kriminalist." *Pravo*, January 29, 1912, 188–95.

———. "Fet (K stoletiiu so dnia rozhdeniia)." *Rul´*, December 5, 1920, 6.

———. *Iz voiuiushchei Anglii: Putevye ocherki*. Petrograd: "Union," 1916.

———. "Iz vospominanii o teatre (za 35 let)." *Teatr i Zhizn´* (*Theater und Leben*), nos. 1–2 (September 1921): 4–5.

———. "Piatidesiatiletie Literaturnogo Fonda." In *Iubileinyi sbornik Literaturnogo Fonda, 1859–1909*, ed. S. A. Vengerov, 474–87. St. Petersburg: "Obshchestvennaia Pol´za," ca. 1910.

———. *Tiuremnye dosugi*. St. Petersburg: "Obshchestvennaia Pol´za," 1908.

Nabokov, Vladimir. "Diaghilev and a Disciple." Review of *Serge Diaghilev*,

His Life, His Work, His Legend: An Intimate Biography, by Serge Lifar. *The New Republic,* November 18, 1940, 699–700.

———. "The Glasses of St. Joseph." Trans. Dmitri Nabokov. *The Nabokovian* 54 (Spring 2005): 4.

———. "Gogol´." Publ. Aleksandr Dolinin. *Zvezda* 4 (1999): 14–19.

———. *Kak ia liubliu tebia.* Moscow: "Tsentr-100," 1994.

———. "Natasha." Manuscript Division, Vladimir Nabokov Archives, container 19. Library of Congress, Washington D.C.

———. "Natasha." Trans. Dmitri Nabokov. *The New Yorker,* June 9 and 16, 2008, 54–60.

———. "On Generalities." Publ. Aleksandr Dolinin. *Zvezda* 4 (1999): 12–14.

———. "Peter in Holland." Trans. Dmitri Nabokov. *The Nabokovian* 51 (Fall 2003): 4.

———. *Rasskazy. Priglashenie na kazn´. Roman. Esse, interv´iu, retsenzii.* Moscow: "Kniga," 1989.

———. "Revolution." Trans. Dmitri Nabokov. *Paris Review* 175 (Fall/Winter 2005): 171–73.

———. "Tolstoy." Trans. Dmitri Nabokov. *New York Review of Books* 35, no. 3 (March 3, 1988): 6.

———. *Tragediia gospodina Morna. P´esy. Lektsii o drame.* St. Petersburg: "Azbuka-klassika," 2008.

———. "Ut pictura poesis." Trans. Dmitri Nabokov. *The Nabokovian* 51 (Fall 2003): 28–31.

Nicol, Charles. "Music in the Theater of the Mind: Opera and Vladimir Nabokov." In *Nabokov at the Limits: Redrawing Critical Boundaries,* ed. Lisa Zunshine, 21–41. New York and London: Garland, 1999.

———. "Nabokov and Science Fiction: 'Lance.'" *Science-Fiction Studies* 14, no. 1 (March 1987): 9–20.

Nicol, Charles, and Gennady Barabtarlo, eds. *A Small Alpine Form: Studies in Nabokov's Short Fiction.* New York and London: Garland, 1993.

Niqueux, Michel. "*Ekphrasis* et fantastique dans *la Vénitienne* de Nabokov ou l'Art comme envoûtement." *Revue des Études Slaves* 72, nos. 3–4 (2000): 475–84.

Proffer, Carl R., ed. *A Book of Things About Vladimir Nabokov.* Ann Arbor, Mich.: Ardis, 1974.

Proffer, Ellendea, comp. and ed. *Vladimir Nabokov: A Pictorial Biography.* Ann Arbor, Mich.: Ardis, 1991.

Raguet-Bouvart, Christine. "European Art: A Framing Device?" In *Nabokov at the Limits: Redrawing Critical Boundaries,* ed. Lisa Zunshine, 183–212. New York and London: Garland, 1999.

Riaguzova, L. N. "'Prizma' kak universal´naia kategoriia v khudozhestvennoi sisteme V. V. Nabokova." In *Nabokovskii sbornik: Iskusstvo kak priem,* ed. M. A. Dmitrovskaia, 19–29. Kaliningrad: Izdatel´stvo Kaliningradskogo gosudarstvennogo universiteta, 2001.

Ronen, Omry. "Emulation, Anti-Parody, Intertextuality, and Annotation." *Facta Universitatis,* series Linguistics and Literature, 3, no. 2 (2005): 161–67.

———. "The Triple Anniversary of World Literature: Goethe, Pushkin, Nabokov." In *Nabokov at Cornell,* ed. Gavriel Shapiro, 172–81. Ithaca, N.Y., and London: Cornell University Press, 2003.

Roth, Phyllis A., ed. *Critical Essays on Vladimir Nabokov.* Boston: G. K. Hall, 1984.

Rydel, Christine A. "Nabokov and Tiutchev." In *Nabokov at Cornell,* ed. Gavriel Shapiro, 123–35. Ithaca, N.Y., and London: Cornell University Press, 2003.

Sbrilli, Antonella. "Le mani fiorentine di Lolita: Coincidenze warburghiane in Nabokov (e viceversa)." *La Rivista di Engramma* 43 (September 2005): 1–21. www.engramma.it/engramma_v4/rivista/saggio/43/043 _sbrilli_nabokov.html.

Schiff, Stacy. *Véra (Mrs. Vladimir Nabokov).* New York: Modern Library, 2000.

Schlögel, Karl. "Stadtwahrnehmung: Nabokov und die Taxifahrer." In his *Berlin Ostbahnhof Europas: Russen und Deutsche in ihrem Jahrhundert,* 159–76. Berlin: Siedler Verlag, 1998.

Senderovich, Savely, and Yelena Shvarts. "Starichok iz evreev (kommentarii k *Priglasheniiu na kazn´* Vladimira Nabokova)." *Russian Literature* 43, no. 3 (1 April 1998): 297–327.

———. "Tropinka podviga (Kommentarii k romanu V. V. Nabokova 'Podvig')." *Nabokovskii vestnik* 4 (1999): 140–53.

Shapiro, Gavriel. *Delicate Markers: Subtexts in Vladimir Nabokov's "Invitation to a Beheading."* Middlebury Studies in Russian Language and Literature 19. New York: Peter Lang, 1998.

———. "*Lolita* Class List." *Cahiers du Monde Russe* 37, no. 3 (July–September 1996): 317–35.

———. "Nabokov and Comic Art." In *Nabokov at the Limits: Redrawing Crit-*

ical Boundaries, ed. Lisa Zunshine, 213–34. New York and London: Garland, 1999.

———. "Nabokov and Comic Art: Additional Observations and Remarks." *The Nabokovian* 59 (Fall 2007): 21–31.

———. "Nabokov and Early Netherlandish Art." In *Nabokov at Cornell,* ed. Gavriel Shapiro, 241–50. Ithaca, N.Y., and London: Cornell University Press, 2003.

———. "Nabokov and the 'Other Shores.'" In *The Russian Emigration: Literature, History, Chronicle of Films,* ed. V. Khazan, I. Belobrovtseva, and S. Dotsenko, 109–16. Jerusalem, Israel: The Hebrew University of Jerusalem; Tallinn, Estonia: Tallinn Pedagogical University, 2004.

———. "Nabokov and *The World of Art.*" *Slavic Almanac* 6, no. 9 (2000): 35–52.

———, ed. *Nabokov at Cornell.* Ithaca, N.Y., and London: Cornell University Press, 2003.

———. "Nabokov's Allusions: Dividedness and Polysemy." *Russian Literature* 43, no. 3 (April 1, 1998): 329–38.

———. "Otgoloski *Tiuremnykh dosugov* V. D. Nabokova v *Priglashenii na kazn'.*" *Cahiers de l'Émigration Russe* 5 (1999): 67–75.

———. "References to Russian Art in *The Defense.*" *The Nabokovian* 50 (Spring 2003): 58–62.

———. "Setting His Myriad Faces in His Text: Nabokov's Authorial Presence Revisited." In *Nabokov and His Fiction: New Perspectives,* ed. Julian W. Connolly, 15–35. Cambridge: Cambridge University Press, 1999.

Shrayer, Maxim D. "The Perfect Glory of Nabokov's Exploit." *Russian Studies in Literature* 35, no. 4 (Fall 2000): 29–41.

———. *The World of Nabokov's Stories.* Austin: University of Texas Press, 1999.

Sistematicheskii katalog biblioteki Vladimira Dmitrievicha Nabokova. St. Petersburg: "Tovarishchestvo Khudozhestvennoi Pechati," 1904.

Sistematicheskii katalog biblioteki Vladimira Dmitrievicha Nabokova: Pervoe prodolzhenie. St. Petersburg: "Tovarishchestvo Khudozhestvennoi Pechati," 1911.

Skonechnaia, Ol'ga. "Nabokov v Tenishevskom uchilishche." *Nashe nasledie* 1 (1991): 109–12.

Smirnov, Igor, ed. *Hypertext "Otchaianie"/Sverkhtekst "Despair": Studien zu Vladimir Nabokovs Roman-Rätsel.* Munich: Otto Sagner, 2000.

Stark, Vadim, publ. "Perepiska Vladimira Nabokova s M. V. Dobuzhin-skim." *Zvezda* 11 (1996): 92–108.

———. "Ut pictura poesis: Nabokov-risoval´shchik." *Vyshgorod* 3 (1999): 116–38.

Sweeney, Susan Elizabeth. "'Ballet Attitudes': Nabokov's *Lolita* and Petipa's *The Sleeping Beauty.*" In *Nabokov at the Limits: Redrawing Critical Boundaries,* ed. Lisa Zunshine, 111–26. New York and London: Garland, 1999.

———. "Looking at Harlequins: Nabokov, the *World of Art* and the Ballets Russes." In *Nabokov's World,* ed. Jane Grayson, Arnold McMillin, and Priscilla Meyer, 2 vols., 2:73–95. New York: Palgrave, 2002.

Tammi, Pekka. "*Glory.*" In *The Garland Companion to Vladimir Nabokov,* ed. Vladimir E. Alexandrov, 169–78. New York and London: Garland, 1995.

———. *Problems of Nabokov's Poetics: A Narratological Analysis.* Helsinki: Suomalainen Tiedeakatemia, 1985.

———. "The St. Petersburg Text and Its Nabokovian Texture." In his *Russian Subtexts in Nabokov's Fiction: Four Essays,* 67–90. Tampere Studies in Literature and Textuality. Tampere, Finland: Tampere University Press, 1999.

Terekhov, A. "Neizdannoe stikhotvorenie V. Nabokova." *Rossiiskii literaturovedcheskii zhurnal* 11 (1997): 316–26.

Toker, Leona. "Between Allusion and Coincidence: Nabokov, Dickens and Others." *Hebrew University Studies in Literature and the Arts* 12, no. 2 (Autumn 1984): 175–98.

———. "Lichnoe i chastnoe v avtobiografii Vladimira Nabokova: 'mirazh prinimaemyi za landshaft.'" *Revue des Études Slaves* 72, nos. 3–4 (2000): 415–21.

———. *Nabokov: The Mystery of Literary Structures.* Ithaca, N.Y., and London: Cornell University Press, 1989.

Urban, Thomas. *Vladimir Nabokov: Blaue Abende in Berlin.* Berlin: Propyläen Verlag, 1999.

Verizhnikova, T. F. "Vladimir Nabokov i iskusstvo knigi Anglii rubezha vekov: 'Khram Shekspira' v biblioteke V. D. Nabokova." *Nabokovskii vestnik* 1 (1998): 201–8.

Virolainen, Maria. "Angloiazychnoe tvorchestvo Nabokova kak inobytie russkoi slovesnosti." In her *Istoricheskie metamorfozy russkoi slovesnosti,* 422–55. St. Petersburg: "Amfora," 2007.

Wetzsteon, Ross. "Nabokov as Teacher." *TriQuarterly* 17 (Winter 1970): 240–46.

Zimmer, Dieter E. *A Guide to Nabokov's Butterflies and Moths.* Hamburg: n.p., 2001.

———. "*Mary.*" In *The Garland Companion to Vladimir Nabokov,* ed. Vladimir E. Alexandrov, 346–58. New York and London: Garland, 1995.

———. *Nabokovs Berlin.* Berlin: Nicolai, 2001.

Zunshine, Lisa, ed. *Nabokov at the Limits: Redrawing Critical Boundaries.* Border Crossings 4. New York and London: Garland, 1999.

WORKS ON OTHER SUBJECTS

Abramov, L. Ia. et al., eds. *Shakhmatnyi slovar'.* Moscow: "Fizkul'tura i sport," 1964.

Alberti, Leon Battista. *On Painting.* Trans. John R. Spencer. New Haven, Conn.: Yale University Press, 1956.

Alderson, Simon. "*Ut pictura poesis* and Its Discontents in Late Seventeenth- and Early Eighteenth-Century England and France." *Word and Image* 11, no. 3 (July–September 1995): 256–63.

Andersen, Hans Christian. *The Complete Andersen.* Trans. Jean Hersholt. 6 vols. New York: Limited Editions Club, 1949.

Anderson, Roger, and Paul Debreczeny, eds. *Russian Narrative and Visual Art: Varieties of Seeing.* Gainesville: University Press of Florida, 1994.

Asvarishch, Boris I. "Friedrich's Russian Patrons." In *The Romantic Vision of Caspar David Friedrich,* ed. Sabine Rewald, 19–40. New York: Metropolitan Museum of Art, 1990.

Barolsky, Paul. "Leonardo, Satan, and the Mystery of Modern Art." *Virginia Quarterly Review* 74, no. 3 (Summer 1998): 393–414.

———. *Walter Pater's Renaissance.* University Park and London: Pennsylvania State University Press, 1987.

Barron, Stephanie, and Wolf-Dieter Dube. *German Expressionism: Art and Society.* London: Thames and Hudson, 1997.

Bathrick, David. "Max Schmeling on the Canvas: Boxing as an Icon of Weimar Culture." *New German Critique* 51 (Autumn 1990): 113–36.

Behr, Shulamith. *Expressionism.* London: Tate Gallery, 1999.

Bennett, Virginia. "The Russian Symbolists and John Ruskin's Aesthetics."

Paper presented at the annual meeting of the American Association of Teachers of Slavic and East European Languages (AATSEEL), Philadelphia, December 28, 2004.

Benois, Alexander [Benua, Aleksandr]. *Istoriia russkoi zhivopisi v XIX veke.* 1902. Reprint, Moscow: "Respublika," 1995.

———. *Istoriia zhivopisi.* 4 vols. St. Petersburg: "Shipovnik," 1912.

———. "Khudozhestvennye pis'ma: Muter." *Rech´,* July 23 (August 5), 1909, 2.

———. *Moi dnevnik, 1916–1917–1918.* Moscow: Russkii put´, 2003.

———. *Moi vospominaniia.* 2 vols. Moscow: Nauka, 1990.

———. *Vozniknovenie "Mira Iskusstva."* 1928. Reprint, Moscow: "Iskusstvo," 1994.

Białostocki, Jan. "Man and Mirror in Painting: Reality and Transience." In his *The Message of Images: Study in the History of Art,* 93–107. Vienna: Istituto per le Ricerche di Storia dell'Arte, 1988.

Bidney, Martin. *Patterns of Epiphany: From Wordsworth to Tolstoy, Pater, and Barrett Browning.* Carbondale and Edwardsville: Southern Illinois University Press, 1997.

Borowitz, Helen Osterman. *The Impact of Art on French Literature: From de Scudéry to Proust.* Newark: University of Delaware Press, 1985.

Bowlt, John E. *The Silver Age: Russian Art of the Early Twentieth Century and the "World of Art" Group.* Newtonville, Mass.: Oriental Research Partners, 1979.

Boym, Svetlana. *The Future of Nostalgia.* New York: Basic Books, 2001.

Bredius, Abraham, ed. *The Paintings of Rembrandt.* Vienna: Phaidon Verlag, 1936.

Bülow, Kjeld. *George Grosz: A Bibliography and Other Check Lists.* Copenhagen: Booktrader, 1993.

Callahan, Virginia Woods. "Alciato's Quince-Eating Bride, and the Figure at the Center of Bellini's *Feast of the Gods.*" *Artibus et Historiae* 35 (1997): 73–79.

Carter, David G. "Reflections in Armor in the *Canon van der Paele Madonna.*" *Art Bulletin* 36, no. 1 (March 1954): 60–62.

Cassirer, Ernst. *The Individual and the Cosmos in Renaissance Philosophy.* Trans. Mario Domandi. New York: Harper and Row, 1963.

Chaddock, Bruce E. "Authorial Presence and the Novel." Ph.D. diss., Cornell University, 1974.

Chernowitz, Maurice E. *Proust and Painting.* New York: International University Press, 1945.

Chugunov, G. I. *Mstislav Valerianovich Dobuzhinsky.* Leningrad: "Khudozhnik RSFSR," 1984.

———, comp. *Vospominaniia o Dobuzhinskom.* St. Petersburg: "Akademicheskii proekt," 1997.

Chukovsky, Kornei. *Dnevnik 1901–1929.* 2nd ed. Moscow: Sovremennyi pisatel´, 1997.

Collier, Peter. *Proust and Venice.* Cambridge: Cambridge University Press, 1989.

Contini, Roberto. "Portrait of a Young Roman Woman (Dorothea)." In *Sebastiano del Piombo 1485–1547,* ed. Giuseppe Scandiani, 144–45. Rome: Federico Motta Editore, 2008.

Cossio, Manuel Bartolomé. *El Entierro del Conde de Orgaz.* Madrid: Victoriano Suárez, 1914.

———. *El Greco.* 2 vols. Madrid: Victoriano Suárez, 1908.

Crone, Anna Lisa, and Jennifer Jean Day. *My Petersburg / Myself: Mental Architecture and Imaginative Space in Modern Russian Letters.* Bloomington, Ind.: Slavica, 2004.

Crowe, Joseph Archer, and Giovanni Battista Cavalcaselle. *A History of Painting in Italy.* 6 vols. New York: Charles Scribner's Sons, 1903–14.

Daniel, Sergei. "The Art of Claude Lorrain as a Cultural Phenomenon." In *Claude Lorrain: Painter of Light,* by Sergei Daniel and Natalia Serebriannaya, 7–31. Bournemouth, Eng.: Parkstone; and St. Petersburg: Aurora, 1995.

Dante Alighieri. *The Divine Comedy.* Trans. John D. Sinclair. 3 vols. New York: Oxford University Press, 1979.

de Grummond, Nancy Thomson. "VV and Related Inscriptions in Giorgione, Titian, and Dürer." *Art Bulletin* 57, no. 3 (September 1975): 346–56.

de Jonge, C. H. *Delft Ceramics.* Trans. Marie-Christine Hellin. London: Pall Mall, 1970.

Diagilev, Sergei. "Slozhnye voprosy." *Mir iskusstva* 1–2 (1899): 1–16, and 3–4 (1899): 37–61.

Dinesen, Isak. *Ehrengard.* New York: Random House, 1963.

Dobuzhinsky, Mstislav. "Beseda s M. V. Dobuzhinskim." Massapequa, N.Y., November 19, 1957. Dobuzhinsky Papers, box 4. Bakhmeteff Archive, Columbia University Library, New York City.

————. "Mir Iskusstva." 1942. Dobuzhinsky Papers, box 4. Bakhmeteff Archive, Columbia University Library, New York City.

————. "Oblik Peterburga." Publ. Galina Glushanok. *Zvezda* 5 (2003): 101–7.

————. *Pis´ma.* St. Petersburg: Izdatel´stvo "Dmitri Bulanin," 2001.

————. "Susal´nyi fil´m." 1947. Dobuzhinsky Papers, box 5. Bakhmeteff Archive, Columbia University Library, New York City.

————. *Vospominaniia.* Moscow: Nauka, 1987.

————. "Zapozdalyi venok na mogilu druga: K. A. Somov." N.d., 18 pages. Dobuzhinsky Papers, box 5. Bakhmeteff Archive, Columbia University Library, New York City.

Doherty, Brigid. "Berlin Dada: Montage and Embodiment of Modernity, 1916–1920." Ph.D. diss., University of California, Berkeley, 1996.

Duffy, Stephen. *Paul Delaroche, 1797–1856: Paintings in the Wallace Collection.* London: Trustees of the Wallace Collection, 1997.

Durham, John I. *The Biblical Rembrandt: Human Painter in a Landscape of Faith.* Macon, Ga.: Mercer University Press, 2004.

Dyer, T. F. Thiselton. *The Folk-Lore of Plants.* London: Chatto and Windus, Piccadilly, 1889.

Erpel, Fritz. *Die Selbstbildnisse Rembrandts.* Berlin: Henschelverlag, 1969.

Etkind, Mark. *A. N. Benua i russkaia khudozhestvennaia kul´tura.* Leningrad: "Khudozhnik RSFSR," 1988.

Ettlinger, Leopold D., and Helen S. Ettlinger. *Raphael.* Oxford: Phaidon, 1987.

Fagan, Louis Alexander. *Raffaello Sanzio, His Sonnet in the British Museum.* London: Fine Art Society, 1884.

Fedorov-Davydov, A. A. *Isaak Il´ich Levitan.* 2 vols. Moscow: "Iskusstvo," 1966.

Fedorova, V. I. *V. V. Maté i ego ucheniki.* Leningrad: "Khudozhnik RSFSR," 1982.

Flavell, M. Kay. *George Grosz: A Biography.* New Haven, Conn., and London: Yale University Press, 1988.

Forsh, Ol´ga, and S. P. Iaremich. *Pavel Petrovich Chistiakov.* Leningrad: Izdanie komiteta populiarizatsii khudozhestvennykh izdanii pri gosudarstvennoi akademii istorii material´noi kul´tury, 1928.

Fourest, Henry Pierre. *Delftware: Faience Production at Delft.* Trans. Katherine Watson. New York: Rizzoli, 1980.

Freedman, Luba. *The Classical Pastoral in the Visual Arts.* Hermeneutics of Arts 1. New York: Peter Lang, 1989.

———. *Titian's Portraits Through Aretino's Lens.* University Park: Pennsylvania State University Press, 1995.

Friedrich, Otto. *Before the Deluge: A Portrait of Berlin in the 1920's.* New York: Harper and Row, 1972.

Gaehtgens, Thomas W., and Kurt Winkler, eds. *Ludwig Justi: Werden—Wirken—Wissen: Lebenserinnerungen aus fünf Jahrzehnten.* 2 vols. Berlin: Nicolai, 2000.

Geller, Leonid, ed. *Ekfrasis v russkoi literature: Trudy Lozannskogo simpoziuma.* Moscow: "MIK," 2002.

Gershenzon-Chegodaeva, N. M. *Pervye shagi zhiznennogo puti (vospominaniia docheri Mikhaila Gershenzona).* Moscow: Zakharov, 2000.

Gessen, I. V. *Gody izgnaniia: Zhiznennyi otchet.* Paris: YMCA, 1979.

Gogol, Nikolai. *The Complete Tales of Nikolai Gogol.* Ed. Leonard J. Kent. 2 vols. Chicago and London: University of Chicago Press, 1985.

Gordon, Donald E. *Ernst Ludwig Kirchner.* Cambridge, Mass.: Harvard University Press, 1968.

Gowing, Lawrence. "The Modern Vision." In *Places of Delight: The Pastoral Landscape,* by Robert C. Cafritz, Lawrence Gowing, and David Rosand, 182–248. Washington, D.C.: Phillips Collection in association with National Gallery of Art, 1988.

Grabar´, Igor´, ed. *Istoriia russkogo iskusstva.* 6 vols. Moscow: Izdanie I. Knebel´, 1909–16.

———. "Otvet g. Zhanu Broshe." *Mir iskusstva* 10 (1899), "Khudozhestvennaia khronika" section: 116–17.

Grosz, George. *The Autobiography of George Grosz: A Small Yes and a Big No.* Trans. Arnold J. Pomerans. London and New York: Allison and Busby, 1982.

Gruyer, François Anatole. *Raphaël, peintre de portraits, fragments d'histoire et d'iconographie sur les personnages représentés dans les portraits de Raphael.* 2 vols. Paris: Librairie Renouard, 1881.

Guasti, Cesare. *Le rime di Michelangelo Buonarroti, pittore, scultore e architetto.* Florence: F. Le Monnier, 1863.

Gusarova, Alla. *"Mir iskusstva."* Leningrad: "Khudozhnik RSFSR," 1972.

———, comp. *Mstislav Dobuzhinsky: Zhivopis´, grafika, teatr.* Moscow: "Izobrazitel´noe iskusstvo," 1982.

Hagstrum, Jean H. *The Sister Arts: The Tradition of Literary Pictorialism and English Poetry from Dryden to Gray.* Chicago: University of Chicago Press, 1958.

Hamilton, George Heard. *The Art and Architecture of Russia.* New York: Penguin Books, 1983.

Hartlaub, Gustav Friedrich. *Zauber des Spiegels: Geschichte und Bedeutung des Spiegels in der Kunst.* Munich: R. Piper, 1951.

Hazlitt, William. "On a Landscape of Nicholas Poussin." In his *Complete Works,* ed. P. P. Howe, 21 vols., 8:168–74. London and Toronto: J. M. Dent and Sons, 1930–34.

Heckscher, William S. "Erwin Panofsky: A Curriculum Vitae." In Erwin Panofsky, *Three Essays on Style,* ed. Irving Lavin, 169–97. Cambridge, Mass.: MIT Press, 1995.

Heffernan, James A. W. *Museum of Words: The Poetics of Ekphrasis from Homer to Ashbery.* Chicago and London: University of Chicago Press, 1993.

Hirst, Michael. *Sebastiano del Piombo.* Oxford: Oxford University Press, 1981.

Hofstede, Justus Müller. "Der Künstler in Humilitas-Gestus: Altniederländische Selbstporträts und ihre Signifikanz im Bildkontext: Jan van Eyck—Dieric Bouts—Hans Memling—Joos van Cleve." In *Autobiographie und Selbstportrait* [sic] *in der Renaissance,* ed. Gunter Schweikhart, 39–69. Cologne: Walther König, 1998.

Horne, Herbert Percy. *Alessandro Filipepi, Commonly Called Sandro Botticelli, Painter of Florence.* London: George Bell and Sons, 1908.

Huebner, Friedrich Markus. "Der Expressionismus in Deutschland, 1920." In *Expressionismus: Der Kampf um eine literarische Bewegung,* ed. Paul Raabe, 133–46. Zurich: Arche Verlag, 1987.

Hurley, Ann, and Kate Greenspan, eds. *So Rich a Tapestry: The Sister Arts and Cultural Studies.* Cranbury, N.J.: Associated University Presses, 1995.

Iaremich, S. P. *Mikhail Aleksandrovich Vrubel´: Zhizn´ i tvorchestvo.* Moscow: Izdanie I. Knebel´, 1911.

Il´in, Nikolas, and Natal´ia Semenova. *Prodannye sokrovishcha Rossii.* Moscow: Trilistnik, 2000.

Ivanov, Georgy. *Sobranie sochinenii v trekh tomakh.* Moscow: "Soglasie," 1994.

Janson, H. W. *Apes and Ape Lore in the Middle Ages and the Renaissance.* London: Warburg Institute, University of London, 1952.

Jensen, Jens Christian. *Adolph Menzel.* Cologne: DuMont Buchverlag, 1982.

Jungić, Josephine. "Prophecies of the Angelic Pastor in Sebastiano del Piombo's *Portrait of Cardinal Bandinello Sauli and Three Companions.*" In *Prophetic Rome in the High Renaissance Period,* ed. Marjorie Reeves, 345–70. Oxford: Clarendon, 1992.

Kadi, Simone. *La peinture chez Proust et Baudelaire.* Paris: La Pensée Universelle, 1973.

Kaganov, Grigory. *Images of Space: St. Petersburg in the Visual and Verbal Arts.* Trans. Sidney Monas. Stanford, Calif.: Stanford University Press, 1997.

Keisch, Claude, and Marie Ursula Riemann-Reyher, eds. *Adolph Menzel, 1815–1905: Between Romanticism and Impressionism.* New Haven, Conn.: Yale University Press, 1996.

Kennedy, Janet. *The "Mir Iskusstva" Group and Russian Art.* New York: Garland, 1977.

Khagi, Sofya. "Silence and the Rest: The Inexpressible from Batiushkov to Tiutchev." *Slavic and East European Journal* 48, no. 1 (Spring 2004): 41–61.

Knust, Herbert. "George Grosz: Literature and Caricature." In *Montage, Satire and Cultism: Germany Between the Wars,* ed. Herbert Knust, 20–49. Champaign: University of Illinois Press, 1975.

Kondakov, S. N., comp. *Spisok russkikh khudozhnikov k iubileinomu spravochniku Imperatorskoi Akademii Khudozhestv.* 1914. Reprint, Moscow: "Antik-Biznes-tsentr," 2002.

Konechnyi, Al´bin. "'Peterburg s togo berega' (v memuarakh emigrantov 'pervoi volny')." *Blokovskii sbornik* 13 (1996): 128–46.

Kovarsky, Vera. "M. V. Dobujinsky—Pictorial Poet of St. Petersburg." *Russian Review* 19, no. 1 (January 1960): 24–37.

Kris, Ernst, and Otto Kurz. *Legend, Myth, and Magic in the Image of the Artist.* New Haven, Conn., and London: Yale University Press, 1979.

Landow, George P. *The Aesthetic and Critical Theories of John Ruskin.* Princeton, N.J.: Princeton University Press, 1971.

Lapshin, V. P. *Khudozhestvennaia zhizn´ Moskvy i Petrograda v 1917 godu.* Moscow: "Sovetskii khudozhnik," 1983.

Lapshina, Natalia. *"Mir iskusstva."* Moscow: "Iskusstvo," 1977.

Leck, Ralph M. *Georg Simmel and Avant-Garde Sociology: The Birth of Modernity, 1880–1920.* Amherst, N.Y.: Humanity Books, 2000.

Lee, Rensselaer Wright. *Ut Pictura Poesis: The Humanistic Theory of Painting.* New York: W. W. Norton, 1967.

Leikind, O. L., K. V. Makhrov, and D. Ia. Severiukhin, comps. *Khudozhniki Russkogo Zarubezh´ia, 1917–1939.* St. Petersburg: "Notabene," 1999.

Levey, Michael. "Botticelli and Nineteenth-Century England." *Journal of the Warburg and Courtauld Institutes* 23, nos. 3–4 (1960): 291–306.

Levin, David M. *The Philosopher's Gaze.* Berkeley: University of California Press, 1999.

Levinson-Lessing, V. F. "Pervoe puteshestvie Petra I za granitsu." In *Kul´tura i iskusstvo petrovskogo vremeni,* ed. G. N. Komelova, 5–36. Leningrad: "Avrora," 1977.

———. "S. P. Iaremich (1869–1939)." *Soobshcheniia Gosudarstvennogo Érmitazha* 2 (1940): 26–27.

Lifar´, Sergei. *Diagilev.* St. Petersburg: "Kompozitor," 1993.

Lightbown, Ronald W. *Sandro Botticelli: His Life and Work.* 2 vols. Berkeley: University of California Press, 1978.

Lloyd, Jill. *German Expressionism: Primitivism and Modernity.* New Haven, Conn., and London: Yale University Press, 1991.

Löffler, Fritz. *Otto Dix: Life and Work.* Trans. R. J. Hollingdale. New York: Holmes and Meier, 1982.

Long, Rose-Carol Washton, ed. and annot. *German Expressionism: Documents from the End of the Wilhelmine Empire to the Rise of National Socialism.* New York: G. K. Hall, 1993.

Loss, Archie K. *Joyce's Visible Art: The Work of Joyce and the Visual Arts, 1904–1922.* Ann Arbor, Mich.: UMI Research, 1984.

MacDonogh, Giles. *Berlin.* New York: St. Martin's, 1998.

Makovsky, S. K. *Grafika M. V. Dobuzhinskogo.* Berlin: "Petropolis," 1924.

———. "Maliavin." *Zhar-ptitsa* 10 (1923): 2–5.

———. "Portrety S. A. Sorina." *Zhar-ptitsa* 8 (1922): 2–6.

———. *Stranitsy khudozhestvennoi kritiki.* 2 vols. St. Petersburg: "Panteon," 1909.

Manin, Vitaly. *Russkii peizazh.* Moscow: "Belyi gorod," 2001.

Martin, Louis. "Panofsky and Poussin in Arcadia." In his *Sublime Poussin,* 104–19. Stanford, Calif.: Stanford University Press, 1999.

Mayer, August L. *El Greco.* Berlin: Klinkhardt und Biermann, 1931.

Mazauric, Claude, et al. *Charlotte Corday: Une Normande dans la Révolution.* Versailles: Musée Lambinet, 1989.

McCloskey, Barbara. *George Grosz and the Communist Party: Art and Radical-*

ism in Crisis, 1918 to 1936. Princeton, N.J.: Princeton University Press, 1997.

McTighe, Sheila. *Nicolas Poussin's Landscape Allegories*. Cambridge: Cambridge University Press, 1996.

Mel´nikov, V. L. "N. K. Rerikh i izdatel´stvo 'Svobodnoe Iskusstvo' (1916–1917)." *Peterburgskii Rerikhovskii sbornik* 1 (1998): 293–340.

Menzel, Wolfgang. *Christliche Symbolik*. 2 vols. Regensburg, Ger.: G. Joseph Manz Verlag, 1854.

Mets, A. G. *Osip Mandel´shtam i ego vremia*. St. Petersburg: "Giperion," 2005.

Michaud, Philippe-Alain. *Aby Warburg and the Image in Motion*. Trans. Sophie Hawkes. New York: Zone Books, 2004.

Mitchell, W. J. T., ed. *Landscape and Power*. Chicago and London: University of Chicago Press, 1994.

Mommsen, Theodor E. "Football in Renaissance Florence." *Yale University Library Gazette* 16, no. 1 (July 1941): 14–19.

Murphy, Jonathan Paul. *Proust's Art: Painting, Sculpture and Writing in "À la recherche du temps perdu."* New York: Peter Lang, 2001.

Muther, Richard. *The History of Modern Painting*. 4 vols. London: J. M. Dent, 1907.

———. *Istoriia zhivopisi v XIX veke*. Trans. Zinaida Vengerova. 3 vols. St. Petersburg: "Znanie," 1899–1902.

Naftulin, Lawrence. "A Note on the Iconography of the van der Paele Madonna." *Oud Holland* 86, no. 1 (1971): 3–8.

Nicholas of Cusa. *The Vision of God*. Trans. Emma Gurney Salter. New York: E. P. Dutton, 1928.

Ovid. *Fasti*. London: Penguin Books, 2000.

Panofsky, Erwin. *Early Netherlandish Painting*. 2 vols. Cambridge, Mass.: Harvard University Press, 1953.

———. *"Et in Arcadia ego:* On the Conception of Transience in Poussin and Watteau." In *Philosophy and History: Essays Presented to Ernst Kassirer,* ed. Raymond Klibansky and Herbert James Paton, 223–54. Oxford: Clarendon, 1936.

———. "Et in Arcadia ego: Poussin and the Elegiac Tradition." In his *Meaning in the Visual Arts: Papers in and on Art History,* 295–320. Garden City, N.Y.: Doubleday Anchor Books, 1955.

———. "Jan van Eyck's *Arnolfini Portrait*." *Burlington Magazine* 64 (1934): 117–28.

Parrot, Nicole. *Mannequins*. Paris: Editions Colona, 1981.

Petrova, Yevgenia, ed. *The World of Art: On the Centenary of the Exhibition of Russian and Finnish Artists, 1898*. St. Petersburg and Helsinki: Palace Editions, 1998.

Philostratus, *Imagines;* Callistratus, *Descriptions*. Trans. Arthur Fairbanks. New York: G. P. Putnam's Sons, 1931.

Polonsky, Rachel. *English Literature and the Russian Aesthetic Renaissance*. New York: Cambridge University Press, 1998.

Posse, Hans. *Die Gemäldegalerie des Kaiser-Friedrich-Museums*. 2 vols. Berlin: Julius Bard Verlag, 1909.

Praz, Mario. "'Ut Pictura Poesis.'" In his *Mnemosyne: The Parallel Between Literature and the Visual Arts*, 3–28. Princeton, N.J.: Princeton University Press, 1970.

Proust, Marcel. *Remembrance of Things Past*. Trans. C. K. Scott Moncrieff and Terence Kilmartin. 3 vols. New York: Vintage Books, 1982.

Pruzhan, Irina. *Konstantin Somov*. Moscow: "Izobrazitel´noe iskusstvo," 1972.

Pushkin, Alexander. *The Complete Works of Alexander Pushkin*. Ed. Iain Sproat et al. 15 vols. Norfolk, Eng.: Milner, 1999–2003.

———. *Polnoe sobranie sochinenii*. 17 vols. Moscow and Leningrad: Izda-tel´stvo Akademii Nauk SSSR, 1937–59.

Rand, Richard, with contributions by Antony Griffiths and Colleen M. Terry. *Claude Lorrain—The Painter as Draftsman: Drawings from the British Museum*. New Haven, Conn., and London: Yale University Press; and Williamstown, Mass.: Sterling and Francine Clark Art Institute, 2006.

Reeh, Henrik. *Ornaments of the Metropolis: Siegfried Kracauer and Modern Urban Culture*. Cambridge, Mass.: MIT Press, 2004.

Rewald, Sabine, with essays by Ian Buruma and Matthias Eberle. *Glitter and Doom: German Portraits from the 1920s*. New York: Metropolitan Museum of Art, 2006.

Robillard, Valerie, and Els Jongeneel, eds. *Pictures into Words: Theoretical and Descriptive Approaches to Ekphrasis*. Amsterdam: VU University Press, 1998.

Rosand, David. "Giorgione, Venice, and the Pastoral Vision." In *Places of Delight: The Pastoral Landscape*, by Robert C. Cafritz, Lawrence Gowing, and David Rosand, 21–81. Washington, D.C.: Phillips Collection in association with National Gallery of Art, 1988.

Rosenberg, Jakob, Seymour Slive, and E. H. ter Kuile. *Dutch Art and Architecture: 1600 to 1800*. Harmondsworth, Eng.: Penguin Books, 1966.

Rosenblum, Robert. "Friedrichs from Russia: An Introduction." In *The Romantic Vision of Caspar David Friedrich,* ed. Sabine Rewald, 3–17. New York: Metropolitan Museum of Art, 1990.

Rowe, Dorothy. *Representing Berlin: Sexuality and the City in Imperial and Weimar Germany.* Aldershot, Eng., and Burlington, Vt.: Ashgate, 2003.

Rubins, Maria. *Crossroad of Arts, Crossroad of Cultures: Ecphrasis in Russian and French Poetry.* New York: Palgrave, 2000.

Rumold, Rainer. *The Janus Face of the German Avant-Garde: From Expressionism Toward Postmodernism.* Evanston, Ill.: Northwestern University Press, 2002.

Rusakova, A. A. *Simvolizm v russkoi zhivopisi.* Moscow: "Iskusstvo," 1995.

Russell, H. Diane. *Claude Lorrain, 1600–1682.* Washington, D.C.: National Gallery of Art, 1982.

Russkaia akademicheskaia shkola zhivopisi v XVIII veke. Moscow and Leningrad: OGIZ, 1934.

Sabarsky, Serge. *George Grosz: The Berlin Years.* New York: Rizzoli, 1985.

Schama, Simon. *Rembrandt's Eyes.* New York: Alfred A. Knopf, 1999.

Schapiro, Meyer. "'Muscipula Diaboli,' The Symbolism of the Mérode Altarpiece (1945)." In his *Late Antique, Early Christian and Mediaeval Art,* 1–19. New York: George Braziller, 1979.

———. *Romanesque Art.* New York: George Braziller, 1977.

Schleinitz, Rotraud. *Richard Muther—Ein provokativer Kunstschriftsteller zur Zeit der Münchener Secession.* Hildesheim: Georg Olms Verlag, 1993.

Schmeling, Max. *Max Schmeling: An Autobiography.* Trans. George B. von der Lippe. Chicago: Bonus Books, 1998.

Schouvaloff, Alexander. *Léon Bakst: The Theatre Art.* London: Sotheby's Publications, 1991.

Schroth, Sarah. *"Burial of the Count of Orgaz." Studies in the History of Art* 11 (1982): 1–17.

S(c)hruba, Manfred. *Literaturnye ob´edineniia Moskvy i Peterburga 1890—1917 godov.* Moscow: Novoe literaturnoe obozrenie, 2004.

Schuster, Peter-Klaus, ed. *George Grosz: Berlin–New York.* Berlin: Ars Nicolai, 1994.

Schwarz, Daniel R. *Reconfiguring Modernism: Explorations in the Relationship Between Modern Art and Modern Literature.* New York: St. Martin's, 1997.

Schwarz, Heinrich. "The Mirror in Art." *Art Quarterly* 15, no. 2 (Summer 1952): 97–118.

Schweizer, Niklaus R. *The Ut Pictura Poesis Controversy in Eighteenth-Century England and Germany.* Bern: Herbert Lang, 1972.

Selz, Peter. *Max Beckmann.* New York: Abbeville, 1996.

Severiukhin, D. Ia., and O. L. Leikind. *Zolotoi vek khudozhestvennykh ob˝edinenii v Rossii i SSSR (1820–1932).* St. Petersburg: Izdatel´stvo Chernysheva, 1992.

Shapiro, Gavriel. *Nikolai Gogol and the Baroque Cultural Heritage.* University Park: Pennsylvania State University Press, 1993.

Shapiro, Marianne. "Ecphrasis in Virgil and Dante." *Comparative Literature* 42, no. 2 (Spring 1990): 97–115.

Shcheglov, Iu. K. *Romany I. Il´fa i E. Petrova: Sputnik chitatelia.* 2 vols. Vienna: Wiener Slawistischer Almanach, 1990–91.

Shcherbatov, Prince Sergei. *Khudozhnik v ushedshei Rossii.* New York: Izdatel´stvo imeni Chekhova, 1955.

Shestakov, Viacheslav. *Iskusstvo i mir v "Mire iskusstva."* Moscow: "Slavianskii dialog," 1998.

Sidorov, A. A. *Russkaia grafika nachala XX veka.* Moscow: "Iskusstvo," 1969.

Simmel, Georg. "The Metropolis and Mental Life." In *The Sociology of Georg Simmel,* ed. and trans. Kurt H. Wolff, 409–24. New York: Free Press of Glencoe, 1964.

———. "The Stranger." In *The Sociology of Georg Simmel,* ed. and trans. Kurt H. Wolff, 402–8. New York: Free Press of Glencoe, 1964.

Sindalovsky, Naum. *Peterburg v fol´klore.* St. Petersburg: "Letnii Sad," 1999.

Sobol´, S. L. *Istoriia mikroskopa i mikroskopicheskikh issledovanii v Rossii v XVIII veke.* Moscow and Leningrad: Izdatel´stvo Akademii Nauk SSSR, 1949.

Springer, Peter. *Hand and Head: Ernst Ludwig Kirchner's "Self-Portrait as Soldier."* Trans. Susan Ray. Berkeley: University of California Press, 2002.

Steward, Barbara. *The Symbolic Rose.* New York: Columbia University Press, 1960.

Stoichita, Victor I. *The Self-Aware Image: An Insight into Early Modern Meta-Painting.* Cambridge: Cambridge University Press, 1997.

Summer, Susan Cook. "The Poet of St. Petersburg." *Columbia Library Columns* 33, no. 2 (February 1984): 3–11.

Svetlov, S. F. *Peterburgskaia zhizn´ v kontse XIX stoletiia (v 1892 godu).* St. Petersburg: "Giperion," 1998.

Tatar, Maria. *Lustmord: Sexual Murder in Weimar Germany.* Princeton, N.J.: Princeton University Press, 1995.

Tatarinov, Vladimir. "Grafika Dobuzhinskogo." Review of *Grafika Dobuzhinskogo,* by Sergei Makovsky. *Zhar-ptitsa* 13 (1925): 33–34.

Thompson, G. R. *The Art of Authorial Presence: Hawthorne's Provincial Tales.* Durham, N.C., and London: Duke University Press, 1993.

Tintner, Adeline R. *Henry James and the Lust of the Eyes: Thirteen Artists in His Work.* Baton Rouge: Louisiana State University Press, 1993.

Vaiskopf, Mikhail. *Pisatel' Stalin.* Moscow: Novoe literaturnoe obozrenie, 2001.

Valkenier, Elizabeth Kridl. *Valentin Serov: Portraits of Russia's Silver Age.* Evanston, Ill.: Northwestern University Press, 2001.

Van Dam, Jan Daniel. *Delffse Porceleyne: Dutch Delftware 1620–1850.* Amsterdam and Zwolle: Rijksmuseum and Uitgeverij Waanders, 2004.

Vasari, Giorgio. *Lives of the Most Eminent Painters, Sculptors and Architects.* Trans. Gaston du C. de Vere. 10 vols. London: Macmillan and Medici Society, 1912–14.

Vassiliev, Alexandre. *Beauty in Exile.* New York: Harry N. Abrams, 2000.

Vengerov, S. A., ed. *Russkaia literatura XX veka (1890–1910).* 3 vols. Moscow: "Mir," 1914–16.

Vogt, Paul. *Expressionism: German Painting 1905–1920.* Trans. Antony Vivis and Robert Erich Wolf. New York: Harry N. Abrams, 1980.

Volpe, Carlo, and Mauro Lucco. *L'opera completa di Sebastiano del Piombo.* Milan: Rizzoli, 1980.

Vydrin, I. I., comp. *A. N. Benua i M. V. Dobuzhinsky: Perepiska (1903–1957).* St. Petersburg: Izdatel´stvo "Sad iskusstv," 2003.

Vydrin, I. I., and V. P. Tret´iakov, comps. *Stepan Petrovich Iaremich.* St. Petersburg: Izdatel´stvo "Sad iskusstv," 2005.

Wachtel, Andrew Baruch. *The Battle for Childhood: Creation of a Russian Myth.* Stanford, Calif.: Stanford University Press, 1990.

Ward, John L. "Disguised Symbolism as Enactive Symbolism in Van Eyck's Paintings." *Artibus et Historiae* 29 (1994): 9–53.

Warner, Malcolm. "John Everett Millais, *Christ in the Carpenter's Shop (Christ in the House of His Parents),* 1849–50." In *The Pre-Raphaelites,* ed. Leslie Parris, 77–79. London: Tate Gallery, 1994.

Watts, Pauline Moffitt. *Nicolaus Cusanus: A Fifteenth-Century Vision of Man.* Leiden: E. J. Brill, 1982.

Weinstein, Joan. *The End of Expressionism: Art and the November Revolution in*

Germany, 1918–19. Chicago and London: University of Chicago Press, 1990.

Westermann, Mariët. *Rembrandt.* London: Phaidon, 2000.

White, Michael. "The Grosz Case: Paranoia, Self-Hatred and Anti-Semitism." *Oxford Art Journal* 30, no. 3 (2007): 431–53.

Whitford, Frank. *The Berlin of George Grosz.* New Haven, Conn., and London: Yale University Press, 1997.

Willett, John. *Expressionism.* London: Weidenfeld and Nicolson, 1970.

Winkler, Kurt. "Ludwig Justi—Der Konservative Revolutionär." In *Avantgarde und Publikum: Zur Rezeption avantgardistischer Kunst in Deutschland 1905–1933,* ed. Henrike Junge, 173–85. Cologne: Böhlau Verlag, 1992.

Wittkower, Rudolf. *Art and Architecture in Italy, 1600 to 1750.* 1958. Reprint, Harmondsworth, Eng.: Penguin Books, 1985.

Wolfradt, Willi. *Caspar David Friedrich und die Landschaft der Romantik.* Berlin: Mauritius Verlag, 1924.

Woods-Marsden, Joanna. *Renaissance Self-Portraiture: The Visual Construction of Identity and the Social Status of the Artist.* New Haven, Conn., and London: Yale University Press, 1998.

Zamiatin, Evgeny. *A Soviet Heretic: Essays by Yevgeny Zamyatin.* Ed. and trans. Mirra Ginsburg. Chicago: University of Chicago Press, 1970.

Zhukovsky, V. A. *Sobranie sochinenii v chetyrekh tomakh.* Moscow and Leningrad: Gosudarstvennoe izdatel´stvo khudozhestvennoi literatury, 1959–60.

Zil´bershtein, I. S., and A. N. Savinov, eds. *Aleksandr Benua razmyshliaet . . .* Moscow: "Sovetskii khudozhnik," 1968.

Zil´bershtein, I. S., and V. A. Samkov, comps. *Sergei Diagilev i russkoe iskusstvo.* 2 vols. Moscow: "Izobrazitel´noe iskusstvo," 1982.

Zöllner, Frank. "'Ogni Pittore Dipinge Sé': Leonardo da Vinci and 'Auto-mimesis.'" In *Der Künstler über sich in seinem Werk,* ed. Matthias Winner, 137–60. Weinheim, Ger.: VCH, Acta Humaniora, 1992.

Index

277

About the Author

Gavriel Shapiro is a professor in the department of Russian at Cornell University. He is the author of *Nikolai Gogol and the Baroque Cultural Heritage* (1993), *Delicate Markers: Subtexts in Vladimir Nabokov's "Invitation to a Beheading"* (1998), and the editor of *Nabokov at Cornell* (2003).